THE INTERNET ELECTION

Communication, Media, and Politics

Series Editor
Robert E. Denton, Jr., Virginia Tech

This series features a range of work dealing with the role and function of communication in the realm of politics, broadly defined. Including general academic books and texts for use in graduate and advanced undergraduate courses, the series encompasses humanistic, critical, historical, and empirical studies in political communication in the United States. Primary subject areas include campaigns and elections, media, and political institutions. *Communication, Media, and Politics* books will be of interest to students, teachers, and scholars of political communication from the disciplines of communication, rhetorical studies, political science, journalism, and political sociology.

Recent Titles in the Series

For more information on these and other titles in the series,
visit www.rowmanlittlefield.com.

THE INTERNET ELECTION
Perspectives on the Web in Campaign 2004

Edited by
Andrew Paul Williams and
John C. Tedesco

ROWMAN & LITTLEFIELD PUBLISHERS, INC.
Lanham • Boulder • New York • Toronto • Oxford

ROWMAN & LITTLEFIELD PUBLISHERS, INC.

Published in the United States of America
by Rowman & Littlefield Publishers, Inc.
A wholly owned subsidiary of The Rowman & Littlefield Publishing Group, Inc.
4501 Forbes Boulevard, Suite 200, Lanham, Maryland 20706
www.rowmanlittlefield.com

P.O. Box 317, Oxford OX2 9RU, UK

British Library Cataloguing in Publication Information Available

Library of Congress Cataloging-in-Publication Data

The Internet election : perspectives on the Web in campaign 2004 / edited by
  Andrew Paul Williams and John C. Tedesco.
    p. cm.
  Includes bibliographical references and index.
  ISBN-13: 978-0-7425-4095-8 (cloth : alk. paper)
  ISBN-10: 0-7425-4095-2 (cloth : alk. paper)
  ISBN-13: 978-0-7425-4096-5 (pbk. : alk. paper)
  ISBN-10: 0-7425-4096-0 (pbk. : alk. paper)
    1. Internet in political campaigns—United States. 2. Internet—Political aspects—
United States. 3. Presidents—United States—Election—2004. 4. United States—
Politics and government—2001–   . 5. Political campaigns—United States. 6.
Presidential candidates—United States.   I. Williams, Andrew Paul, 1967–   .
II. Tedesco, John C.
JK2281.I57 2006
324.973'0931—dc22

                                                                              2006001184

Printed in the United States of America

∞™ The paper used in this publication meets the minimum requirements of American
National Standard for Information Sciences—Permanence of Paper for Printed Library
Materials, ANSI/NISO Z39.48-1992.

Contents

Acknowledgments

W<small>E ARE GRATEFUL</small> for the support and guidance of many of our colleagues and friends who have helped us compile this manuscript. Our colleague Robert E. Denton, Jr., is the first person we must thank for his continued strong and generous support. In addition to Bob's wonderful support as a departmental colleague and personal friend, in his role as editor for Rowman & Littlefield's Communication, Media, and Politics series he helped provide us with valuable perspective and insight at various phases of the book's development. Bob's high standards and impressive contributions not only as an editor, but also as a model department citizen are inspirational.

We are fortunate to be members of an international research team of scholars who share our passion for political communication. Our colleagues on the Uvote2004 team, led by Lynda Lee Kaid, offer not only their friendship but also a helping hand in data collection efforts for various projects we share in common. We thank Lynda, Mitchell McKinney, Dianne Bystrom, John Balloti, Mary Banwart, Diana Carlin, Mike Chanslor, Colleen Connolly-Ahern, Paul D'Angelo, Elizabeth Dudash, Frank Esser, Joe Foote, April Franklin, Kim Gaddie, Rob Gobetz, Georgine Hodgkinson, Alison Howard, Karla Larson Hunter, Amy Jasperson, Tom Johnson, Anne Johnston, Clifford Jones, Spiro Kiousis, Stephanie Greco Larson, Yang Lin, Michael McDevitt, Charlton McIlwain, Lori Melton McKinnon, Jerry Miller, J. Gregory Payne, Tom Reichert, Terry Robertson, Laura Roselle, Julia Spiker, James Tomlinson, Kaye Trammell, Tim Vercellotti, Barbara Walkosz, Scott Wells, and Robert Wicks.

We end with a special note of thanks to Lynda Lee Kaid. Lynda guided us as our doctoral adviser, provided us with much career inspiration, and is a dear friend. Her generosity, inclusive nature, and integrity are deeply appreciated. We are truly blessed to have had Lynda share so much of her energy and passion with us over the years, and it is largely her encouraging collaborative research that has led us to edit this volume, which draws work from numerous talented scholars.

Introduction

Andrew Paul Williams and John C. Tedesco

SIGNIFICANT SHIFTS in citizens' and candidates' uses of the Internet for political information and communication led us to characterize the 2004 U.S. presidential election as the "Internet Election." Reinforcement of the "Internet Election" is found in multiple sources, including Pew Internet & American Life Project reports about the 2004 campaign (i.e., "Far More Voters Believe Election Outcome Matters: But Many Already Wary of Negative Tone" and "Voters Liked Campaign 2004, But Too Much 'Mud-Slinging'"), showing that (1) 63 million online political news consumers used the Internet for political information, (2) 43 million discussed politics via e-mail, and (3) 13 million used the Internet to make campaign contributions or arrangements for volunteer efforts. While many Americans participated in more than one of the above online political activities, 75 million Americans participated in at least one of these Web opportunities. Increases in Internet access since 1996, and expansion since 2000 both in users and uses of online political information, have transformed the Web's political news consumer profile such that it now more closely resembles the profile of the American voter. Pew's findings (2004) also demonstrate that more than half the online news consumers (52%) indicated that information from the Internet helped in their vote decision making. Furthermore, approximately a quarter of online political news consumers credited the Internet with encouraging them to vote and determining for whom they would vote.

Whereas the growth in numbers of online political news consumers helps support the case for classification of 2004 as the Internet Election, the changing uses of the Internet by campaigns and citizens may be more significant.

Critics of the Internet have challenged users and crafters to identify ways to capitalize on the Internet's interactive potential. Citizen use of chat rooms, e-mail, and meet-up forums for political mobilization made a noticeable impact in 2004. Web logs—now well known as blogs—also played an important role in providing citizens a voice during the campaign. Notable organizations such as MoveOn.org and Meetup.com generated much attention for their use of the Web for mobilization and citizen advertising. Jibjab.com brought a new style of entertainment parody to the Web, while FactCheck.org offered online users a nonpartisan analysis of a variety of candidate messages. Candidate advances in online fund-raising, certainly led by Howard Dean's successes, also marked a significant online advance for the 2004 campaign. Strategic political marketing and audience segmentation for e-mail messages and online volunteer mobilization networks also marked advances for candidate Web uses. While blogs were a common feature of candidate sites, control of comment postings by the campaigns created a fabricated sense of dialogue between the campaigns and citizens. Chapters in *The Internet Election* address many of these online advances and provide broad description and analysis of the Web in campaign 2004.

In chapter 1, Clifford Jones sets a legal context for the book by exploring rules governing the application of the Federal Election Campaign Act (FECA) to the Internet. Candidate advertising, e-mail, Web sites and hyperlinks, and blogs are analyzed under the current FECA rules as well as rule-making possibilities beyond 2004. Steven Schneider and Kirsten Foot (chapter 2) present a comprehensive analysis of candidate Web pages by comparing sites from 2000 and 2004. Schneider and Foot's contribution is guided by their quest to explore the evolution of candidate Web strategies according to their organizing matrix, which categorizes Web features within informing, involving, connecting, or mobilizing functions. The gendering of candidates on campaign Web sites is explored by Mary Banwart (chapter 3) using the webstyle concept she developed and implemented during analysis of campaigns during 2000. By examining three gubernatorial and ten U.S. Senate races featuring opposing female and male major party candidates, Banwart compares presentation differences for verbal, nonverbal, production, and interactive messages. Christopher Hull presents an empirical investigation into the role of the Internet in the Iowa caucuses from 1996 to the present in chapter 4. Using exposure to candidate Web sites, campaign e-mail contact, online support registration, and online news consumption, Hull explores whether Internet usage was significantly different among Howard Dean supporters.

Lynda Lee Kaid's chapter on political advertising (chapter 5) examines the content of online advertisements during 2004. Kaid demonstrates that, despite efforts to limit campaign spending and soft money contributions, the 2004 presidential campaign witnessed record spending on political spots and created an unprecedented negative environment for electoral politics. Kaid discusses a wide range of online ads, from those by candidates and parties to those by independent groups and individual voters. The online advertising story in 2004 is one of the most interesting stories of the election. Chapter 6 presents one of the first systematic investigations of candidate e-mail message strategies. Andrew Paul Williams offers a unique look at candidate self-referential and opponent-based framing in e-mail messages from Bush and Kerry. Williams signed up to receive e-mail notices from both candidates through the lens of a Florida resident. Williams's look at the messages sent to voters in the battleground state of Florida offers readers analysis of the advantages and missed opportunities in this political marketing opportunity for candidates.

Monica Postelnicu, Justin Martin, and Kristen Landreville assess the role of campaign Web sites in promoting candidates and attracting campaign resources (chapter 7). These authors compare and assess Bush's and Kerry's official Web sites along dimensions of issue promotion, image promotion, fundraising, and voter mobilization. In chapter 8, Jennifer Stromer-Galley and Andrea Baker present a rich description of Dean blog posts and citizen comments with a critical investigation of blog interactivity. Stromer-Galley and Baker, through their analysis of the hype, hope, reality, and joys and sorrows of the Dean Internet strategy, consider whether Dean interacted *at* citizens or *with* citizens. Blogs were certainly an interesting and novel feature of campaign 2004. Kaye Trammell's chapter follows Stromer-Galley and Baker's and continues the examination of blogs in the 2004 campaign. Chapter 9 traces the historical evolution of blogs and compares Bush's and Kerry's use of blogs during the general election phase. Blog tools and features are described and analyzed for both leading presidential candidates. Trammell concludes her chapter with a prediction about the role of blogs in future campaigns.

Barbara Kaye and Thomas Johnson, in chapter 10, extend their research on uses and gratifications among politically interested Internet users during the two weeks before and two weeks after the 2004 presidential election. Those motivated to go online to communicate with others were found to use interactive features of the Web—such as blogs, e-mail lists and bulletin boards, chat rooms, and instant messaging—to a greater extent than those users only seeking information. Convenience was sited as a primary reason for heavy use of the Web for political information, while contact with like-minded political users was a primary incentive for use of interactive chat Web features.

Chapter 11 takes the Internet Election into a unique direction through examination of Internet whispering campaigns. The whispering campaigns—specifically as they related to the spread of online rumors about a wide array of Teresa Heinz Kerry's personal, business, and financial influence—were abundant in message boards and online networks. Ashli Quesinberry Stokes presents interesting evidence of the negative rhetorical strategies used throughout the whispering campaigns and constructs an analysis of their use to discredit the Kerry campaign and provide fuel to Bush supporters. The final chapter of the book presents an analysis of the impact of Web interactivity and its potential for mobilizing and engaging young adult voters. John Tedesco uses an online experiment to demonstrate differences in young adult evaluations of and reactions to political Web sites containing interactive opportunities for young adults to participate in campaign dialogue. Chapter 12 closes with the optimistic finding that young adults feel a stronger sense of internal efficacy when sites they visit provide them a forum for voicing their ideas and opinions.

While developments in 2004 demonstrated a dramatic shift in the users and uses of the Internet for online campaigning, we wonder whether these developments will be seen in historical context as the major shift in Internet politics or simply the beginning of an online political revolution. We hope you find the chapters full of interesting description and analysis and hope the authors engage and trigger research ideas of your own.

1

Campaign Finance Reform and the Internet: Regulating Web Messages in the 2004 Election and Beyond

Clifford A. Jones

JUST AS AL GORE DID NOT REALLY INVENT the Internet, the 2004 elections did not really mark the discovery of the Internet as a campaign tool by politicians. The major campaigns used candidate Web sites in 1996, and both Jesse Ventura in 1998 and John McCain in 2000 made increased use of the Internet. Nonetheless, the 2004 elections saw the most significant employment of the Internet in campaigns to date in terms of both depth and scope. Indeed, it is difficult to see any reason other than the potential for stifling regulation discussed below why the quantum increases in Internet-based election campaigning seen since about 1996 will not live long and prosper.

The growth in Internet campaigning has not occurred in a vacuum, but in a period of burgeoning online population and use. In 1996, Internet adoption in the United States was about 23% of the population, but by 2004 it had grown to 61% of the adult population (Rainie, Cornfield, and Horrigan 2005). Rainie, Cornfield, and Horrigan (2005: i) reported that in the 2004 elections,

Fully 75 million Americans—37% of the adult population and 61% of online Americans—used the internet to get political news and information, discuss candidates and debate issues in emails, or participate directly in the political process by volunteering or giving contributions to candidates. The online political news consumer population grew dramatically from previous election years (up from 18% of the U.S. population in 2000 to 29% in 2004), and there was an increase of more than 50% between 2000 and 2004 in the number of registered voters who cited the internet as one of their *primary* sources of news about the presidential campaign.

Political Campaign Functions on the Internet in 2004

The ways in which 63 million political "online news consumers" (those who used the Internet for three types of actions) used the Internet in the 2004 elections were catalogued by Rainie, Cornfield, and Horrigan (2005: ii):

1. 34 million researched candidate positions on issues.
2. 32 million got or sent e-mail with jokes about the election.
3. 31 million went online to find out how candidates were doing in opinion polls.
4. 25 million used the Internet to check the accuracy of claims made by or about the candidates.
5. 20 million researched candidate voting records.
6. 19 million watched video clips about the candidates or the election.
7. 18 million took online polls.
8. 17 million sent e-mails about the campaign to groups of family members or friends as part of listservs or discussion groups.
9. 16 million found out about the endorsements or ratings of candidates by organizations.
10. 14 million got information about when or where to vote.
11. 14 million signed up for e-mail newsletters or other online alerts to get the latest news about politics.
12. 7 million signed up to receive e-mail from the presidential campaigns.
13. 6 million joined political discussions and chat groups.
14. 4 million contributed money to a candidate online.
15. 4 million signed up online for campaign volunteer activities such as helping to organize a rally, registering voters, or getting people to the polls on Election Day.

While no one suggests that the Internet has actually displaced more traditional forms of campaign organization, communication, and fund-raising, these surveys indicate that the Internet now strongly supplements these methods and in some areas provides innovative uses not previously feasible. An early frontrunner who faded abruptly, Howard Dean, based his campaign strategy on identification with the Internet as a promoter and reviver of democracy (Trippi 2004). Cornfield (2005) credits the following, among others, as innovations of the Dean campaign: (1) news-pegged fund-raising appeals, where e-mail appeals are tied to a campaign event or a need to respond immediately to an opponent's political ad; (2) "meet-ups" and other net-organized local gatherings, where the word goes out on the net for aficionados of anything, even campaigns, to gather at a stated time and place to discuss shared interests; (3) blogging (covered in detail in subsequent chapters), in which the now-famous on-line diaries are used to organize everything from handwritten letter campaigns to Iowa and New Hampshire voters to call-ins to talk shows to correct perceived unfair media coverage ("Dean Defense Forces"); and (4) online referenda, such as the faux referendum to provide political cover for Dean's decision to opt out of the presidential public financing system, in which yes voters received a reply thanking them—along with a request for money. While the Dean campaign and others in 2004 certainly made greater use of the Internet than had candidates in previous elections, so had John McCain in 2000 and Jesse Ventura in 1998, and in the 1996 campaign, both the Clinton–Gore and Dole–Kemp campaigns used Web sites to distribute information, solicit volunteers, and highlight campaign activities (Center for Democracy and Technology 1999).

From among the myriad Internet-based campaign functions, several stand out as actual and potential subjects of campaign finance regulation. All political uses of the Internet do not have implications for campaign finance law, but at least the following have the potential to: creating a Web site, linking or hyperlinking, blogging, e-mail, fund-raising, and online advertising, including banner ads and online spots or videos. Some have implications for campaign finance law for different reasons, including who is doing it and on what basis rather than what is done. These will be discussed in more detail below.

A Brief History of Campaign Finance Regulation and the Internet

The Federal Election Campaign Act of 1971 (FECA 1971–2002) provided the first serious attempt to regulate federal elections. It has been amended several times, most substantially in 1974 (following the Watergate scandal involving the Nixon administration), in 1976 after several provisions were declared unconstitutional in *Buckley*, and most recently in March 2002, by the Bipartisan Campaign Finance Reform Act (BCRA). The BCRA amendments to FECA became effective on November 6, 2002, immediately following the 2002 elections. FECA's key elements include:

a. Required disclosure of amounts and sources of contributions to candidates and political committees and disclosure of independent expenditures. Reports are filed with the Federal Election Commission (FEC), and they are publicly available over the Internet at www.fec.gov. The BCRA amendments (2002) added new disclosure requirements concerning "electioneering communications," discussed below.

b. Contribution limits. Specific limits were set in the 1974 law at $1,000 per election (primary and general elections counted separately) to federal candidates by individuals, $20,000 per year on contributions to national political parties, and $5,000 per year to state and local parties. Effective with the BCRA amendments in 2002, the limits on contributions to candidates rose to $2,000 per election, and the limits are now indexed to inflation so they automatically will increase in the future (e.g., to $2,100 in 2005–2006). Under the BCRA amendments, the limits on contributions increase to $25,000 per year ($26,700 in 2005–2006) in the case of national parties and to $10,000 per year in the case of state or local parties. Aggregate contribution limits rose under BCRA from $25,000 per year to $95,000 per two-year election cycle ($101,400 in 2005–2006), of which only $37,500 may be contributed to candidates (distinct from parties) over the two years ($40,000 in 2005–2006).

c. Limits on contributions by political action committees (PACs) of $5,000 per election to candidates, and annual limits on contributions by PACs of $5,000 to other outside PACs and state and local parties and $15,000 annually to national parties. There is no annual aggregate limitation on PAC contributions. These limits are not indexed to inflation.

d. Expenditure limits (now invalid): limits on total candidate spending and on spending of candidate's personal funds. These rules were declared unconstitutional in *Buckley* (1976). Accordingly, candidates may spend unlimited amounts of personal funds. However, in BCRA (2002), it is provided (Sections 304 and 318) that Senate and House candidates running against candidates proposing to spend substantial amounts of personal funds will be allowed to receive contributions in excess of the contribution limits up to six times the normal limits and have limits on party "coordinated" expenditures removed. This so-called "Millionaires Provision" was challenged as unconstitutional in *McConnell v. Federal Election Commission* (2003), a lawsuit by U.S. Senator Mitch McConnell and others, but the Court did not decide the issue.

e. Limits on expenditures for radio and television advertising by candidates. These specific limits were eliminated in the 1974 amendments, but general expenditure limits remained until declared unconstitutional in *Buckley* (1976). They are no longer in force.

f. Limits on "independent" expenditures ($1,000) advocating or opposing election of a candidate. These were declared unconstitutional in *Buckley* (1976) and are no longer in force. However, independent expenditures over $1,000 must be disclosed by filing reports with the FEC.

g. Bans on corporate and labor union contributions, except through PACs. PACs are generally organized by employers (often, but not always, corporations) or labor unions, or they may be "nonconnected." A corporate or union PAC may solicit contributions from its employees or members, which are then pooled and contributed to political candidates. These funds are not considered corporate or union funds (i.e., general treasury funds derived from profits or union dues) and do not violate the statutes prohibiting such contributions. Contributions to PACs by employees or union members are voluntary. FECA 1971 created the framework that allowed PACs to exist. Prior to FECA, statutory bans on direct contributions to candidates for federal office by corporations and labor unions, still in effect today, were already in place. Corporations and labor unions are also banned from making expenditures from corporate/union treasuries intended to influence federal elections: both contributions and expenditures are banned. Corporations and labor unions may make "issue" advertisements so long as they fall short of expressly advocating the election or defeat of federal candidates, as such ads are not considered intended to influence the outcome of federal elections.

h. Created the FEC.

i. Established a system of partial public funding of presidential campaigns and party conventions funded by a voluntary "tax check-off" system in which taxpayers may designate on their federal income tax returns that $3.00 (originally $1.00) of their tax liability should go to the Presidential Election Campaign Fund.

Buckley involved a constitutional challenge to certain provisions of the Federal Election Campaign Act Amendments of 1974 (FECA 1974), which *inter alia* placed limits on the amount of funds candidates could spend in support of their elections, limits on the amount of funds that could be expended by independent persons supporting or opposing candidates, and limits on expenditures by candidates of their personal funds in support of their elections. These limits on campaign expenditures by candidates and others were held to "heavily burden core First Amendment expressions" because they represented "substantial rather than merely theoretical restraints on the quantity and diversity of political speech" (*Buckley* 1976: 19). Accordingly, they were unconstitutional as violations of the First Amendment.

The relationship between political communication in the modern age and the raising and spending of money had by the time of *Buckley* assumed constitutional dimensions:

[V]irtually every means of communicating ideas in today's mass society requires the expenditure of money. The distribution of the humblest handbill or leaflet entails printing, paper, and circulation costs. Speeches and rallies generally necessitate hiring a hall and publicizing the event. The electorate's increasing dependence on television, radio, and mass media for news and other information has made these expensive modes of communication indispensable instruments of effective political speech. (*Buckley* 1976: 19)

The *Buckley* framework for regulating political communication, now essentially in place for nearly thirty years, in effect lays down a model of political speech based on the factual premise (true at the time and essentially true now except for a major development—the Internet) that mass media are expensive and that all aspects of the expenditure of money in political campaigns require regulation. As will be noted below, this model does not really fit the Internet, where the marginal or incremental cost of e-mail and hyperlinks is often essentially zero.

As the above description suggests, however, political speech is rarely directly regulated, but for the most part is indirectly regulated by a combination of limits on the amounts of monetary or other contributions that lawfully can be made to federal candidates and parties, requirements that contributions and expenditures in campaigns for federal office be disclosed, and outright bans on certain corporate and union contributions, speech, and expenditures. Two aspects of this complex statutory scheme require some elaboration because of their implications for Internet usage in campaigns: the definition of contributions and expenditures, especially in the context of bans on corporate and labor unions, and the concepts of public communications and electioneering communications, all of which are defined in the statute in a technical sense.

First, the definition of what constitutes a "contribution" to a political candidate (or party) is extremely broad, encompassing "any gift, subscription, loan, advance, or deposit of money or *anything of value* made by any person for the purpose of influencing any election for Federal office" (FECA 2 U.S.C. Sec. 431(8); emphasis added). The definition of *expenditure* is comparably broad: "any purchase, payment, distribution, loan, advance, deposit, or gift of money or *anything of value*, made by any person for the purpose of influencing any election for Federal office" (FECA 2 U.S.C. Sec. 431(9); emphasis added).

The broad sweep of these definitions includes much more that mere gifts of money or expenditures of money. Preparing a Web site for a candidate or party might be a gift of something of value, as might providing a hyperlink to a candidate's Web site. The difficulty of deciding what the value is can be put aside for the moment: if someone creates a Web site on the union's computer or provides a hyperlink from a corporate or union Web site, it may be a *corporate* or *union* "contribution" or "expenditure," which may be illegal regardless of amount. If the combination of hardware, software, server time or space, or ISP charges exceeds the relevant contribution or expenditure threshold, then these contributions may be illegal, whether corporate or union. If an expenditure and the value is over the relevant expenditure threshold, sometimes as little as $250, then expenditure reports may have to be filed with the Federal Election Commission, which may incur legal or accounting costs, and those reports may have to be filed for a two-year election cycle. There are exceptions to these contribution limits and disclosure requirements, but it is easy to see that ordinary citizens' Web activities can generate substantial engagement with campaign finance rules without their realizing it.

The second area requiring some investigation is activities that are more directly communicative but that might also run afoul of other aspects of the campaign finance rules. Simple acts such as sending an e-mail to one thousand of your closest friends containing a candidate's spot ad, or even providing the link to one, or just commenting on one of the candidates could be illegal campaign communications, as could placing a banner ad on a Web site. And, if you do it on the company or union computer, on company time, or even on a home computer or laptop provided by your company or university, or using the company network or ISP, you may be back into prohibited corporate or union activity.

The keys here are the FECA-defined acts of "public communication" (FECA 2 U.S.C. Sec. 431(22)) and "electioneering communication" (FECA 2 U.S.C. Sec. 434(f)). A "public communication" at present means a communication "by means of any broadcast, cable, or satellite communication, newspaper, magazine, outdoor advertising facility, mass mailing, or telephone bank to the general public, or any other form of general public political advertising." Notably absent from the statute is any reference to the Internet. The FEC's regulations—current implementing rules—expressly provided that "The term public communication shall not include communications over the Internet" (11 C.F.R. Sec. 100.26, 2002). Under FEC regulations, advertising conveyed over the Internet thus has so far been exempt from certain rules, such as disclaimer requirements, the so-called "stand by your ad" provisions now familiar to all who enjoyed the 2004 television spot ad experience: "I'm John Kerry, and I approve this ad, message, etc." In 2004, a federal judge struck down this blanket Internet exemption contained in the FEC rules, but not the statute, as unauthorized by Congress (*Shays, et al. v. FEC* 2004). As of May 2005, the FEC is engaged in a "rule-making proceeding" to draft new rules governing the application of FECA to the Internet. Until new rules are adopted, the old rules (e.g., the blanket exemption from the definition of a "public communication") remain in effect. This may change for the 2006 elections.

Normally, individuals may make advertising or other expenditures that expressly advocate the defeat or election of candidates without limit, although expenditures in excess of $1,000 must be reported to the FEC. Corporations or unions may not make ads that *expressly* advocate election or defeat of particular candidates, but may (except as noted below) do so in the form of "issue" ads, so long as express advocacy is avoided. If coordinated with candidates, union or corporate expenditures of this type can be considered (illegal) campaign contributions by the corporation or union. However, the BCRA changed these rules by prohibiting "electioneering" communications by corporations or unions.

Under FECA (2 U.S.C. Section 434(f)), the term "electioneering communication" means "any broadcast, cable, or satellite communication which":

(I) refers to a clearly identified candidate for Federal office;
(II) is made within—
(aa) 60 days before a general, special, or runoff election for the office sought by the candidate; or
(bb) 30 days before a primary or preference election, or a convention or caucus of a political party that has authority to nominate a candidate, for the office sought by the candidate; and
(III) in the case of a communication which refers to a candidate for an office other than President or Vice President, is targeted to the relevant electorate. (FECA 2002)

By restricting "electioneering communications" to "broadcast, cable, or satellite," the statutory term excludes spots or other communications delivered via the Internet, as well as in newspapers, magazines, or any other place besides radio or television. Other than this, electioneering communications are distinguished from public communications by the fact that they occur within a specific time frame (thirty days before a primary or sixty days before the general election), that they refer to a federal candidate (by audio or video means), and that they are "targeted" to the electorate of a nonpresidential candidate (the whole country is the electorate for presidential candidates). Electioneering communications need not expressly promote, attack, support, or oppose ("PASO" in FEC jargon) a candidate to be covered.

The importance of a message being categorized as an electioneering communication includes the fact that such messages are banned for corporations or labor unions even when they avoid express advocacy. The importance of being "public communications" affects whether or not Internet ads can be placed on Web sites by corporations or labor unions acting in coordination with candidates (which otherwise might be considered illegal contributions to the candidates) and whether or not state parties can use "soft money" (money raised outside the restrictions of federal law but lawfully under state law) to "PASO" federal candidates. The major purpose of the BCRA amendments ostensibly was to eliminate parties' use of "soft money" in federal elections, and the amendments' sponsors have claimed that exempting the Internet from these rules would restore the use of soft money in federal campaigns (McCain et al. 2005).

The consequences of Internet-based conduct that unknowingly blunders into the campaign finance regulation arena can be substantial, especially for individuals lacking ready access to lawyers seasoned in the morass of detailed statutes [234 pages], rules [516 pages plus 702 pages of explanations and justifications], advisory opinions of the FEC [over 1,300] and court decisions [over 350] interpreting the statutes and regulations that make up campaign finance law (Morris 2005). Up to this point, the burden has been relatively light, as the discussion in the next part of this chapter shows. However, that state of affairs is likely to change in at least some respects in the next two years, as noted in the final section of the chapter.

Web Messages in the 2004 Election: The Legal Environment

Advertising

The 2004 election took place under the FEC's post-BCRA regulations (2002b), which expressly excluded communications delivered over the Internet from the definition of "public communications." Thus, advertising videos (spots) or banner ads delivered from or placed on Web sites or servers were virtually unrestricted by most of the campaign finance regulatory regime. However, while advertising on the net seems to have reached its high-water mark to date in the 2004 elections, it apparently accounted for a relatively small percentage of political advertising. One firm, PQ Media, projected in August 2004 that Internet political advertising would reach $25.3 million (out of $2.68 billion overall) in 2004, an increase of 853% over 2000 (Gonsalves 2004).

Cornfield (2004) reported that the main presidential candidates spent only $2.66 million on Internet banner ads between January 2004 and August 2004, compared to $330 million on television advertising between March 3 and September 20, 2004, a ratio greater than one hundred to one. However, this Pew study captured only banner ads, not spots delivered via e-mail or distributed via campaign Web sites. Moreover, since one of the attractions of Internet ads is that they are cheap compared to spots broadcast on television networks, the comparison is more like apples to oranges. While there can be little doubt that more money was spent on television ads than on Internet ads, no attempt was made to measure the reach of Internet ads or make any comparison of effectiveness. The Pew study looked only at the presidential campaigns, not spending in all races as projected by the PQ Media study, so the two cannot be directly compared.

The Pew study also did not measure political advertising on the net by other groups than the campaigns. In fact, the most interesting Web-based political communications in 2004 were by noncampaign groups such as the now famous Jib-Jab video sung to the tune of "This Land Is Your Land, This Land Is My Land," the equally famous but less humorous Swift Boat Veterans for Truth Internet ads, and the "Bush in 30 Seconds" contest for amateur Web videos held by MoveOn.org (Darr and Barko 2004). Unless stifled by new legislation or rules, such Web-based communications by campaigns and others seem sure to grow in future elections.

E-mail

As an Internet-based communication, e-mail was generally exempt from campaign finance regulation in 2004. The FEC regulations (2002b, 11 C.F.R. Section 100.27) specifically exempt e-mail or communications over the Internet from the definition of "mass mailings." However, there is an exception if a political committee as defined in the FECA makes "soft money" disbursements for "general public political advertising"; in this case, the political committee is required to attach statements of sponsorship—who paid for the ads and who sponsored them—to certain e-mails (amounting to five hundred or more substantially similar unsolicited e-mails) and the political committee's Web site. This is because for this specific purpose (political committees spending soft money on advertising), though not generally, Internet communications are considered general public political advertising (FECA, 2 U.S.C. Section 441d (a); Bauer 2004). In 2004, the Bush campaign used e-mail to send links to Web-based videos to its e-mail list of six million subscribers (Aboud 2004). In addition, PACs who send out over one hundred substantially similar e-mails in a one-year period that contain express advocacy for (or against) a candidate are required to disclose the source/sponsorship of the communication (FEC 1999d), and groups who are not PACs but also engage in express advocacy may be well advised to adhere to this ruling, even though it may not technically apply to them. Text messages sent to cell phones are not subject to this requirement because the sponsorship information would leave no room for the message (FEC 2002a, AO 2002-9, *Target Wireless*).

Web Sites and Hyperlinks

Although political candidates were required to post sponsorship information on their Web sites, what about ordinary citizens who created Web sites or provided links to information, fund-raising appeals, and so forth? Such sites and links were not directly regulated, but the regulatory issue for these types of activities was whether maintaining such sites and links constituted providing "anything of value" as a contribution or expenditure. Early FEC advisory opinions had indicated an intent to regulate. In 1995, the FEC ruled that a Web site run by a PAC and distributing information was a form of general public political advertising (FEC 1995).

In 1998, an individual voter (Leo Smith) who created a Web site to help support a candidate and criticize the Republican Congress was told by the FEC in an advisory opinion that his Web site was a form of general public political advertising, that it was something of value that expressly advocated the election of a candidate, that he must disclose his full name and indicate whether it was authorized by the campaign, and that if the cost of the Web site exceeded $250 it would have to be reported as an independent expenditure (if independent) or as an in-kind contribution to the candidate (if he coordinated with the official campaign). If the site was a contribution, it was limited in amount (along with any other contributions) to a maximum of $1,000 (FEC 1998a).

In another 1998 proceeding, the FEC's General Counsel concluded that a link on a corporate Web site to a campaign Web site (the candidate owned the company, and the corporate URL was the candidate's name) was an illegal corporate contribution because the link was "something of value" that gave additional exposure to the general public and was tantamount to advertising (FEC 1998b). The FEC rejected the argument that since the link was free of charge it should not be considered an in-kind contribution, since paid hyperlinks were often found on the Web, and just because it was free did not mean it lacked value. This was consistent with an earlier ruling in which online provider CompuServe offered to provide free Web sites and member accounts to all federal candidates on a nonpartisan basis to facilitate posting of candidate position papers and responses to voter questions. The FEC ruled that this would constitute illegal corporate contributions since CompuServe did not qualify for the media exemption (FEC 1996).

More recently, at least in a nonpartisan context, the FEC ruled that the State of Minnesota could provide links on the secretary of state's Web site to all candidates for office on a nonpartisan, uniform basis without being deemed to make a contribution (FEC 1999a). The FEC found that this qualified as a specific nonpartisan activity exemption designed to encourage individuals to vote or register to vote. More broadly, the FEC now seems to have concluded in a series of advisory opinions that if the Web site is nonpartisan, whether nonprofit or for-profit, and offers equal access to candidates and does not advocate or oppose the election of candidates for federal office, it is neither a contribution nor an expenditure (FEC 1999c; 1999b). In addition, the FEC has held that a nonprofit, nonpartisan corporation's studying of the impact of

Internet advertising by exposing randomly selected viewers to political spots advocating the election of candidates, even though this provided free advertising, did not constitute a contribution—although the commissioners could not agree on why it was not (FEC 2000).

While these more recent opinions are somewhat encouraging, they are not of general application and do not bind the FEC in future cases. They are applications of FEC policy to particular facts and thus do not provide legal certainty. The FEC began a rule-making procedure in 2001–2002 to study the application of FECA to the Internet more broadly, but decided in 2002 not to proceed until more time (before the election) and resources were available. A new proceeding is underway at present.

Bloggers, Corporations, Unions, and the Media Exemption

The level of political blogging that occurred in the 2004 election gives rise to several issues. Some bloggers were nothing more than individuals holding forth on the issues or candidates. Others were online magazines or periodicals such as *Salon* or *Slate*. Others were paid by campaigns, such as the Dean presidential campaign or the Thune senatorial campaign in South Dakota, to blog their opinions (Hasen 2005). Some bloggers may have been incorporated for a variety of reasons, such as to take advantage of the liability limitations attached to such forms of organization, and others may have worked for corporations and blogged on company time or on their own time but used corporate or union facilities such as computers, networks, and Internet services. To the extent that such bloggers may have expressly advocated election of certain candidates or used their sites to distribute campaign materials or links, and to the extent the corporate form or corporate/union facilities were used to engage in blogging, some bloggers may have violated campaign finance laws.

But what about ABC, NBC, *The New York Times*, and the like? They are corporations. They may endorse candidates without limits to the amount they spend. How can they do so legally? They can do so because of the "media exemption" contained in FECA (1971–2002), Section 431(9)(B)(i). The media exemption means that these aspects of the campaign finance laws do not apply to bona fide news stories and commentaries distributed through broadcasting stations, newspapers, magazines, or "other periodical publication" because they are excluded from the definition of "expenditures." But what is a periodical publication? A print magazine such as *Time* clearly is one. An online magazine such as *Slate* almost certainly is. But what about Joe's Blog? If owning a printing press makes you a journalist, does creating a blog make you a journalist? And is every blog a "periodical publication?" And if every blogger is entitled to the media exemption, the media exemption arguably swallows the limits on corporate and union campaign activity (Hasen 2005).

Alternatively, if every blogger is *not* entitled to the media exemption, how comfortable are we in letting the government decide who are the media and who are not? Will not the very fact that the government makes such decisions chill the desire of many to speak, or "blog," out? The National Rifle Association (NRA), a corporation, is already broadcasting a daily news and commentary program, *NRA News*, on satellite radio and claiming the benefit of the press exemption (Hasen 2005). Is there any end? Should there be? In such ways, the Internet is already shaking the foundational premises on which much campaign finance regulation is based. We need to be thinking long and hard about how the Internet fits, or does not fit, the paradigm of campaign finance regulation before "reformers" such as McCain, Feingold, Shays, and Meehan lose the First Amendment in their zeal to restructure the rules governing political communication. They may mean well, but without understanding, such zeal can do much more damage than good. Ordinary citizens who find themselves conducting Internet activity that triggers campaign finance reporting requirements, or two or more individuals who find that their joint efforts have made them a "political committee," are far too likely to react by not participating in the democratic process rather than risk legal violations. This cannot be good for the system.

Beyond 2004: The Urge to Regulate Internet Political Speech Grows

As noted above, the FEC is engaging in a "rule-making" procedure necessitated by the fact that Congressman Shays and others obtained a court ruling (*Shays et al. v. FEC* 2004) that Congress did not intend a blanket exclusion of the Internet from certain campaign finance rules, such as the definition of public communications. If this rule-making procedure goes forward, rules governing the Internet along the lines of the draft rules published by the FEC may be adopted. It is possible that the rule making will by short-circuited by legislation introduced in 2005, in the Senate by Harry Reid (D-Nev.) and in the House of Representatives by Jeb Hensarling (R-Tex.), that would statutorily exempt the Internet from the definition of public communications as used in the FECA, thus vindicating the original FEC regulations. However, it is not yet known if this bill will become law. If not, then the current rule-making proceedings may be very important.

The draft FEC rules, which may change even if final rules are adopted, provide among others the following provisions related to political uses of the Internet. First, the draft rules would amend 11 C.F.R. § 100.26 (the FEC rule invalidated in *Shays*) to include within the definition of "general public political advertising" Internet ads that are placed for a fee on the Web sites of others, such as streaming video in a banner ad or pop-up ads. The FEC's notice asks for comment on whether (unpaid) bloggers should be expressly excluded from the definition of "general public political advertising," but its draft text does not do so.

Second, the draft FEC rules propose to change the disclaimer rules, which may apply if over five hundred substantially similar e-mails are sent, to apply only to situations in which e-mail distribution lists are purchased in a "commercial transaction." In other words, private e-mails not sent to bought e-mail address lists would not have to carry disclaimers identifying the source and contain full street or mailing addresses. However, the draft rules would still require disclaimers on e-mail "public communications" sent by political committees, or e-mails that expressly advocate the election or defeat of a candidate or solicit political contributions.

The draft FEC rules would amend the "coordinated communication" rules (under which a communication coordinated with a corporation might be considered an illegal corporate contribution) so that coordinated messages placed only on the company's own Web site would not be considered contributions, and ads placed on Web sites without fees would not be considered contributions, even if the Web site owner was a corporation or labor union that would otherwise be a prohibited source of contributions. This would alleviate the problem of incorporated bloggers or small firms who put up messages on their own Web sites but would prevent paid ad campaigns sponsored by corporations and placed on others' Web sites.

The draft FEC rules also address the scope of the media exemption and seek to make it clear that the media exemption extends to media activity carried out over the Internet, whether in the form of Web site, e-mail, or other form of Internet communication. The proposed rules would clearly extend the media exemption to online-only publications such as Slate.com, Salon.com, or Drudgereport.com, which lack any other print or broadcasting component. However, the FEC invites comment only on whether the exemption should extend to bloggers or online media that do not have an advertising or subscription-based business model, and does not expressly extend the exemption to them. It remains to be seen whether this will change after public comments are received.

Finally, the proposed rules would amend certain rules affecting the definitions of "contribution" and "expenditure" related to uncompensated independent or volunteer activity using the Internet so that individuals involved in such activity and using computers to which they otherwise already have access (as opposed to purchasing new equipment for that purpose) could engage in Internet-related volunteer activity without being deemed to have made contributions or expenditures. Computers owned by others or publicly accessible computers (e.g., in public libraries) could thus be used without making contributions or expenditures under the proposed rules.

However, if the computer is owned by a corporation or labor union, and is used by a member or employee in order to avoid being an illegal contribution or expenditure, the use must still comply with the current rule that such usage is "occasional, isolated, or incidental." This rule applies whether the usage is during working hours, outside working hours, on the premises, or at home. The corporate employee who takes his company laptop home every night to do political Internet work still likely makes an illegal corporate contribution. The FEC currently has a "safe harbor" rule, under which usage of less than one hour per week or four hours per month is always not a contribution, whether at home or at the office, but anything more runs some risk of not being "occasional, isolated, or incidental." The proposed rule does not change the safe harbor provision.

The FEC is now poised, although somewhat reluctantly, to regulate political Internet usage much more in the years to come. The current draft regulations seem relatively benign, but that could change in the future. It is submitted that the tendency of politicians to regulate anything that affects their reelection chances should be curbed rather than allowed to expand. Political usage of the Internet does not conflict with the goals of campaign finance regulation, and much harm to free expression can result from trying to treat the Internet like broadcasting. Internet politics offer the promise of greater individual participation in elections and political communication, and this should not be curbed. As the Supreme Court noted in *Reno v. ACLU* (1997: 870), "Through the use of chat rooms, any person with a phone line can become a town crier with a voice that resonates farther than it could from any soapbox. Through the use of Web pages, mail exploders, and newsgroups, the same individual can become a pamphleteer." What rational democracy would have it otherwise?

References

Aboud, Alexandra M. 2004. "Bush Team Begins Campaign for Re-election: Uses Traditional and Modern Techniques." March 3. Available at usinfo.state.gov/dhr/Archive/2004/Mar/03-457852.html (accessed May 10, 2005).

Bauer, Robert. F. 2004. *More Soft Money Hard Law*. 2nd ed. Washington, DC: Perkins, Coie.

Buckley v. Valeo. 1976. 424 U.S. 1.

Center for Democracy and Technology. 1999. *Square Pegs and Round Holes: Applying Campaign Finance Law to the Internet—Risks to Free Expression and Democratic Values*. Washington, DC: CDT. Available at www.cdt.org (accessed May 10, 2005).

Cornfield, Michael. 2004. *Presidential Campaign Advertising on the Internet.* Washington, DC: Pew Internet & American Life Project and Pew Research Center for the People and the Press. October. Available at www.pewinternet.org/ (accessed May 10, 2005).

———. 2005. *The Internet and Campaign 2004: A Look Back at the Campaigners.* Washington, DC: Pew Internet & American Life Project and Pew Research Center for the People and the Press. March 6. Available at www.pewinternet.org/ (accessed May 10, 2005).

Darr, Carol, and Julie Barko. 2004. *Under the Radar and over the Top: Independently-Produced Political Videos in the 2004 Presidential Election.* Washington, DC: Institute for Politics, Democracy & the Internet. Available at www.ipdi.org (accessed May 10, 2005).

Federal Election Campaign Act of 1971. 1971–2002. 2 U.S.C. §§ 431 et. seq.

Federal Election Commission. 1995. Advisory Opinion 1995-9.

———. 1996. Advisory Opinion 1996-2, *CompuServe.*

———. 1998a. Advisory Opinion 1998-2, Leo Smith.

———. 1998b. General Counsel Report, Matter Under Review 4340.

———. 1999a. Advisory Opinion 1999-7, *Minnesota Secretary of State.*

———. 1999b. Advisory Opinion 1999-24, *Election Zone.*

———. 1999c. Advisory Opinion 1999-25, *Democracy Net.*

———. 1999d. Advisory Opinion 1999-37, *X-PAC.*

———. 2000. Advisory Opinion 2000-16, *Third Millennium.*

———. 2002a. Advisory Opinion 2002-9, *Target Wireless.*

———. 2002b. Federal Election Commission Regulations. 11 C.F.R. §§ 100.01 et. seq.

Gonsalves, Antone. 2004. "Internet Posts Fastest Growth in Political Spending." August 19. Available at www.techweb.com/wire/30000087 (accessed May 8, 2005).

Hasen, Richard L. 2005. "The Ripple Effects of the FEC's Rules on Political Blogging: Why They Will End Up Undermining Limits on Corporation and Union Campaign Finance Activities." *FindLaw's Writ: Legal Commentary.* April 5. Available at writ.news.findlaw.com/commentary/20050405_hasen.html (accessed May 8, 2005).

McCain, John S., Russell D. Feingold, Christopher D. Shays, and Marty Meehan. 2005. *Letter to Federal Election Commission.* On file with Federal Election Commission. Available at www.fec.gov (accessed May 10, 2005).

McConnell v. Federal Election Commission. 2003. 124 S.Ct. 619.

Morris, John B., Jr. 2005. "Campaign Finance Law and the Internet: Problems Raised for Individuals' Online Political Speech." Available at fec.cdt.org/mockup/Problems_Final.pdf (accessed May 17, 2005).

Rainie, Lee, Michael Cornfield, and John Horrigan. 2005. *The Internet and Campaign 2004.* Washington, DC: Pew Internet & American Life Project and Pew Research Center for the People and the Press. March 6. Available at www.pewinternet.org/ (accessed May 10, 2005).

Reno v. American Civil Liberties Union. 1997. 521 U.S. 844.

Shays, et al. v. Federal Election Commission. 2004. 337 F. Supp.2d 28 (D.D.C.), *appeal filed (on other grounds),* No. 04-5352 (D.C. Cir. Sept. 28, 2004).

Trippi, Joe. 2004. *The Revolution Will Not Be Televised: Democracy, the Internet, and the Overthrow of Everything.* New York: Regan.

2

Web Campaigning by U.S. Presidential Primary Candidates in 2000 and 2004

Steven M. Schneider and Kirsten A. Foot

A S THE INTERNET, and in particular the Web, has emerged into the mainstream of American society, candidates have increasingly sought to capitalize on the opportunities offered by this emerging medium to facilitate their campaigning efforts. In 1996, for most candidates, merely being on the Web, or demonstrating knowledge of the Web, was Web campaigning. Most of the contenders for the contested Republican presidential nomination established Web sites during the campaign, including Bob Dole, Steve Forbes, Lamar Alexander, Phil Gramm, Dick Lugar, Arlen Specter, and Pat Buchanan. Alexander announced his candidacy on America Online, even though 88% of the American households did not have access to the Internet and 70% of the households did not even have a computer (Institute for Politics, Democracy & the Internet 2004; LaPointe 1999). By the time of the general election in 1996, both major party and several minor party presidential candidates had Web sites, as did nearly half of the Senate and about 15% of the House candidates (D'Alessio 2000; Kamarck 1999). Bob Dole, the Republican nominee, attempted to plug his campaign site at the end of his closing remarks during the first presidential debate. Unfortunately for Dole, he missed the final "dot" in his attempt to say www.dolekemp96.org, perhaps creating frustration for the mostly inexperienced group of Web users at the time (Besag 2001; Kamarck 1999; LaPointe 1999). In 1998, although the percentage of candidates with Web sites increased significantly (Kamarck 1999), scholarly analyses concluded that most continued to serve as "virtual billboards" or "brochureware," simply replicating in electronic form materials already distributed in print (D'Alessio 2000; Kamarck 1999; LaPointe 1999; Sadow and James 1999).

In general, Web campaigning prior to 2000 was largely seen as a gimmick, or at best something ancillary to "real" campaigning.

This chapter evaluates the development of Web campaigning practices among candidates seeking elected office in the United States, as manifested in the Web sites of those candidates competing in the presidential primary elections of 2000 and 2004. Presidential primary campaigns in the United States provide an excellent laboratory to observe the evolution of Web campaigning. In most primary campaigns, at least one of the two major parties features a spirited competition for the nomination; thus we have more than two candidates competing for a single office, allowing us to hold office constant and have multiple cases. U.S. presidential primary campaigns are organized around a long run-up to multiple electoral events (primaries and caucuses), providing both an opportunity and an incentive for campaign organizations to develop Web sites featuring state-of-the-art practices. At the same time, given the structure of the campaign (e.g., the focus on Iowa and New Hampshire), multiple campaigns are competing on the same playing field at the same time. U.S. presidential primary campaigns also function as a kind of clearinghouse for political professionals seeking to burnish their skills and credentials for the political marketplace in the coming general election featuring gubernatorial, Senate, and House campaigns. For these reasons, it is reasonable to assume that primary election campaign Web sites, especially as viewed in a common time frame just prior to the New Hampshire primary, should function as a particularly good window through which to view the state of Web campaigning at a particular point in time.

In this chapter, we focus on the Web campaigning practices of the campaign organizations associated with candidates for major party nominations for president in both 2000 and 2004. We explore the extent that Web practices adopted by presidential primary campaign organizations evolved from the 2000 to the 2004 elections in the United States. Our analysis of the Web campaigning practices of campaign organizations is based on observations of the campaign Web sites launched by contenders for major party nominations for president in the period just prior to the first primary, New Hampshire, in both years. To observe Web campaigning practices, we systematically evaluated the Web sites produced by campaign organizations that share a common operational perspective. Each of the campaign organizations analyzed shared (at least in theory) a common purpose: to secure one of the two major party nominations for the U.S. presidency for its candidate. Each of the campaign organizations also shared a common environment: all were engaged in competition for the nomination with other candidates, and all developed a presence on the Web as part of their competition. Taking each set of sites produced for a presidential primary election as a case, we analyze comparatively the

2000 and 2004 presidential primary election cases. By holding the office and competitive level constant, and varying the time across two election cycles, we are able to gauge the evolution or development of presidential campaigns' use of the Web. In comparing the extent to which each set of primary campaigns engaged in various Web campaigning practices, we are able to assess the development of presidential campaigns' use of the Web as a strategic resource during this time period. We suggest that developments in Web campaigning by U.S. presidential campaigns be viewed as harbingers of developments in Web campaigning by other federal and state-level campaigns in the United States, and by campaigns in some other elections outside the United States.

Technology, Campaigning, and the Internet Prior to 2000

Our analysis is grounded in a form of theory development called practice-based theorizing. Using this approach, we seek to understand the evolving relationship between the Web and electoral politics by investigating the Web production practices of campaign organizations. Although we take up questions of why campaigns employ Web practices to varying extents, and offer some potential explanations, we do so through an empirically grounded account of the techniques employed in four Web campaigning practices: informing, involving, connecting, and mobilizing. The conceptualizations of these practices, and the techniques that constitute them, provide frameworks that may be useful in examining other dimensions of the relationship between electoral politics and the Web.

Web production practices both reflect existing offline structures and prior practices and result in a particular online structure. These acts of making in turn enable and constrain actions in ways that may shape future iterations of practices, and thus the evolution of structures, both online and offline. More specifically, the Web practices of campaigns (and other political actors) are shaped by existing (offline) structures and cultural resources in that they reflect political strategies and campaign practices developed over decades of electoral activity. They also manifest technology adoption patterns within sociotechnical organizations or networks that may have deep historical or cultural roots. Concurrently, campaigns' Web practices instantiate an emergent and evolving set of norms and create online structures for political action, some of which may be quite innovative (Schneider and Foot 2002). We conceptualize an "online structure" as a (co)produced electronic space, comprising various html pages, features, links, and texts, providing users opportunities to associate and act. On the Web, relations between Web producers, as well as between producers and users, are enacted and mediated through online structures. Furthermore, each online structure enables and constrains the potential for various kinds of political action, both online and offline.

Web Campaigning Practices

Although electoral campaigns vary considerably in their size, funding, status, and internal structure, as a type of organization they share several characteristics. All have an outward orientation, in that their success depends on informing, persuading, and involving others in the promotion of a candidate. All employ some type(s) of information and communication technology in those actions, whether handwritten flyers, radio advertisements, or Internet applications such as the Web. To understand how Web campaigning developed between 2000 and 2004, we engage in a close analysis of the four specific types of practices on presidential primary sites—informing, connecting, involving, and mobilizing—suggesting that each practice involves a distinct type of relationship between campaign organizations and other political actors. Campaign organizations engage in the practice of informing when online structures are created to support the campaign in presenting information to potential "consumers" or "users." This practice invokes the classic transmission models of communication, in which a communicator or producer transmits a message to a receiver or recipient (Lasswell 1948). Informing was the first campaign practice adapted to the Web, as evidenced by scholarly characterizations of campaign sites produced prior to 2000 as "brochure-ware" (Kamarck 1999) and "virtual billboards" (Sadow and James 1999). Providing basic issue information, such as candidate biography, issue statements, and news or press releases, exemplifies engaging in the Web practice of informing.

Campaigns also engage in the practice of involving, in which the organization provides the online structure facilitating a connection between the user and the campaign. Involving as a campaign practice concerns the opportunity to establish interaction between users and campaign organizations; campaigns usually employ this practice to cultivate supporters. Involving practices on the Web include allowing users to sign up for e-mail lists or to contribute funds to the campaign. The relationship between the producing organization and the actor using the site is reminiscent of the swapping between roles of source/encoder and receiver/decoder envisioned by Schramm (Schramm 1954) in his model of communications (McQuail and Windahl 1981).

The Web practice of connecting involves a campaign in the creation of online structure that serves as a bridge between the user of the site and a "third" political actor. In other words, the campaign organization uses its Web presence to "connect" a site user with another political actor, such as a press organization, a political party, a government agency, or even an electoral opponent. In social network theory, these bridges are the ties between nodes of the network (Granovetter 1973); in our analysis, any other political actor, whether offline or online, constitutes a node to which a campaign Web site may be connected, and the online structure facilitating the connection acts as the tie between nodes. The practice of connecting on the Web is most familiarly invoked using the technique of linking, but our conception is considerably broader in that we suggest campaigns create both cognitive and transversal bridges between users and third actors. Transversal connections provide the online structure to facilitate movement through cyberspace, from one place (e.g., a Web page) to another (Saco 2002), while cognitive connections provide only the mental or psychological bridge, relying on users to complete the connection through either online or offline action.

Additionally, some campaigns engage in the practice of mobilizing—providing online structure facilitating a user's efforts to involve another actor in the goals and objectives of the campaign, mostly to recruit other citizens to support the campaign with funds or votes. In this type of practice, the campaign has moved beyond involving itself with the user and beyond making it possible for the user to become connected with a third party actor. Mobilizing practices include structures allowing individuals to send Web pages to friends, print campaign brochures for offline distribution, and obtain names and telephone numbers of potential supporters to be telephoned or e-mailed.

In summary, these four practices can be viewed as supporting a variety of relationships among three political actors: the site visitor, the campaign organization, and "third" actors such as political parties, news organizations, and other citizens. The practice of informing is a one-way relationship in which the campaign organization functions as the sender and the site visitor functions as the receiver; no exchange relationship is invited or intended. The practice of involving is an attempt to establish interactions between the campaign organization and the site visitor. The practice of connecting positions the campaign organization as a facilitator attempting to establish some form of communication between the site visitor and third actors. The practice of mobilizing takes this one step further and positions the campaign organization as a facilitator attempting to establish some form of communication between site visitors and potential supporters of the campaign.

Comparing Web Sites from 2000 and 2004

Our aim in this analysis was to assess the extent to which campaigns engaged in each of the four Web campaigning practices during the competitive 2000 and 2004 U.S. presidential primary elections. Other research of candidates' use of the Web has proposed and employed various typologies cataloging the range and distribution of features on campaign sites (Benoit and Benoit 2000; D'Alessio 2000; Kamarck 1999; Puopolo 2001). In contrast, this chapter seeks to advance the description of campaign Web site elements by exploring ways candidates used the four primary features detailed previously.

This chapter uses a grounded theory method to advance our previous research on campaign organization Web sites (Foot and Schneider 2002; Schneider and Foot 2002; Stromer-Galley et al. 2001). The grounded theory method resulted in a list of twenty-two features associated with various types of online structures used to facilitate political action.[1] The appendix shows the categories and operational definitions of variables used in this analysis. This chapter describes two sets of campaign Web sites: those produced by the official campaign organizations associated with the significant candidates competing in the two major party presidential primary campaigns in 2000 and those produced by campaigns for candidates competing in 2004.[2] In addition to assessing the extent to which individual campaigns have engaged in specific practices, we have also assessed the extent to which the campaign organizations as a group engaged in these practices in each campaign year. We calculate a cross-site index by dividing the sum of features present across sites for a given campaign by the product of the number of features observed and the number of campaign Web sites examined. For example, if every Web site examined for a given campaign was found to have each feature associated with a given practice, the cross-site index would equal 1.0. The cross-site index is most useful in a comparative context, when sets of sites across two or more elections are assessed.

Campaign Organization Web Strategies

Our analysis of campaign Web sites, showing specific features grouped by Web campaigning practice and indicating the level of adoption of the four practices by individual candidates and the combined sets of candidates from 2000 and 2004, is presented in table 2.1. The presence or absence of each of the twenty-two features assessed is indicated for the eight Web sites produced during the 2000 campaign and the nine sites produced during the 2004 campaign. The density of features present across all four practices clearly increased from 2000 to 2004. In addition, the density of features present is most prominent for the practice of informing and least prominent for the practice of mobilizing.

TABLE 2.1
Presence of Features on Campaign Web Sites Produced by Candidates in Competitive U.S. Presidential Primary Elections, 2000 and 2004

Practice	Feature [• indicates feature was present]	2004 Candidates									2000 Candidates							
		Sharpton	Moseley Braun	Lieberman	Kucinich	Kerry	Gephardt	Edwards	Dean	Clark	McCain	Keyes	Hatch	Gore	Forbes	Bush	Bradley	Bauer
Informing	Issues	•	•	•	•	•	•	•	•	•	•	•	•	•	•	•	•	•
	Campaign News	•	•	•	•	•	•	•	•	•	•	•	•	•	•	•	•	•
	Biography		•	•	•	•	•	•	•	•	•	•	•	•	•	•	•	•
	Speeches		•	•	•	•	•	•	•	•	•	•	•	•	•	•		•
	Photos from campaign events	•	•	•	•	•	•	•	•	•							•	
	Campaign ads			•	•	•		•	•	•	•	•	•	•	•	•	•	
Involving	Online donations	•	•	•	•	•	•	•	•	•	•	•	•	•	•	•	•	•
	Volunteer	•	•	•	•	•	•	•	•	•	•	•	•	•	•	•	•	
	Sign up for email	•	•	•	•	•	•	•	•	•	•	•	•	•	•	•	•	
	Campaign calendar of events	•	•	•	•	•	•	•	•	•	•	•	•	•	•	•	•	
	Store		•	•	•	•	•	•	•	•	•	•	•	•	•	•	•	
Connecting	Endorsements	•	•	•	•	•	•	•	•	•	•	•				•	•	•
	Links to government entities					•		•	•	•				•				
	Links to civic and advocacy groups	•	•			•	•	•	•	•	•		•					
	Links to press organizations	•	•		•	•	•	•	•			•	•					
	Comparison to opponents			•			•								•			
	Links to political parties				•						•	•	•					
Mobilizing	Send links from site	•		•	•	•	•	•	•	•	•	•		•	•	•	•	
	E-paraphernalia				•	•	•	•	•	•	•	•		•	•	•	•	
	Offline distribution of campaign materials		•		•	•		•	•	•			•		•	•	•	
	Letters to editors		•		•	•		•									•	
	Action management site or section				•	•					•							

There is limited variance across the seventeen campaign Web sites evaluated in the level of adoption of the four campaign practices. All but one of the campaigns that established the practice of mobilizing (indicated by asterisks in cells in table 2.1) had established the practices of involving and informing as well. In addition, all but one of the campaigns that established the practice of involving had also established the practice of informing. Six of the seventeen campaigns established the practices of informing and involving and were emergent in the practices of connecting and mobilizing (indicated by the open cells in table 2.1). An additional five campaigns had established the practices of informing, involving, and mobilizing and were emergent on the practice of connecting. The remaining six campaigns had idiosyncratic patterns of adoption.

Table 2.2 provides a summary of these data across the four practices and the two campaign years examined. Overall, across all four practices, the level of adoption increased from 2000 to 2004. In the 2000 election, all of the campaigns were at least emergent adopters of the practices of informing, involving, and connecting. This pattern continued in the 2004 campaign. In addition, in 2004 all campaigns were at least emergent adopters of the practice of mobilizing. In sum, across the seventeen Web sites examined in the two campaigns, all but one of the sites had adopted each of the four practices.

A close look at the extent to which each of the practices was emergent or established provides an indication of the development of Web campaigning between the two campaigns. Recall that an emergent practice is indicated by the presence of at least one feature associated with the practice, while an established practice is indicated by the presence of all or all but one feature associated with the practice. The practice of informing was established in all but two of the sites in 2000 and all but one of the sites in 2004, a slight increase. The cross-site index, a measure of the dispersion of features across all sites, increased marginally from .84 to .88, again indicating a slight shift in the extent to which this practice was part of Web campaigning.

The extent of the practice of involving indicates a sharp increase from 2000 to 2004. In 2000, five of the eight sites observed had established the practice of involving, while in 2004 all of the sites had done so. Involving is the only practice that became ubiquitous among presidential campaign primary sites. The growth in the cross-site index from .6 to .98 is an indication not only that the practice is widespread, but also that the implementation of the specific features associated with involving is nearly ubiquitous as well.

There was only a slight increase from 2000 to 2004 in the proportion of campaign organizations engaging in the practice of connecting. In 2000, all of the campaigns were emergent with respect to this practice. One of the campaign sites had established the practice of connecting in 2004, while the remaining eight sites were emergent. The considerable rise of the cross-site index, from

TABLE 2.2
Level of Adoption and Overall Index by Practice,
U.S. Presidential Primary Candidates in Contested Elections, 2000 and 2004

Practice	2000 Campaign Percent (Number) of Campaigns				2004 Campaign Percent (Number) of Campaigns			
	Not Adopted	Emerging	Established	Cross-Site Index	Not Adopted	Emerging	Established	Cross-Site Index
Informing	0% (0)	25% (2)	75% (6)	.84	0% (0)	11% (1)	88% (8)	.88
Involving	0% (0)	12% (1)	87% (7)	.90	0% (0)	0% (0)	100% (9)	.98
Connecting	0% (0)	100% (8)	0% (0)	.31	0% (0)	88% (8)	11% (1)	.56
Mobilizing	12% (1)	75% (6)	12% (1)	.45	0% (0)	55% (5)	44% (4)	.64

.31 to .56, indicates an increase in the number of connecting features deployed, even though the patterns of adoption of this practice changed only marginally.

The most development across the four practices was related to mobilization. In 2000, one site included no features associated with mobilization, and six of the eight sites observed were emergent on this practice; only one campaign had established the practice. In 2004, mobilization was at least emergent on all sites observed, and four of the nine campaigns had established the practice. The cross-site index more than doubled, from .28 to .64, providing further evidence of significant growth of this practice.

Implications of Web Campaigning in 2000 and 2004

Clearly, campaigns' levels of engagement in each of these four practices of Web campaigning increased between the 2000 and 2004 U.S. presidential primary elections. In 2004, a greater proportion of campaigns used each of the four practices examined on campaign sites than campaigns had during the 2000 campaign. The cross-site index, measuring the dispersion of features across campaign sites, increased for each of the four practices. By 2004, all or nearly all of the campaign sites were fully engaged in the practices of informing and involving, and half were engaged in the practice of mobilizing using the Web. The practice of connecting remained emergent for nearly all campaigns: it was established on only one campaign site in 2004. In this concluding section we consider possible reasons why informing and involving became so well established and connecting and mobilizing remained predominantly emergent in 2000 and 2004.

Informing and involving are core practices for campaigns, and campaigns incur minimal cost and risk in adapting them to the Web. Although there was significant variation in the breadth and depth of information provided within each informing feature on campaign sites within each election and across election years, all seventeen campaigns provided at least half of the informing features we looked for, and most provided all of them. The use of metaphors such as "brochure-ware" and "digital yard signs" in the studies of campaign sites in the 1996 and 1998 U.S. elections cited above demonstrate that informing was the first campaign practice adapted to the Web, and it is certainly the easiest from a technical perspective. Public perception of the Web as an information source may also help explain why campaigns engage extensively in informing.

Similarly, the practice of involving is a long-standing campaign strategy, and adapting it to the Web does not require a rethinking of campaign organization or a release of control. The ubiquity of involving by 2004 may also reflect the donor-driven political culture of electoral politics in the United

States. The contributions of volunteers, both financial and in labor, are fundamental to the life of an electoral campaign in the United States. Offering e-mail updates to site visitors allows a campaign to collect e-mail addresses and, often, other kinds of personal information from site visitors. This information enables campaigns to tailor future requests for donations and volunteer labor in ways that might increase their persuasive power. Thus development of Web site features associated with informing may represent investment in the campaign, whether for the present or the future.

Connecting and mobilizing, unlike informing and involving, represent the emergence of more innovative forms of Web campaigning. We suggest that the extent of connecting remained relatively low in 2004 for several reasons, including campaigns' desires to maintain control of site traffic and presentation, concerns about repurposing of materials by opponents or even supporters, legal concerns, and a general aversion on the part of campaigns to risky behavior. Campaigns are likely to desire to maintain site "stickiness" (Lewin 2003) based on the sense that site visitors, once captured by a specific site, are too valuable to "give away" to another site via a link. It is also conceivable that, from a campaign's perspective, connecting to other political actors gives rise to the possibility that the material ultimately viewed by site visitors clicking on the link will not be the same as was intended when the connection was created. The uncertainty created by a link to another political actor's site may be sufficient to discourage its implementation by some campaigns. Also, the practice of connecting through the technique of linking can place campaign organizations on somewhat uncertain legal terrain. Some campaigns may be wary of copyright infringement, either on their own part or on the part of those organizations to which they connect. Connecting to organizations whose tax status prevents political activity could lead to questions and allegations threatening the independence of those organizations. The possibility of providing links to organizations that may be registered as lobbyists for foreign governments is another legal barrier.

A significant reason for campaigns' wariness in regard to both connecting and mobilizing may be that these practices are perceived by some campaign organizations as risky. Campaigns are inherently risk-averse organizations (Selnow 1998). This risk-aversive behavior is particularly applicable to environments in which the opportunities for rewards are perceived as low. Given a lack of perceived rewards, campaigns have been cautious in their experimentation with connecting and mobilizing. The presidential primary campaign of Howard Dean seemed to have changed this calculus. One of the lasting outcomes of the phenomenal success Howard Dean's campaign experienced online in the lead-up to the 2004 primary may be its catalyzing of both connecting and mobilizing. The online component of the Dean campaign was created as a distributed Web presence, involving multiple sites, many of which were produced by people outside of the official campaign. For example, one part of the Dean campaign Web presence, the fordean.org network of sites, included a single site that connected more than five hundred discussion groups, state and local Dean action coordinators, and Dean supporter Web sites. This extensive use of connecting and mobilizing as Web practices set a new standard for Web campaigning that was, in part, emulated by other campaign organizations in the 2004 presidential primary, and that we should anticipate being replicated in future campaign cycles.

In the future, we expect informing, involving, and mobilizing to become ubiquitous practices among all candidates—not only those running for president, but also those running in other federal, state, and local elections. These practices are natural extensions of traditional campaigning onto the Web, and thus more likely to be adopted broadly across campaigns fairly quickly. However, the adoption of connecting is likely to lag behind until candidates become more comfortable with it or develop risk-management strategies.

Appendix: Operational Definitions of Features

Action management site or section. Presence of link to separate site or section of site to allow visitors to manage their interactions with other citizens on behalf of the campaign.

Biography. Page with the personal/political history of the candidate.

Campaign ads. Online reproduction ads distributed also on TV, radio, print, or other offline media.

Campaign calendar of events. Feature that allows visitors to locate upcoming events on the candidate's schedule.

Campaign news. Section containing news on the campaign's progress.

Compare positions to opponent. Comparison of issue positions with positions of individual explicitly identified as the opponent.

Endorsements. Section dedicated to listing the names and positions of those who have endorsed the candidate.

E-paraphernalia. Electronic, downloadable campaign items such as campaign buttons and bumper stickers.

Issues. Separate section of site that discusses the candidate's assessment of what issues are relevant to the race or the candidate's goals pertaining to those issues.

Letters to the editor. Feature that allows visitors to write letters of support for a candidate and distribute them on site.

Links to civic or advocacy groups. Links to sites produced by civic or advocacy groups: national and state-level nonprofit organizations with a civic, voting, or election emphasis or a legislative or policy agenda.

Links to government entities. Links to any site produced by a U.S. federal, state, or local government agency.

Links to political parties. Links to any national, state, or local chapter of a political party.

Links to press organizations. Links to sites produced by organizations that produce news for public consumption, such as newspapers, news programs, or news magazines.

Offline distribution of campaign materials. Explicit effort on the part of the campaign to get site visitors to distribute site materials to media and other outlets in the visitors' communities.

Online donations. Feature that allows visitors to make credit card or other electronic donations online.

Photographs from campaign events. Photographs of campaign events available online.

Send links from site. Feature that allows visitors to send a link about the campaign site, via e-mail, to a friend.

Sign up for e-mail. Feature that allows visitors to subscribe to the campaign listserv.

Speeches. Text of candidate speeches.

Store. Opportunity for visitors to purchase items related to the campaign.

Volunteer. Feature that provides visitors with the information or tools they need to register as a volunteer for the campaign.

Notes

1. Drawing on our initial work as well as research by other scholars assessing candidate Web sites in the 1998 and 2000 elections (Kamarck 2002; Puopolo 2001), we analyzed 1,168 Web sites produced by campaign organizations competing in races for House, Senate, and governor in 2002. Our analyses, based in part on an assessment of the presence or absence of features that we anticipated finding on the campaign Web sites, include examinations of issue position taking on campaign Web sites (Xenos and Foot 2005) and campaign organizations' patterns of linking to other political sites (Foot et al. 2003).

2. "Significant" candidates were those identified as candidates on the Web sites produced by established press organizations (*Washington Post, New York Times,* and CNN). Candidates were considered to be "competing" if more than one significant candidate was included on the ballot. In the 2000 campaign, a total of eight candidates with campaign Web sites were identified: Gary Bauer, Bill Bradley, George W. Bush, Steve Forbes, Al Gore, Orrin Hatch, Alan Keyes, and John McCain. In the 2004 campaign, a total of nine candidates with campaign Web sites were identified: Wesley Clark, Howard Dean, John Edwards, Dick Gephardt, John Kerry, Denis Kucinich, Joe Lieberman, Carol Moseley Braun, and Al Sharpton.

In the 2000 presidential primary, only one campaign (John McCain's) produced more than one site, whereas in 2004, each of the presidential primary campaigns produced at least two sites. For the purpose of comparing campaigns' Web practices between 2000 and 2004, we based this analysis on the "main" Web site produced for each candidate in both 2000 and 2004. We archived the presidential campaign sites regularly between January and March 2000 and January and March 2004, which enabled us to analyze them retrospectively. Versions of the campaign Web sites posted on the Web just prior to the January primary in 2000 and 2004 were evaluated using a coding protocol developed for use on the 2002 campaign sites, as discussed above. Trained research assistants were employed to evaluate the sites, and measures were used that had undergone extensive reliability testing. Research assistants were instructed to evaluate the front page of each site, and all pages linked from the front page and the first level of internal pages, to determine the presence or absence of twenty-two different features on the sites. Each of the twenty-two features included an explicit operational definition that was provided to the site analysts. For example, the feature labeled "issues" was defined as the presence of an identified section of the Web site that presented the candidate's assessment of which issues were relevant for the race or the candidate's goals pertaining to those issues. The feature labeled "offline distribution of online materials" was defined as an explicit effort on the part of the campaign to encourage and enable site visitors to distribute site materials to media and other outlets in the visitors' communities. (See the appendix for the operational definitions of the twenty-two features assessed in this study.)

This study is based on an assumption that campaigns' practices are inscribed in particular Web site features. Our mapping of practices to features is presented in table 2.1. While this mapping of practices to features is neither exhaustive nor mutually exclusive—we certainly recognize that other features could have been identified or associated with the practices under review, and that some of the features could arguably be said to be indicators of practices other than those we have suggested—we believe our mapping to be a useful starting point to assess the extent to which four Web campaign practices were used during the presidential primary campaigns in 2000 and 2004. The number of features present on a Web site that were associated with a particular practice was used as an indicator of the extent to which a specific campaign engaged in that practice. Campaigns whose Web sites had none of the associated features were determined to have not adopted the practice. Campaigns that produced Web sites including any of the associated features but missing two or more were labeled as emergent adopters of the practice. Those campaigns with Web sites including all or all but one of the associated features were determined to be established in their use of the practice.

References

Benoit, William L., and Pam J. Benoit. 2000. "The Virtual Campaign: Presidential Primary Websites in Campaign 2000." *American Communication Journal* 3 (3).

Besag, D. H. 2001. *An Evaluation of the Web Sites of "Third" Political Parties in the United States of America.* Unpublished manuscript, University of Northumbria at Newcastle, Newcastle, England.

D'Alessio, David. 2000. "Adoption of the World Wide Web by American Political Candidates, 1996–1998." *Journal of Broadcasting and Electronic Media* 44 (4): 556–68.

Foot, Kirsten A., and Steven M. Schneider. 2002. "Online Action in Campaign 2000: An Exploratory Analysis of the U.S. Political Web Sphere." *Journal of Broadcasting and Electronic Media* 46 (2): 222–44.

Foot, Kirsten A., Steven M. Schneider, Meghan Dougherty, Michael Xenos, and Elena Larsen. 2003. "Analyzing Linking Practices: Candidate Sites in the 2002 U.S. Electoral Web Sphere." *Journal of Computer-Mediated Communication* 8 (4).

Fuller, Wayne E. 1972. *The American Mail: Enlarger of the Common Life.* Chicago: University of Chicago Press.

Granovetter, Mark S. 1973. Strength of Weak Ties. *American Journal of Sociology* 78: 1360–80.

Institute for Politics, Democracy & the Internet. 2004. "Pioneers in Online Politics: Nonpartisan Political Web Sites in the 2000 Campaign." Washington, DC: Institute for Politics, Democracy & the Internet.

Kamarck, Elaine C. 1999. "Campaigning on the Internet in the Elections of 1998." In *Governance.com: Democracy in the Information Age,"* edited by Elaine C. Kamarck and Joseph S. Nye, 99–123. Washington, DC: Brookings Institution.

———. 2002. "Political Campaigning on the Internet: Business as Usual?" In *Governance.com: Democracy in the Information Age,"* edited by Elaine C. Kamarck and Joseph S. Nye, 99–123. Washington, DC: Brookings Institution.

Klandermans, Bert, Hanspeter Kriesi, and Sidney Tarrow. 1998. *International Social Movement Research. From Structure to Action: Comparing Social Movement across Cultures.* London: JAI.

LaPointe, Mark E. 1999. *Cyber Campaigning for the United States Senate: A Content Analysis of Campaign Web Sites in the 1998 Senate Elections.* Unpublished manuscript, University of Nevada, Reno.

Lasswell, Harold D. 1948. "The Structure and Function of Communication and Society." In *The Communication of Ideas,* edited by Lyman Bryson, 203–248. New York: Harper and Row.

Lewin, James. 2003. "Is Your Site Sticky?" *Computer World,* 18 March.

McQuail, Denis, and Sven Windahl. 1981. *Communication Models for the Study of Mass Communications.* Harlow, England: Longman.

Puopolo, Sonia T. 2001. "The Web and U.S. Senatorial Campaigns 2000." *American Behavioral Scientist* 44 (12): 2030–47.

Saco, Diana. 2002. *Cybering Democracy: Public Space and the Internet.* Thousand Oaks, CA: Sage.

Sadow, Jeffrey D., and Karen James. 1999. "Virtual Billboards? Candidate Web Sites and Campaigning in 1998." Paper presented at the annual meeting of the American Political Science Association, Atlanta.

Schneider, Steven M., and Kirsten A. Foot. 2002. "Online Structure for Political Action: Exploring Presidential Web Sites from the 2000 American Election." *Javnost* (The Public) 9 (2): 43–60.

Schramm, Wilbur. 1954. "How Communication Works." In *The Process and Effects of Mass Communication*, edited by Wilbur Schramm. Urbana: University of Illinois Press.

Selnow, Gary W. 1998. *Electronic Whistle-Stops: The Impact of the Internet on American Politics.* Westport, CT: Praeger.

Stromer-Galley, Jennifer, Kirsten A. Foot, Steven M. Schneider, and Elena Larsen. 2001. "How Citizens Used the Internet in Election 2000." In *Elections in the Age of the Internet: Lessons from the United States*, edited by Stephen Coleman, 26–35. London: Hansard Society.

Xenos, Michael, and Kirsten A. Foot. 2005. "Politics as Usual, or Politics Unusual: Position-Taking and Dialogue on Campaign Web Sites in the 2002 U.S. Elections." *Journal of Communication* 55 (1): 165–89.

3

Webstyles in 2004:
The Gendering of Candidates on
Campaign Web Sites?

Mary Christine Banwart

THE SELF-PRESENTATION of political candidates has been widely studied through their televised advertising (e.g., Kaid and Davidson 1986; Kaid and Johnston 2001; Kaid and Tedesco 1999). However, only recently have political candidates' campaign Web sites received—or warranted—such attention. Since the 1996 election, candidates' use of the Internet as a political tool has risen dramatically, but understandably. A campaign Web site offers the candidate many of the benefits offered by television campaign advertising, but without the exorbitant expenses or time and length restrictions. As with campaign ads, candidates have full control in design and content of their Web sites and thus full control over how they are presented as candidates. Therefore, the study of candidate self-presentation strategies as used on campaign Web sites recognizes an important tool for campaign message dissemination.

In their study of televised campaign ads, Kaid and Davidson (1986) originally identified the method of candidate self-presentation in advertising as *videostyle*. Further research has explored the influence of gender on candidate videostyle, finding differences—and similarities—in the videostyles of female and male candidates (Banwart 2002; Bystrom 1995; Bystrom et al. 2004). Focusing on the 2000 election cycle, Banwart (2002) adapted the videostyle concept to explore the strategies—*webstyles*—of candidate self-presentation in mixed-gender U.S. House, U.S. Senate, and gubernatorial races via campaign Web sites. While later work has compared the webstyles of U.S. Senate and gubernatorial candidates in mixed-gender races from 2000 to 2002 (Bystrom et al. 2004), the research reported in this chapter extends previous webstyle analyses to explore the use of self-presentation strategies in the 2004 U.S. Senate and gubernatorial mixed-gender races.

Webstyle Consideration

Webstyle and Self-Presentation

Webstyle builds on the conceptual approach of videostyle, which was developed to analyze the style of candidate self-presentation in televised spot ads. Videostyle has traditionally analyzed three components of candidate messages: verbal content, nonverbal content, and production characteristics (Kaid and Davidson 1986). Certain elements of videostyle are not available for analysis in the unique medium of the Internet; however, strong correlations between webstyle and videostyle are obvious in each of videostyle's three categories.

For instance, webstyle verbal content contains elements correlated to videostyle's verbal content, such as the candidate's discussion of issue information and of image information, including his or her attributes and characteristics. Webstyle nonverbal content also includes elements contained in videostyle's nonverbal content, such as the candidate's personal appearance, kinesics, and the environment and objects featured around the candidate in photos or audio/video clips. Additionally, graphics and special effects found in videostyle's production category correlate with the graphics and special effects available for use in candidate Web sites, such as computer graphics.

Webstyle also offers a fourth component that is unique: interactive content. In 2000, the Democracy Online Project reported that the top online campaign practice requested by the public was the provision of interactive opportunities for visitors. As Michael Cornfield, director of the project, stated, "When a campaign extends interactive features to the public, it signals a willingness to listen and learn from the people" (Cornfield 2000: 53). Furthermore, research has suggested that high levels of interaction on campaign Web sites increases perceptions of candidate sensitivity, responsiveness, and trustworthiness (Sundar et al. 1998).

Opportunities for candidates to create interactivity with Web site visitors include e-mail and feedback capability with the campaign/candidate, links to other sites that represent who the candidate is and what he or she supports, a campaign directory listing and capability for online communication, download/printing capability for campaign materials, and the capability to volunteer and donate online. Webstyle therefore makes it possible to evaluate the interactive content of a Web site and the ability for the voter to interact directly and immediately in a way that more traditional self-presentation via television (videostyle) cannot offer.

Webstyles in Mixed-Gender Races

Prior work on candidate webstyles in mixed-gender races (Banwart 2002; Bystrom et al. 2004) suggests that, at least in the 2000 and 2002 election cycles, the self-presentation strategies of female and male candidates were generally very similar. In the 2000 cycle (Banwart 2002), female candidates in U.S. Senate, U.S. House, and gubernatorial races did discuss women's issues more than males, used expert authorities to support their campaign or positions, and were more likely to be viewed in formal attire, to be smiling in photos, and to include a form for contributing. Male candidates discussed defense more often than female candidates, used statistics more often, identified their party on their home page more frequently, and were more likely to be in casual attire in their photos.

In their study of the 2000 and 2002 mixed-gender U.S. Senate and gubernatorial races, Bystrom et al. (2004) argued that again, overall, there were more similarities than differences in female and male candidate webstyles. Female and male candidates did present similar issue agendas and were similar in their emphasis of masculine traits, such as aggressiveness, competency, past performance/success, and experience in politics. Notably, male candidates were more likely to issue a negative attack on their opponents, and female candidates were less likely to emphasize feminine traits such as honesty/integrity, trustworthiness, and being a Washington outsider.

In terms of nonverbal content in 2000 and 2002, Bystrom et al. (2004) determined that female and male candidates were presented in formal attire more than casual, sometimes made eye contact with the viewer through their photos, predominantly smiled when pictured, and generally used compact body language. Likewise, female and male candidates used similar types of graphics in the presentation of their Web sites and were also similar in their use of interactive content. For instance, the most common sections on the Web sites included candidate biography, issues, contributions, getting involved, and a campaign directory for both female and male candidates; both included forms for contributing and volunteering; and both frequently included a link to sign up for e-mail updates. Of note, 50% of female candidates and 46% of male candidates included televised ads on their Web sites in 2000 and 2002. One certain difference did emerge, with male candidates including more main menu links from the home page than female candidates.

Overall, Bystrom et al. (2004) concluded that female and male candidates exhibited far more similarities than differences in their webstyles. One explanation offered was that "Web stereotypes," as opposed to gender stereotypes, shaped the self-presentation strategies of female and male candidates in 2000 and 2002 (Bystrom et al. 2004: 141). Thus, instead of employing strategies in response to socially expected norms that would differ for female and male candidates, the candidates used strategies in response to expectations for the medium, hence the similarity in strategies across gender. Unfortunately, the authors noted an overall lack of attention paid to opportunities for interacting with potential voters.

Webstyles in 2004

With campaign Web sites still in an evolutionary process, there is much to be understood about the strategies used to present a viable candidate image through this channel of political communication. Granted, one caution in placing emphasis on the study of campaign Web sites stems from an apparent lack of attention paid to the sites by voters. Surveys indicate, however, not only that there is an overall increase across election cycles in use of the Internet for researching candidate stands on the issues by those seeking news online (Pew 2003; Pew 2004a), but also that visits to candidate Web sites have increased across election cycles (Pew 2004b). Further, with young voters being encouraged to visit candidate Web sites as part of a process for informing themselves before voting (Butler 2004), and some arguing that visiting candidate Web sites is part of a strategy to counteract bias in the mainstream media (Darnay 2004), it is not unrealistic to expect candidates will respond by advancing the design and message development—and thus self-presentation—strategies on their campaign Web sites.

With that advancement, it is worth continued study to determine whether strategies used by female and male candidates remain more fully influenced by expectations of the medium, as opposed to the influence of gender stereotypes previously observed in televised ads (see, e.g., Bystrom et al. 2004). Consequently, can campaign Web sites remain an equalizing medium of communication?

This current chapter advances the webstyle research to the 2004 election cycle, specifically analyzing the official campaign Web sites of candidates running in mixed-gender U.S. Senate and gubernatorial races. It examines whether there were differences in the verbal content of male and female candidate webstyle in the 2004 campaign Web sites; whether there were differences in the nonverbal content of male and female candidate webstyle in the 2004 campaign Web sites; whether there were differences in the production content of male and female candidate webstyle in the 2004 campaign Web sites; and whether there were differences in the interactivity content of male and female candidate webstyle in the 2004 campaign Web sites.

Evaluating Gender and Webstyle in 2004

Candidate Web Sites in 2004

In the 2004 general election, three gubernatorial and ten U.S. Senate races featured both female and male major party candidates. By using a computer program designed to download Web sites, the twenty-six Web sites were collected for analysis.[1] The fundamental evaluation method used in this chapter was first developed as an analysis of videostyle (Kaid and Davidson 1986; Kaid and Johnston 2001) in which verbal, nonverbal, and production content was examined. Bystrom (1995) further expanded videostyle to identify the influence of gender in videostyles. Building on this prior work, this chapter examines verbal Web content, nonverbal Web content, and interactive Web site content.[2]

Verbal Content

In an examination of the differences in the verbal content of female and male candidate campaign Web sites, verbal content variables were examined. Such variables included issues discussed, character traits emphasized, types of appeals, and the negative/positive focus of the candidates.

Issues Discussed

In 2004, the most common issues discussed included education (females 100%; males 92%) and the economy (females 92%; males 100%). Taxes, health care, and job growth also received frequent attention (see table 3.1). Overall, both female (54%) and male candidates (69%) were most likely to list over ten topical issues in their issues section.

TABLE 3.1
Most Frequently Discussed Issues on
Candidate Web Sites by Gender

Female Candidate Sites	*Male Candidate Sites*
Education (100%)	Economy (100%)
Economy (92%)	Education (92%)
Health Care (92%)	Environment (92%)
Taxes (85%)	Taxes (92%)
Job Growth (85%)	Health Care (92%)
Senior Citizen Issues (85%)	Unemployment (85%)
Homeland Security (85%)	Job Growth (85%)

Note: Percentages indicate frequencies within gender.

TABLE 3.2
Number of Issues Discussed by Category

	Female (n=13)		Male (n=13)	
	#	%	#	%
Feminine Issues				
7–9 discussed	1	8%	4	31%
4–6 discussed	11	85%	7	54%
1–3 discussed	1	8%	2	15%
Masculine Issues				
10–12 discussed	4	31%	5	39%
7–9 discussed	5	39%	5	39%
4–6 discussed	3	23%	7	54%
1–3 discussed	0	0%	2	15%

Note: Percentages indicate frequencies within gender.

A total of nine "feminine" issues and twelve "masculine" issues were coded for in the chapter,[3] and in order to examine issue discussion categorically, the actual numbers of feminine and masculine issues discussed were compared (see table 3.2). Both female (85%) and male candidates (54%) were most likely to discuss between four and six feminine issues. However, 69% of female and 77% of male candidates were likely to discuss more than seven masculine issues on their Web sites.

Image Content

The two most common image/character traits (see table 3.3) emphasized by female and male candidates included cooperation with others (females 85%;

TABLE 3.3
Character Traits Emphasized on Candidate Web Sites

Female Candidate Sites	Male Candidate Sites
Cooperation with others (85%)	Cooperation with others (100%)
Honesty/integrity (85%)	Honesty/integrity (100%)
Of the people (85%)	Leadership (92%)
Experience in politics (77%)	Qualified (92%)
Leadership (77%)	Competent (85%)
Past performance (77%)	Experience in politics (85%)
Qualified (77%)	Knowledgeable (85%)
	Of the people (85%)
	Past performance (85%)

Note: Percentages indicate frequencies within gender.

TABLE 3.4
Number of Character Traits Discussed by Category

	Female (n=13)		Male (n=13)	
	#	%	#	%
Feminine Issues				
4–5 discussed	7	54%	6	46%
1–3 discussed	6	46%	7	54%
Masculine Issues				
6–8 discussed	4	31%	6	46%
4–5 discussed	5	39%	6	46%
1–3 discussed	3	23%	0	0%

Note: Percentages indicate frequencies within gender. One Web site (8%) for females and one for males did not include an emphasis on any masculine traits.

males 100%) and honesty/integrity (females 85%; males 100%). In addition, females frequently emphasized that they were "of the people" (85%); males emphasized their leadership (92%) and that they were qualified (92%).

The "feminine" and "masculine" traits[4] were then collapsed into their respective categories and frequency of emphasis was compared (see table 3.4). Of the eight feminine traits for which the sites were coded, female candidates were only slightly more likely to emphasize four or more traits (54%) than were male candidates (46%). However, 69% of female candidates and 92% of male candidates were likely to emphasize over four masculine traits.

Appeal Strategies

Also included in the verbal content analysis of the Web sites was the candidates' use of appeal strategies. Incumbent, challenger, feminine, and masculine appeals were coded on each site. With regard to incumbent and challenger strategies, all female candidate Web sites and 92% of male candidate Web sites employed incumbent strategies, and all female and male Web sites employed challenger strategies. Ninety-two percent of female and 85% of male candidates used feminine strategies, whereas 92% of female and male candidates used masculine strategies.

Attack and Group Appeals

In order to analyze attack appeals, the presence of a negative attack, who issued the attack, and the strategy used in making the attack were coded. Female candidates did include an attack on their opponent in a majority of their sites (67%), and yet only 39% of male candidates included an attack. In these instances, the female (88%) and male candidates (100%) were likely to issue the attacks themselves; in other words, the attack was not credited to a specific source. Female candidates predominantly used a negative association as their strategy for attacking (67%), whereas male candidates were split between using negative association (39%) and guilt by association (39%).

In terms of group appeals, male candidates were more likely to include sections targeting specific voter demographics. For instance, 31% of male candidates included a section for women voters, 46% included a section for veterans, 23% included a section for senior citizen voters, and 39% included a section for young voters. Female candidates were most likely to include a section for veterans (23%), followed by senior citizens (15%), young voters (15%), and women (8%). Of note, 23% of female and 15% of male candidates identified their party affiliation on their home page, and a strong majority of female (85%) and male (100%) candidates identified the office they were seeking on their Web site.

Nonverbal Content

To evaluate whether there were nonverbal differences between female and male candidate Web sites, the nonverbal elements coded for included candidate attire, facial expressions, body language, eye contact, setting of photographs, and who was shown in the photographs. Female candidates were more likely to be pictured in formal attire (100%) on their Web site than casual (54%),[5] as were male candidates (formal attire 100%; casual attire 69%).

With regard to facial expressions, female (92%) and male (92%) candidates were most frequently smiling in their Web site photos. Female candidate Web sites (58%) generally used photos in which the candidate sometimes made eye contact with the viewer, whereas male candidates (62%) almost always made eye contact with the viewer. Overall, male candidate body language was more likely to be compact (54%) and female candidate photos showed a mixture of compact and expansive body language (67%).

When people other than the candidate or opponent were present in photos on the site, men were included in photos on 83% of female candidate sites and women were featured in photos on 75% of female candidate sites. The photos on 85% of male candidate sites featured men, and photos on 85% of their sites included women. Male candidate sites were more likely to include photos of their family (62%), compared to female candidate sites (42%), although children who were not family were in photos on 50% of female candidate sites and on only 39% of male candidate sites. Senior citizens and minorities were also present in the photos on female and male candidate sites, with 67% of female and 54% of male sites posting photos that included seniors and 58% of female and 62% of male sites posting photos that included minorities. The dominant setting of photos for both female (50%) and male (54%) was an outside shot.

Production Content

In regard to the differences in production content used on the Web sites, variables used to analyze this content were use and type of graphics on the home page. All female and male candidate Web sites did include graphics on the home page; candidate-related graphics were most frequently used (females 100%; males 77%), followed by district/state graphics (females 92%; males 77%) and general campaign-related graphics (females 75%; males 85%).

Interactive Content

In order to evaluate whether the interactive content on female and male candidate Web sites differed, variables related to links, downloadable materials, inclusion of videos, and use of forms for contributing, volunteering, and getting involved were analyzed. Thirty-nine percent of female and male candidates included over ten main menu links to different sections of their Web sites. Female (39%) and male candidates (23%) most frequently included eight to ten main menu links, whereas 15% of female and 31% of male candidates included five to seven main menu links. The most common sections to which viewers were linked from the main menu included (see table 3.5): a "get involved" section (females 100%; males 100%), candidate biography (females 92%; males 100%), an issues section (females 100%; males 92%), a contribution section (females 92%; males 100%), news coverage about the candidate (females 92%; males 92%), and a campaign directory (females 85%; males 92%).

Throughout the Web sites, candidates were likely to encourage feedback through a link to e-mail the campaign. Eighty-five percent of female and 100% of male candidates included such a link from their biography section; 92% of female and male candidates included the link from their issues section; 85% of female and 69% of male sites included the link from the location where they discussed upcoming events; 77% of females and 85% of males included a feedback link from their campaign directory section; and 77% of females and 92% of males included a specific feedback link from their "get involved" section.

In the issues section, 54% of female and 31% of male candidates provided links to more detailed information about their issues stands; 31% of females

TABLE 3.5
Interactive Strategies Used by Gender on Candidate Web Sites

Home Page Links	Female (n=13)		Male (n=13)	
	#	%	#	%
Candidate bio section	12	92%	13	100%
New content	8	62%	9	69%
Issue section	13	100%	12	92%
Calendar of events	7	54%	8	62%
Contribution section	12	92%	13	100%
Campaign directory	11	85%	12	92%
Get involved section	13	100%	13	100%
Breaking news	10	77%	8	62%
Link for media	2	15%	3	23%
Links section	2	15%	0	0%
News coverage of candidate	12	92%	12	92%
News coverage of opponent	4	31%	3	23%
Site search engine	1	8%	2	15%

Note: Percentages indicate frequencies within each category.

and 15% of males included additional links to press coverage on those issues; and only 15% of females and 8% of males included links to legislation they sponsored or cosponsored on those issues. Only one female candidate (8%) included a link for a viewer to request the candidate make a special appearance at an event, although 23% of male candidates offered this option through their site. Similarly, few candidates were willing to provide links for contacting a campaign coordinator in a constituent's region (females 8%; males 15%). However, providing information about the traditional methods for contacting a campaign was popular. Most candidates provided information for contacting the campaign such as a mailing address (females 85%; males 100%), a phone number (females 92%; males 100%), a fax number (females 77%; males 77%), and an e-mail address (females 77%; males 77%). Obtaining information about specific individuals was more difficult, as only 23% of female and 39% of male candidates provided a list of key campaign contacts and 8% of female and 39% of male candidates provided names of local campaign coordinators.

For those seeking to get involved in the campaign, 92% of female and 69% of male candidates provided forms on their sites that could be completed and sent either through traditional mail or electronically to the campaign. Not all candidates offered online forms for contributing on their site, with only 77% of female and male sites offering such an option. Few candidates provided talking points to their viewers from their section encouraging involvement (females 15%; males 8%), and 23% of female and 15% of male candidates provided the ability to print or download campaign distribution materials.

The devotion of a special section for linking viewers to external sites—a "links" section—was largely avoided in the Web sites analyzed, with only 23% of female and 15% of male candidate sites offering such a section. When they did offer external links, female candidates predominantly featured links to governmental Web sites (46%), followed by national party sites (31%) and state party sites (31%); male candidates were most likely to offer links to governmental Web sites (15%) and special interest sites (15%).

Candidates also made communication from other outlets available on their Web sites for viewers, specifically, televised spot ad videos (females 92%; males 69%) and their transcripts (females 31%; males 8%), speech transcripts (females 46%; males 31%), and documentation for the content of televised advertising run during the election (females 39%; males 39%). In addition, various items available for downloading were available. Thirty-one percent of female candidates and 23% of male candidates had desktops available to download from their Web sites, and 23% of females and 15% of males had screensavers available for downloading. Bumper sticker images could be downloaded from 23% of both female and male candidate Web sites, while 23% of female and 8% of male candidate sites included campaign press releases that could be downloaded. Almost all female (92%) and male candidates (92%) included a method by which viewers could sign up for e-mail updates.

Gendered Webstyles?

The purpose of this chapter is to analyze systematically female and male webstyles—self-presentation strategies—on 2004 campaign Web sites. The Web sites analyzed were created by candidates running in mixed-gender races at two levels of office—gubernatorial and U.S. Senate. Based on the results of this content analysis, more similarities than differences continue to exist in the presentation of female versus male candidates on campaign Web sites. Such a finding offers continuing indicators that strategies developed for campaign Web sites remain more closely aligned with expectations for the medium as opposed to expectations for the candidate due to gender.

Verbal Content

In 2004, the verbal content of female and male candidate Web sites reflected similar issue agendas and similar image agendas. Notably, education, health care, taxes, and senior citizen issues have remained at the top of female candidate Web site issue agendas for the past three election cycles, whereas education, the environment, taxes, and health care have remained at the top of male candidate Web site issue agendas. Although the top issues discussed by female and male candidates on their Web sites in 2000 and 2002 were predominantly "feminine," it is worth noting that in 2004 a number of "masculine" issues received greater attention. While taxes had been an issue of focus in 2000 and 2002, in 2004 the economy, unemployment, and homeland security were more frequently mentioned.

When the issues are collapsed categorically as "feminine" and "masculine" issues, it does become clear that male candidates were more likely to discuss a broader range of feminine issues than were female candidates. Fully 85% of female candidates discussed from four to six feminine issues, and only one female candidate discussed from seven to nine feminine issues; 31% of male candidates discussed from seven to nine feminine issues and 54% discussed from four to six feminine issues. Even though a greater number of "masculine" issues were included in the coding, 70% of female candidates still discussed over seven "masculine" issues, as did 78% of male candidates. Many of these "masculine" issues could be addressed within the same discussion, as did Inez Tenenbaum (D-S.C.), and thus constitute the seeming emphasis. For instance, within the topic of "Keeping Us Safe," Tenenbaum included homeland security, the war in Iraq, the war on terror, and her "tough stance on crime." Under the topic of "Creating Jobs," Tenenbaum identified issues of concern such as unemployment, international trade, and taxes. Thus, while certain issues may receive greater attention within a given election cycle and ultimately result in a seeming emphasis of "feminine" or "masculine" issue discussion, the context in which the discussion is framed should be included within the analysis to help moderate an inflated categorical effect.

As with the candidates' issue agendas, the image agendas established by the candidates in 2004 were similar. Of note, the trait of cooperating with others definitively increased in emphasis in 2004 compared to the previous two election cycles, as did the trait of honesty. The emphasis on cooperation with others seemed to surpass specific issues or topics, however. For instance, Barbara Mikulski's (D-Md.) Web site offered that she would "work with any President of the United States to defend our country against terrorism," and that she has "worked with local and state fire officials." George Nethercutt (R-Wash.) emphasized that he had "fostered partnerships," had "worked to empower farmers," and had "join[ed] with others to found" an organization to prevent child abuse. While this strategy has been identified as a component of a "feminine style" (Campbell 1989), perhaps the media's attention on the political divisiveness among the major parties encouraged the candidates to emphasize that they can in fact "play well with others" and thus would put the interests of the constituents first.

With regard to the amount of emphasis placed on "feminine" traits—number of traits emphasized—it is worth noting that, although female and male candidates were rather equally divided, incumbent candidates (63%) were more likely to emphasize over four feminine traits, and open-race candidates were more likely to emphasize less than four feminine traits; challenger candidates were as likely to emphasize more than four as to emphasize less than four. Open-race candidates (70%) and challenger candidates (88%) were most likely to emphasize between four and eight masculine traits, whereas incumbent candidates (63%) were most likely to emphasize only four or five masculine traits. Therefore, in mixed-gender races it appears that incumbent candidates emphasize feminine and masculine traits in balance on their Web sites, while perhaps not surprisingly, challenger candidates place more overall emphasis on masculine traits; however, candidates in mixed-gender open races appear to prefer emphasizing the masculine traits of toughness and aggressiveness and offer less attention to an image of trustworthiness and being sensitive.

An analysis of the appeal strategies from 2004 suggests that candidates are using a wide range of strategies on their Web sites and doing so frequently. Almost all sites employed incumbent and challenger strategies, as well as feminine and masculine strategies. The unlimited space and therefore extensive textual development on a campaign Web site allow a candidate to employ a number of approaches that a thirty-second advertisement could never produce effectively. For instance, Barbara Boxer (D-Calif.) could at once employ incumbent, challenger, feminine, and masculine strategies by using a section of the site to emphasize her accomplishments (e.g., securing funding to improve her state's highways), while devoting a section to comparing her opponent's stands to her own (e.g., "Boxer v. Jones"), offering personal experiences to support her candidacy (e.g., she is running to protect the American dream because her mother was an immigrant and she attended public schools), and using statistics to support her stands (e.g., an act she authored reduced dolphin deaths "from over 100,000 per year to less than 2,000 per year"). Web sites therefore offer candidates an opportunity to maximize their appeal to voters, simultaneously drawing from the most effective and appropriate strategies in each category.

Although male candidates have been more likely to issue negative attacks on their Web sites in past election cycles, in 2004 female candidates frequently (67%) included such attacks. This trend is not unexpected as female candidates have recently been more likely to issue attacks against their male opponents in their advertising (Banwart 2002; Bystrom and Kaid 2002).

While several female candidates included specific sections dedicated to their opponents—"Why Alaska Can't Afford Tony Knowles," "Boxer v. Jones," "Isakson Fact Check"—others included their attacks within press-related materials. While such a strategy might lessen attack-related backlash, the use of a specific section not only indicates a willingness to stand one's ground but to be up front and open about any attack; in other words, viewers can expect negative comments when entering that section and can therefore make a choice as to whether or not they expose themselves. The popularity of such sections has increased in the past three years among candidates in mixed-gender races, and undoubtedly they are here to stay. However, with such sections involving less production and drama than attacks in televised ads, candidates concerned with appearing too vicious or shrill might let their Web site do the talking.

In 2004, more candidates used their Web sites to target key voter groups than in past elections; however, still less than half of female and male candidates made use of this targeting feature. The identification of candidate party on the Web site's home page continues to decrease among candidates in mixed-gender races, although most of the candidates are very clear about the office they are seeking. Of those identifying party, female incumbents, male challengers, and open-race candidates were most at ease in identifying their affiliation. Regardless, over three-quarters of female and male candidates elected to not identify themselves, a majority that clearly seeks to appear "unattached," if in name only.

Nonverbal Content

The nonverbal content of the 2004 female and male candidate Web sites was also strikingly similar and repeated consistent trends from previous election cycles. Overall, female and male candidates were pictured in formal attire, smiling, in an outside setting, and most frequently with other men and women in their photos, as well as—and in fewer numbers—senior citizens, children, and minorities. One difference does continue to emerge in nonverbal content, that of family photos. Female candidates, whether on their Web sites or in their televised ads (Bystrom et al. 2004), remain more hesitant than male candidates to remind voters of their family obligations, which can overshadow their emphasis on past experience (Witt, Paget, and Matthews 1995). However, an institutional expectation exists that a family photo be present in the candidate bio section of the Web site (Davis 1999). As over 40% of female candidates have obliged in the past two election cycles, this offers some support for the notion that Web stereotypes can overcome gender stereotypes.

Production Content

In the widespread use of graphics on candidate Web sites, candidate graphics were the most frequently used type. In their banner at the top of the site, candidates frequently featured photo collages of themselves. Doris Haddock (D-N.H.), known as the ninety-year old candidate "Granny D," featured a color head-and-shoulders shot of herself along with a series of blue-shaded photos of her on the campaign trail. In his banner, Kit Bond (R-Mo.) also included five photos of himself from the campaign trail, with well-known political leaders, that blended together at the edges to create a consistent thread. Often the outline or image of the candidate's state was included on the home page, and graphics highlighting attributes for which a state was known were also featured. The most common campaign-related graphic in 2004 was the American flag, certainly strategically included to represent patriotism and remind voters of the candidate's support for the country.

Interactive Content

Web sites for candidates in mixed-gender races have largely institutionalized the inclusion of a "get involved" section, candidate biography section, contribution section, campaign directory section, and issues section. Female and male candidates also frequently encourage feedback from visitors by placing feedback links throughout the Web site. However, female and male candidates are hesitant to provide information for contacting specific individuals in the campaign. While this may seem savvy on the campaign's behalf—campaign staff are not individually deluged with e-mail, and the Web site does not require updating when certain staff leave a campaign—the inability to personalize correspondence or know to whom you should direct a question may suggest inquiries and comments are not welcome or there is no guarantee that the attempt to reach out will actually reach anyone. Either way, although general contact information is available, the interaction does not appear genuinely encouraged with an anonymous design.

As technological advances continue, female and male candidates have become more likely to make volunteering and contributing just a click away. In 2004, a strong majority of female and male candidates included volunteer forms and contribution forms on their Web sites, registering a certain increase from the previous two election cycles (Bystrom et al. 2004). Most certainly in an attempt not to provide their opponent with any additional edge, female and male candidates did not provide many downloadable get-out-the-vote materials—such as talking points, letters to the editor, phone bank information—for their supporters. However, the notion of a candidate store is gathering momentum.

Among those who did provide downloadable materials, such as desktops, screensavers, and bumper sticker images, two also featured cyber "store fronts." For instance, Inez Tenenbaum (D-S.C.) featured "InezWare," which included Web banners, instant messaging icons, and printable signs. Barbara Boxer (D-Calif.) featured "The Boxer Store," which sold T-shirts, "Boxer Victory Packs," "Boxer shorts," a night shirt so "You'll Sleep Better at Night," a cap, bumper stickers, and campaign lapel buttons. Such brand marketing and the ability to reach out to voters in an enterprising manner may very well become an added feature of numerous enterprising candidate Web sites.

The increase in the presence of televised ads posted on campaign Web sites is notable in terms of interactive content. In 2000 and 2002 combined, 50% of female and 46% of male candidates posted at least some televised ads on their Web sites. The increase of 92% and 69% for female and male candidates, respectively, in 2004 is indicative of the cost-effective outlet Web sites offer traditional forms of campaign messages. Although candidates do not yet post debate clips or clips from news conferences, the likelihood we'll see a growing number of video-related materials on candidate Web sites in upcoming elections is strong, and this is yet one more way to reach the all-important voter with a carefully scripted and designed message.

Conclusion

The webstyles of female and male candidates in mixed-gender U.S. Senate and gubernatorial races were generally similar. Candidates continue to use their Web sites to talk about a range of issues, develop a candidate image, use a variety of appeal strategies, and initiate what must be considered "tentative" interaction with visitors. Further, certain issue-related and image-related agendas appear to be establishing consistency across gender and across campaign cycles. While continued attention is undoubtedly warranted, these findings suggest that the strategies employed by candidates on their Web sites remain largely responsive to institutional expectations rather than socialized gender expectations.

Therefore, it is fitting to highly recommend that political candidates embrace the opportunities presented by their campaign Web sites. Not only has Web site technology developed as a tremendously useful tool for organizing volunteers and disseminating unfiltered information, but also it can clearly be developed as an anchor for the campaign in terms of fully and accurately representing who the candidate is as a viable political leader. Further, it can offer uniquely valuable opportunities for interacting with and thus energizing voters. The attention of female candidates in particular to the use of Web sites is important, as these findings suggest a campaign Web site can offer the most ungendered of expectations and requirements of any venue on the campaign trail.

Notes

1. Candidates running for U.S. Senate and gubernatorial seats in mixed-gender races in 2004 included:

Office	Candidate Names		State
Governor:	Ruth Ann Minner (D)	Bill Lee (R)	Delaware
	Claire McCaskill (D)	Matt Blunt (R)	Missouri
	Christine Gregoire (D)	Dino Rossi (R)	Washington
U.S. Senate:	Barbara Boxer (D)	Bill Jones (R)	California
	Barbara Mikulski (D)	E. J. Pipkin (R)	Maryland
	Betty Castor (D)	E. J. Pipkin (R)	Maryland
	Blanche Lincoln (D)	Jim Holt (R)	Arkansas
	Denise Majette (D)	Johnny Isakson (R)	Georgia
	Doris R. Haddock (D)	Judd Gregg (R)	New Hampshire
	Patty Murray (D)	George Nethercutt (R)	Washington
	Inez Tenenbaum (D)	Jim DeMint (R)	South Carolina
	Nancy Farmer (D)	Kit Bond (R)	Missouri
	Lisa Murkowski (R)	Tony Knowles (D)	Alaska

2. Two coders—one female and one male—received two hours of training, conducted by the author, in which the coders became familiar with the coding instrument, the codebook, and the procedures for coding, and coded a political candidate's Web site separate from this sample. Coders were then assigned eight Web sites from the sample (approximately 31% of the total sample) to be coded and analyzed for intercoder reliability. To test for intercoder reliability on the candidate Web sites and appropriateness of the training session and coding instrument, Holsti's formula (North et al. 1963) was used.

$$R = \frac{2(C_{1,2})}{C_1 + C_2}$$

$C_{1,2}$ = # of category assignments both coders agree on
$C_1 + C_2$ = total category assignments made by both coders

The intercoder reliability across all categories was calculated at .88. Coders were then assigned random sets of the Web sites to code.

3. "Feminine" issues were education/schools, health care, senior citizen issues, poverty/homelessness, welfare, environment, drugs/drug abuse, ethics/moral decline, and women's issues. "Masculine" issues were taxes, budget/deficit, unemployment,

cost of living, recession/depression, immigration, economy in general, crime/prison, defense, international issues, and homeland security.

4. "Feminine" traits were honesty/integrity, cooperation with others, Washington outsider, sensitive/understanding, trustworthy. "Masculine" traits were toughness/ strength, past performance, aggressive/fighter, competent, leadership, experience in politics, knowledgeable/intelligent, action-oriented.

5. Betty Castor's Web site included a photo and graphics on the home page that were not available after her Web site was captured, and therefore were unavailable for coding purposes.

References

Banwart, Mary C. 2002. *Videostyle and Webstyle in 2000: Comparing the Gender Differences of Candidate Presentations in Political Advertising and on the Internet.* Doctoral dissertation, University of Oklahoma, Norman.

Butler, Callie E. 2004. "Know Before You Go to Vote." *Sidelines Online.* 7 October. Available at www.mtsusidelines.com/media/paper202/news/2004/10/07/Opinions/ Know-Before.You.Go.To.Vote-744870.shtml.

Bystrom, Dianne G. 1995. *Candidate Gender and the Presentation of Self: The Videostyles of Men and Women in US Senate Campaigns.* Doctoral dissertation, University of Oklahoma, Norman.

Bystrom, Dianne G., Mary Banwart, Lynda Lee Kaid, and Terry A. Robertson. 2004. *Gender and Political Candidate Communication: VideoStyle, WebStyle, and NewsStyle.* New York: Routledge.

Bystrom, Dianne G., and Lynda Lee Kaid. 2002. "Are Women Candidates Transforming Campaign Communication? A Comparison of Advertising Videostyles in the 1990s." In *Women Transforming Congress,* edited by Cindy S. Rosenthal. Norman: University of Oklahoma Press.

Campbell, Karlyn K. 1989. *Man Cannot Speak for Her: A Critical Study of Early Feminist Rhetoric.* Westport, CT: Praeger.

Cornfield, Michael. 2000. *The Civic Web: Online Politics and Democratic Values.* Lanham, MD: Rowman & Littlefield.

Darnay, Keith. 2004. "Election Winners and Losers from an Online Perspective." *Bismarck Tribune,* 7 November, 1E.

Davis, Richard. 1999. *The Web of Politics: The Internet's Impact on the American Political System.* New York: Oxford University Press.

Kaid, Lynda Lee, and Dorothy K. Davidson. 1986. "Elements of Videostyle: Candidate Presentation through Television Advertising." In *New Perspectives on Political Advertising,* edited by Lynda Lee Kaid, Dan Nimmo, and Keith R. Sanders, 184–209. Carbondale: Southern Illinois University Press.

Kaid, Lynda Lee, and Anne Johnston. 2001. *Videostyle in Presidential Campaigns: Style and Content of Televised Political Advertising.* Westport, CT: Praeger/ Greenwood.

Kaid, Lynda Lee, and John C. Tedesco. 1999. "Presidential Candidate Presentation: Videostyle in the 1996 Presidential Spots." In *The Electronic Election*, edited by Lynda Lee Kaid and Dianne Bystrom, 209–222. Mahwah, NJ: Erlbaum.

North, Robert C., Ole Holsti, M. George Zaninovich, and Dina A. Zinnes. 1963. *Content Analysis: A Handbook with Applications for the Study of International Crisis.* Evanston, IL: Northwestern University Press.

Pew Research Center for the People and the Press. 2003. "Political Sites Gain, but Major News Sites Still Dominant: Modest Increase in Internet Use for Campaign 2002." Pew Research Center for the People and the Press. Available at www.people-press.org (accessed January 5, 2003).

———. 2004a. "Far More Voters Believe Election Outcome Matters: But Many Already Wary of Negative Tone." Pew Research Center for the People and the Press. Available at www.people-press.org (accessed March 25, 2004).

———. 2004b. "Voters Liked Campaign 2004, but Too Much 'Mud-Slinging.'" Pew Research Center for the People and the Press. Available at www.people-press.org (accessed November 11, 2004).

Sundar, Shyam S., Kenneth M. Hesser, Sriram Kalyanaraman, and Justin Brown. 1998. "The Effect of Website Interactivity on Political Persuasion." Paper presented at the International Association for Media and Communication Research Convention, Glasgow, Scotland.

Witt, Linda, Karen M. Paget, and Glenna Matthews. 1995. *Running as a Woman: Gender and Power in American Politics.* New York: Free Press.

4

Online Organization:
Dean, Kerry, and Internet Politicking in the 2004 Iowa Caucus

Christopher C. Hull

FORMER VERMONT GOVERNOR HOWARD DEAN took to the stage defeated on January 19, 2004, after having reportedly led into battle the largest Internet army ever assembled in politics. If the "Dean Scream" he let out was any indication, online organization's perceived potential to transform American politics took a lashing in the 2004 Iowa Caucus. But was it really online organization that was defeated on that caucus night, or the hype around Dean's Internet crew?

It is clear the Internet played a crucial role in helping Dean raise upward of $50 million when in the grip of his early e-mentum, and in enabling Senator John Kerry (D-Mass.) to raise $26 million in the two months after his Iowa Caucus victory as well.[1] It's also clear that online fund-raising was already having a significant impact as early as 2000, when Senator John McCain (R-Ariz.) rode an electric surge out of New Hampshire that ultimately shorted out before he could reach the nomination.

But what about Dean's vaunted online organization? Did it desert him in the first battle it faced? This chapter will explore that question empirically, attempting to tease out the various Iowa Caucus impacts of basic Web site visits, campaign e-mail contact, online visitors signing up as supporters, use of the Internet to read articles on a candidate, and Dean's online tool of choice, MeetUp.com.

Old and New Tactics

As we have seen, a number of excellent empirical studies have fixed especially on a "voter's-eye view" of the Iowa Caucus, with a view to discovering what motivates caucus-goers' vote choices (Stone 1982; Stone and Abramowitz 1983; Abramowitz and Stone 1984; Stone, Rapoport, and Abramowitz 1992; Mayer 2000). Advocates of Iowa's role in the primary process have pointed to the importance of "time on task" in person, pressing the flesh, in boosting Iowa outcomes.[2] And, of course, there are the discussions in the main, overarching work on the caucus of how organization tends to dominate caucus outcomes (Winebrenner 1998).

But what about the role of the Internet in retail politics, in Iowa and elsewhere? Did 2004 demonstrate that Iowa's old-style political machinery overpowered the nascent online political revolution? Or did other less-hyped online organizations help other candidates keep up? And more specifically, what role did different Internet tactics play in caucus success, controlling for the old-style organization of rallies, phone banks, and canvassing, as well as press, television ad spending, number of days spent in Iowa, and other factors we would expect to influence caucus outcomes?

What makes the caucus a perfect testing ground for online organization is the weight given old-style grassroots organization in winning it. Based in part on those studies, it is worth applying our "candidate's-eye view" model of the caucus to the further question of how new Internet tactics are affecting its outcomes.

Adding Internet Factors to the Picture

The bulk of the Internet data below comes from an original survey conducted by the author in the month leading up to the 2004 Iowa Caucus. The survey asked active Iowa Republicans and Democrats (former caucus-goers and those voting in the last two primary elections, respectively), regarding each 1996, 2000, and 2004 candidate:

- Whether they had signed up online as a supporter of the candidate
- Whether they had received an e-mail from the candidate
- Whether they had visited the candidate's Web site, and
- Whether they had read an Internet news story or commentary on the candidate

Looking back to 2000 and 1996 is admittedly suspect. On one hand, Internet data from those years—especially 1996—are rarer than hen's teeth, to adopt the

Iowa argot. Finally, asking Republicans about the 2000 cycle in 2004 makes some sense, since it was the latest caucus race for them. The caucus time of 2004 was naturally an important point in the campaign for the Democrats as well.

Finally, I also gathered publicly available MeetUp.com data on supporters in the thirteen Iowa communities where the Web site facilitates local meetings.

The Evolution of Iowa Caucus Internet Activity since 1996

How active an online campaign have caucus candidates run in the past, and how has that evolved through 2004? Before we ask what precise role each Internet tactic had in influencing caucus performance, let us look back at the evolution of Internet activity to the extent we have data on it, and then examine more closely what each 2004 candidate did online.

Comparing the Democrats in 2000 and 2004 and the Republicans in 1996 and 2000 can give us some useful insights. For instance, the average percentage of candidates' supporters signing up online actually declined from 2000 to 2004.

However, this is mainly because in 2000 only two Democratic candidates contested the caucuses, Vice President Al Gore and former U.S. Senator Bill Bradley. In 2004, there were eight major Democratic candidates on the ballot on caucus day, and of those, three did not seriously compete in Iowa, namely General Wesley Clark, Reverend Al Sharpton, and U.S. Senator Joseph Lieberman. Clark's Iowa supporters had a relatively deep reach into his Internet organization, but Sharpton and Lieberman's total lack of effort on that front pulls down the overall number below the 2000 average.

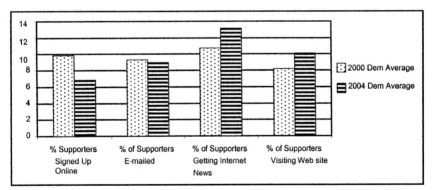

FIGURE 4.1
Supporters' Candidate-Specific Internet Activity: Democratic Averages, 2000 vs. 2004
Note: Average percentages of 2000 and 2004 Democratic candidates' supporters in the survey reporting that they signed up online as the candidate's supporter, received e-mail from the candidate, read Internet news articles on the candidate, and visited the candidate's Web site.

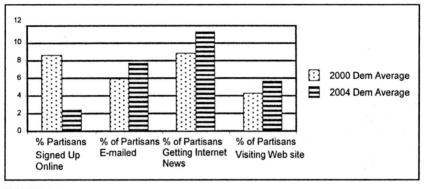

FIGURE 4.2
All Party Activists' Candidate-Specific Internet Activity: Democratic Averages, 2000–2004
Note : Average percentages of those surveyed in 2000 and 2004 reporting that they signed up online as the
candidate's supporter, received e-mail from the candidate, read Internet news articles on the candidate,
and visited the candidate's Web site.

For the same reason, it is remarkable that the percentage of supporters receiving e-mail dropped only slightly, while the percentage of supporters gathering news about their favored candidate online and those visiting their candidate's Web site increased significantly.

Internet activity among all the party activists surveyed shows an even
starker pattern (figure 4.2). Average percentages of all partisans signing up for
each candidate was unsurprisingly much lower in 2004 than it was in 2000.
This makes sense if only because the field is broader, so the pool of partisans
was split eight ways, rather than two.

That said, note the increase in the three non–mutually exclusive Internet
activities. The survey suggests a 31% increase in the average proportion of
party activists getting e-mail from a given candidate, despite the fact that
again several candidates did not actively compete in Iowa. Likewise, there appears to have been a 28% increase in party activists getting news on any given
candidate and a 34% increase in visiting any given candidate's Web site. These
figures suggest important increases in Internet activity among Iowa's Democratic activists.

Of course, the 1996 to 2000 change in Internet activity that took place is far
greater. As noted above, it may be that these differences are due to a simple
lack of recollection, as well as fundamental differences in how candidates used
the Internet between the two cycles. Regardless, the differences are substantial
and worth examining.

The number of candidates works in the opposite direction for the GOP—
since there were six candidates in 2000, as opposed to nine in 1996, we would
expect that signing up online, the mutually exclusive factor, would increase

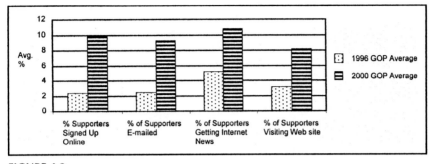

FIGURE 4.3
Increases in Internet Activity 1996–2000, Candidate-Specific Internet Activity Averages
Note: Average percentages of 1996 and 2000 Republican candidates' supporters in the survey reporting that
 they signed up online as the candidate's supporter, received e-mail from the candidate, read Internet news
 articles on the candidate, and visited the candidate's Web site.

proportionately more between the two years. We would also expect that the
lower-tier candidates in 1996 would pull the overall average down. So I will
look at just the top six candidates in 1996 against the candidates in 2000, to
make a more valid comparison.

The increases in supporters' Internet activity were dramatic between 1996
and 2000. The average percentage of supporters who signed up online spiked
318%. The average proportion of supporters saying they were e-mailed by
their favored candidate shot up 280%. Those who reported finding news articles online about the candidate they backed increased 106%, while the average proportion of supporters reporting having visited the candidate's Web site
swelled 162%.

But the 1996–2000 increases in party activist penetration of average
candidate-specific Internet activity are startling. The average percent of all partisans for each given candidate reporting that they signed up online—not the
total percent signing up for any candidate—exploded by 2276%. The average

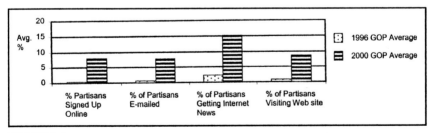

FIGURE 4.4
Increases in Internet Activity 1996–2000, Party Activists' Candidate-Specific Averages
Note: Average percentages of 1996 and 2000 Republican candidates' supporters in the survey reporting that
 they signed up online as the candidate's supporter, received e-mail from the candidate, read Internet news
 articles on the candidate, and visited the candidate's Web site.

percentage of activists saying they had been e-mailed by a given candidate increased 1081%; the average proportion of activists who sought out information on a given candidate online went up 525%; and the average percentage visiting each candidates' Web site rose 885%.

Here is the grain of salt, revisited. We cannot tell how much of the difference between 1996 and 2000 is real, how much is faulty memory, and how much is a transformation in the political role of the Internet between the two cycles. It will be crucial to approach the 1996 data with great care when estimating Internet effects on candidate performance.

Regardless, the hoary, old-school Iowa Caucus, along with the rest of the nation, has sparked a digital revolution. It is difficult to describe the degree to which the last eight years have changed the amount of e-politicking going on in the Hawkeye State.

A Snapshot of 2004 Online Forces

From an Iowa Democrat's point of view, what did things look like online in 2004? First of all, available to the public was the MeetUp.com data showing that Howard Dean was building a massive online organization. On MeetUp, activists for a panoply of causes organize themselves by locality. The Web site allows them to choose from a limited set of official MeetUp locations and set a date and time for anyone interested to gather together and help out. Dean's Web site explicitly drove supporters to MeetUp to organize themselves, pushing power down out of the campaign and into the hands of his supporters at the local level.

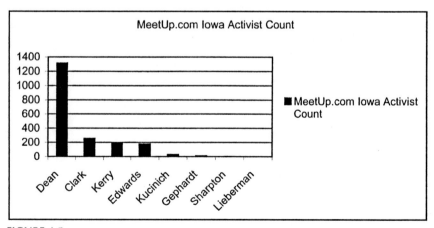

FIGURE 4.5
2004 Democratic Candidates' MeetUp.com Iowa Activist Count

Anyone can go to MeetUp and see the exact number of supporters signed up to be notified of meet-ups on any given cause in a given locality. Using that information, the news media could see that Dean's organization had swelled far beyond that of his competitors. Gathering these data for the thirteen localities in Iowa and adding them together gives one a precise picture of how much MeetUp organization each 2004 candidate had.

Obviously Howard Dean was far out in front of the rest of the 2004 candidates in using MeetUp. But the survey of activist Iowa Democrats found that Dean's Internet activity, while substantial, was not unchallenged. As figure 4.6 demonstrates, both Kerry's and Clark's pools of supporters had levels of Internet activity rivaling Dean's (though not surpassing it).

A higher proportion of Clark's (few) supporters had visited their candidate's Web site (23.5%) than had Dean's supporters (16.3%). The Kerry campaign had e-mailed nearly as many of its supporters (16.5%) as Dean's had (19.8%). Only with respect to signing up online did the Dean camp (16.3%) far outdistance supporters of Clark (11.8%) and Kerry (9.2%).

Clark supporters' Internet savvy, evidenced by their lead in percentage of getting online news on their candidate, was not translated into much impact, because of their tiny numbers. When comparing the Internet activity of all Iowa Democrats surveyed, it becomes clear that Dean was challenged meaningfully

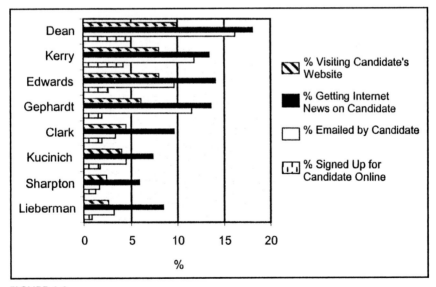

FIGURE 4.6
2004 Candidates' Supporters' Internet Activity
Note : Percentages of 2004 Democratic candidates' supporters in the survey reporting that they signed up online as the candidate's supporter, received e-mail from the candidate, read Internet news articles on the candidate, and visited the candidate's Web site.

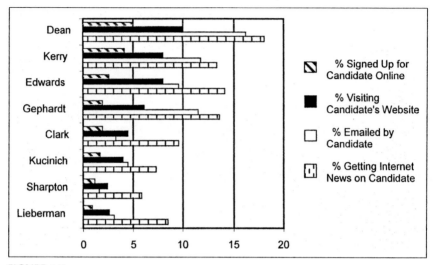

FIGURE 4.7
All 2004 Democratic Activists' Candidate-Specific Internet Activity
Note : Percentages of those surveyed in 2000 and 2004 reporting that they signed up online as the candidate's supporter, received e-mail from the candidate, read Internet news articles on the candidate, and visited the candidate's Web site.

only by Kerry and the dark horse candidate (and second-place Iowa finisher) John Edwards, though Dick Gephardt had a respectable showing.

One in twenty of the activist Iowa Democrats surveyed had signed up as an online supporter of Howard Dean, a pretty remarkable figure—yet John Kerry's online effort was not that far behind, 4.2% to Dean's 5%. Just under one in ten had visited Dean's site (9.9%), but nearly as many had visited Kerry's and Edwards's (8% for each). Dean had more aggressively reached out to Iowa Democrats on e-mail, with 16.2% of those surveyed saying they had been contacted by the Vermonter. That said, Kerry and Gephardt also spammed Iowa, with 11.8% and 11.5% of those surveyed saying those campaigns had been in touch with them via e-mail.

The bottom line is that Dean did not walk away with the Internet organization prize in 2004, contrary to popular belief. It is correct that he won it, but it is entirely incorrect to assume other campaigns were inactive online. Before we estimate what impact online organization had on the 2004 caucus, we would be wise to jettison the misperception that Dean's loss was also a loss for Internet organizing writ large.

And the Hawkeye State saw a lot of Internet organizing in 2004. Nearly one fifth of all Iowa Democrats surveyed had signed up online as a supporter of one candidate or another. The survey sample admittedly was of active partisans— Democrats who had voted frequently in recent elections. However, considering that caucus turnout normally peaks at 10% of registered partisans, and that most Iowa party activists are older and less Internet savvy more generally, 20% of Democrats surveyed is a lot of Iowa Internet activists.

Some Tentative Conclusions about Online Organization

We now have a clearer understanding of how Dean lost Iowa, given a presumably valuable online organization. It appears as though, rather than having unquestioned superiority online, Dean had serious Internet rivals pressing to surpass him. Though his online organization was stronger than that of any other candidate in the field, the differential was not large enough to lift him closer to the front of the pack. Caucus victor John Kerry was busily building quite an online organization himself, for instance.

Howard Dean had every reason to howl on that stage in Iowa. Having raised a bumper crop of cash and amassed an online army, he still went down to defeat. But other candidates, including the eventual nominee, had reason to howl, with glee, since their online organizations served them well.

Dean's defeat notwithstanding, online organizational activity seems to matter, even when tested in an old-style retail politics state such as Iowa. It may be worth more investigation when considering future models of electoral performance.

Notes

This chapter relies on the analysis of an earlier paper by the author, "e-Organization: The Role of Online Organization in the 2004 Iowa Caucus," paper presented to the Midwest Political Science Association, Section 12: Elections and Voting Behavior, Panel 5, Candidate.com: Campaigning on the Internet, April 15, 2004, and American Political Science Association Political Communication Pre-Conference, Chicago, September 1, 2004.

1. Jim VandeHei and Thomas B. Edsall, "Kerry Capitalizing on Party Resources to Fill Coffers," *Washington Post*, March 19, 2004, A6. Note that March 4 was two days after Super Tuesday, not the next day.

2. "Time on task" in the caucus is the term used by David Yepsen of the Des Moines *Register*.

References

Abramowitz, Alan I., and Walter J. Stone. 1984. *Nomination Politics: Party Activists and Presidential Choice*. New York: Praeger.

Abramowitz, Alan I., John McGlennon, Ronald B. Rapoport, and Walter J. Stone. 2001. "Activists in the United States Presidential Nomination Process, 1980–1996." Inter-university Consortium for Political and Social Research 6143, Second ICPSR Version.

Adkins, Randall E., and Andrew J. Dowdle. 2001. "How Important Are Iowa and New Hampshire to Winning Post-reform Presidential Nominations?" *Political Research Quarterly* 54 (2): 431–44.

Bartels, Larry M. 1989. "After Iowa: Momentum in Presidential Primaries." In *The Iowa Caucuses and the Presidential Nominating Process*, edited by Peverill Squire, 121–48. Boulder, CO: Westview.

Brady, Henry E. 1989. "Is Iowa News?" In *The Iowa Caucuses and the Presidential Nominating Process*, edited by Peverill Squire, 89–119. Boulder, CO: Westview.

Hull, Christopher C. 2004 "Explaining Vote Share in the 2004 Iowa Caucus: A Candidate's-Eye-View Empirical Assessment." Paper Presented at the annual meeting of the American Political Science Association, Chicago, September.

Mayer, William G. 1996. "Forecasting Presidential Nominations." In *Pursuit of the White House—How We Choose Our Presidential Nominees*, edited by William G. Mayer. Chatham, NJ: Chatham House.

———, ed. 2000. *In Pursuit of the White House 2000—How We Choose Our Presidential Nominees*. New York: Chatham House.

———. 2000. "Caucuses: How They Work, What Difference They Make." In *In Pursuit of the White House 2000—How We Choose Our Presidential Nominees*, edited by William G. Mayer. New York: Chatham House.

Squire, Peverill. 1989. "Iowa and the Nomination Process." In *The Iowa Caucuses and the Presidential Nominating Process*, edited by Peverill Squire, 1–18. Boulder, CO: Westview.

Stone, Walter J. 1982. "Party, Ideology, and the Lure of Victory: Iowa Activists in the 1980 Prenomination Campaign." *Western Political Quarterly* 35: 527–38.

Stone, Walter J., and Alan I. Abramowitz. 1983. "Winning May Not Be Everything but It's More Than We Thought: Presidential Party Activists in 1980." *American Political Science Review* (77): 945-56.

Stone, Walter J., Ronald B. Rapoport, and Alan I. Abramowitz. 1989. "How Representative Are the Iowa Caucuses?" In *The Iowa Caucuses and the Presidential Nominating Process*, edited by Peverill Squire, 19–49. Boulder, CO: Westview.

———. 1992. "Candidate Support in Presidential Nomination Campaigns: The Case of Iowa in 1984." *Journal of Politics* 54: 1074–97.

Stone, Walter J., and Ronald B. Rapoport. 1994. "Candidate Perception among Nomination Activists: A New Look at the Moderation Hypothesis." *Journal of Politics* 56: 1034–52.

Winebrenner, Hugh. 1998. *The Iowa Caucuses: The Making of a Media Event.* 2nd ed. Ames: Iowa State University Press.

Wolfinger, Raymond E. 1989. "Who Is Vulnerable to the Iowa Caucuses?" In *The Iowa Caucuses and the Presidential Nominating Process*, edited by Peverill Squire, 163–68. Boulder, CO: Westview Press.

5

Political Web Wars:
The Use of the Internet for
Political Advertising

Lynda Lee Kaid

POLITICAL TELEVISION ADVERTISING REMAINS the most important method through which candidates for major political offices in the United States communicate their messages directly to potential voters. Despite the stated attempts of new campaign finance regulations to restrict the availability of soft money for political party advertising and to reduce negative advertising by imposing more explicit restrictions on sponsorship identification (BCRA 2002; Jones and Kaid 2004; Kaid and Jones 2004), the 2004 presidential campaign recorded the highest expenditures on political advertising and the most negative advertising environment in the history of presidential politics (Kaid and Dimitrova 2005). However, the 2004 campaign was also the battleground for a new and vigorous type of political advertising.

In 2004, political advertising on the Internet became a significant contributor to the weaponry of candidates, parties, independent groups, and even individual voters. "Web-based commercials, used sparingly in 2000, have come of age this year. Web ads combine the precision of direct marketing, the dramatic power of video, and the cost-effectiveness and 'viral' distribution potential of the Internet," proclaims the American Museum of the Moving Image on its Web module, *The Living Room Candidate* (2004). This chapter describes the "political Web wars" of 2004, discussing how the candidates and their supporters and detractors used the Internet to communicate directly with voters.

The Web Environment for Political Advertising

Over the past decade, as Internet availability and use have grown, participants in all aspects of the political process have recognized the Web's potential as a new channel for information and persuasion. As the 2004 presidential campaign evolved into its general election phase in the spring of 2004, there were approximately 729 million Internet users around the world (Global Reach 2004), and the Nielsen//NetRatings (2004a) announced that 75% of Americans, or 204.3 million, had home Web access.

Women are a larger proportion of Web surfers; 82% of women, or 34.6 million, between the ages of thirty-five and fifty-four have Internet access, and 77% of them surf the Web. However, 80% of men in the thirty-five to fifty-four age group have access to the Internet, and 76% of them are Web users (Cornfield 2004). Web use is also skewed toward the young, educated, and professional population (Manatt 2004).

Those who follow politics online are more politically active than the general public (Nielsen//NetRatings 2004b). According to the Institute for Politics, Democracy & the Internet Project (McCullagh 2004), Internet users who follow politics online are much more likely to attend political meetings, contact politicians directly, attend a politician's speech or rally, and be active members of an advocacy group.

Early political success stories on Web campaigning were achieved by John McCain in the 2000 primaries (Tomlinson 2003) and in 2004 by the Howard Dean campaign, which used the online approach to raise money, distribute information, and organize supporters, serving as a model for the other campaigns going into the 2004 general election (Cone 2004).

Spending on Web Advertising

While no one suggests that spending for Web advertising approached the $547 million spent on television advertising in the 2004 presidential campaigns, presidential candidates began spending modest amounts on Web advertising during the primary/caucus phase. In the last quarter of 2003, all political candidates in the United States spent $300,000 in online advertising (Kaye 2004). Edwards, Kerry, Kucinich, and Dean all used some Web advertising in the primaries. Independent groups also used Web advertising to get their messages out. Still, all together, these early efforts were characterized as "chump change" in February 2004 (Kaye 2004).

However, as the campaign neared its end in November, the media tracking group TNS documented that $4.2 million had been spent in online advertising in the presidential campaign (TNS 2004). The Bush campaign spent most of its online ad money on local media sites, such as a Fox TV station site in Portland, Oregon; Kerry spent heavily on the *San Francisco Chronicle* Web site ("Bush, Kerry Don't Spend" 2004). Overall comparisons indicate that the Kerry campaign spent three times as much on Internet advertising ($1.3 million) as the Bush campaign ($449,000). The Republican National Committee ($487,000) balanced part of this differential by outspending the Democratic National Committee ($257,000). The independent 527 groups (tax-exempt political organizations that are not regulated by the Federal Election Commission in regard to contribution limits) also invested in online advertising, but at a lesser rate than in their television campaign advertising (Cornfield 2004).

Advantages and Disadvantages of Web Advertising

Political practitioners and scholars have identified a number of reasons for the increased use of Web advertising in political campaigns. Some of these advantages are straightforward and easy to understand. First, of course, Web ads are much cheaper to produce and to distribute than their television counterparts (American Museum of the Moving Image 2004; "Cyber Ads" 2004; Faler 2004a). A second and related advantage is the speed of response and rebuttal made possible by direct access to the Web for immediate distribution (Schroeder 2004). In the 1980s and 1990s, electronic video production allowed candidates and their media producers to shorten dramatically the time required to design, develop, and produce responses to the ads of their opponents. Assuming a campaign could buy or redirect its television time, overnight or twenty-four-hour responses became possible. Today, Web production techniques, combined with inexpensive digital video technologies and free distribution capability, have made that process almost instantaneous.

A third advantage to Web political advertising is that, like television ads, ads placed on commercial sites can reach a broad spectrum of citizens who are not necessarily seeking out political information. Leon Festinger's original conceptualization of the selective exposure theory predicted that individuals will not seek out information that is counter to their beliefs (Bryant and Zillman 1985; Festinger 1957).

One of the earliest documented advantages of television advertising in political campaigns was that television tended to overcome prior predispositions and resulted in almost universal exposure to a candidate's message, regardless of the leanings of individual audience members (Atkin et al. 1973; Kaid 2004; Surlin and Gordon 1976). Although Web advertising on broad general access sites may reach large numbers of individuals, the Web (or the mouse, like the television's remote control) has given some of this access decision back to the receiver. Nonetheless, some observers suggest that Web viewers are focused on their screens and often "simply cannot avoid the advertising that is presented to them," and studies show that 60% admit they would be "likely to notice an online ad for a candidate" (Schroeder 2004: 38).

The Pew Internet & American Life Project also reports that Internet political news use seems to overcome some aspects of selective exposure. In fact, 31% of news users say they get political information from sites that do not have a particular viewpoint; and while 26% say they go to sites that share their viewpoints, 21% go to sites that "challenge their point of view" (Rainie, Cornfield, and Horrigan 2005: 9).

Like television ads, Web advertising may reap credibility benefits from the surrounding programming or content environment in which the advertising appears. On this score, Web advertising has benefited from the ability to place the ads on the news sites of television stations and newspapers. Thus the candidate or group ads often run side by side with news stories, lending credibility and blurring the distinctions between news and advertising (Krebs 2004). Although many news sites, as well as Google and Yahoo!, accept political advertising, their policies about placement and content vary widely, but there can be no doubt that the online news environment is a desirable one for the placement of political ads. The Web sites of major news organizations (such as CNN or *The New York Times*), commercial news sites (such as AOL or Yahoo!), and local news organizations are the most heavily used online political sources (Rainie, Cornfield, and Horrigan 2005).

Another advantage of political advertising on the Web is that it can be targeted to segmented publics. While television time buying has certainly become a sophisticated endeavor with the capability of targeting segments of the population who watch particular programming, targeting on the Web can happen at the individual level. For instance, Google has the ability to sell political advertising that can be targeted to specific individuals based on key word searches at a very cost-effective rate between one cent and one dollar per click, depending on the popularity of the keyword used in the targeting (Chisolm 2004). *The Washington Post*, on whose Web site Kerry advertised frequently, can target ads to those with particular gender, income, and other selective personal characteristics (Faler 2004c). Thus a young mother with children who accesses a particular page on a site might see an ad about the candidate's education positions, while an older male businessman reading the same page might see an ad about the candidate's position on taxes or the economy.

This individualized capability of the Web also empowers individuals to become more involved in its content (Baker 2002), while at the same time providing anonymity. An individual can access sites or promulgate his/her own advertising messages without subjecting himself/herself to the insecurities and stereotypical responses that might result from knowledge of the individual's gender, race, or physical characteristics (Kang 2000; Poster 1997). Some Web ads have incorporated interactive elements and humor to get users more involved (American Museum of the Moving Image 2004). For example, a Web ad from the Republican National Committee (RNC) was formulated as a movie trailer that spoofed Kerry's alliance with world leaders. The video was called "John Kerry, International Man of Mystery." The RNC also produced online attack games such as "Kerryopoly," which parodied Kerry's wealthy lifestyle.

Advertising on the Web also gives candidates, parties, and interest groups a great deal of control over their messages ("Cyber Ads" 2004). For instance, broadcast advertising is subject to very limited time requirements (usually, specific spot lengths of thirty or sixty seconds or short programs of five minutes). Little variation from the prescribed times is possible when buying broadcast time. Related to the control factor is that, in 2004 at least, the Federal Election Commission (FEC) did not consider Web advertising subject to most of the requirements of the BCRA legislation. Particularly significant was that Web advertising did not have to provide the "stand by your ad" disclaimer made personally by the candidate and required for television commercials (McCullagh 2004). Some observers believe that this exemption from the disclaimer rule has resulted in Web ads that have less accountability, and thus in more harsh, negative attacks (McCullagh 2004).

Under the FEC's original interpretation of BCRA, independent advocacy groups were also allowed to "coordinate" their online advertising with candidates without the ads counting as "contributions" to the campaign (McCullagh 2004). Most other types of political advertising cannot be coordinated. This provides another potential type of control for the candidates who value the ability to ensure that ads, whether from the campaign or supporting groups, have consistent messages.

Lest Web political advertising seems like the best of all possible worlds for a political campaign, disadvantages should be remembered. First, of course, the audience for Web ads does not yet reach the levels that television can deliver at any one time. Access issues remain. Thus, the avenues for participation on the Internet are not open to everyone, due to technological and availability issues (Cho et al. 2003; Hindman 2000; Papacharissa 2002).

Another consideration is that the freedoms and controls available on the Internet are a two-edged sword for candidates. On the one hand, the control over a candidate's own ads and even the potential for some coordination with independent groups is all very well and good. On the other hand, opponents have that same control. The low cost of production and time availability on the Internet is another mixed blessing. It costs the opponent and his/her supporters

very little to produce humorous and ridicule-laden Web ads that would be un-
thinkable on the high-dollar television medium.

Types of Political Advertising on the Web

Political advertising on the Internet can take many forms and provide many avenues for a candidate to inform and persuade voters. An examination of the
ways in which Web advertising was used in the 2004 campaign suggests five different categories: (1) use of Web sites as political advertisements, (2) message
ads originally disseminated in other communication channels that are transferred to the Web as a channel for additional distribution, (3) fund-raising appeals, (4) original message ads formulated specifically for the Web environment, and (5) blog ads.

Web Sites as Political Advertising

As noted in the *Handbook of Political Communication Research*, "in many
ways Web sites can be viewed as a form of political advertising" (Kaid 2004:
180). The use of a campaign Web site as an advertisement for the candidate
was one of the first ways in which political advertising took root on the Web.
Internet sites function as forms of political advertising in that they host limitless and detailed information about the campaign, and they serve as vehicles
for access to more traditional advertising materials. In fact, candidates often
develop more than one Web site, assigning particular promotional materials
to Web sites that are targeted to appeal to voters with certain issue concerns or
particular demographic characteristics.

Ads Transferred from Other Channels for Distribution on the Web

Candidates, groups, and parties often load their political ads (from print or
broadcast channels) onto the Web to provide additional distribution and enhance the repeat audience for the ads. Ads for which expensive airtime has
been purchased are limited in their "play" time by budgetary constraints and
by time available for purchase on television and cable stations. The same ad
loaded on the Web site of a candidate, party, or third-person individual or
group can provide many more "plays" at little incremental cost. Kerry, Bush,
their national parties, and many advocacy groups took advantage of this type
of Web advertising during the 2004 campaign. Not only could a user see a
given Kerry ad on the candidate's official Web site, but the user could also see
the evolution, usually chronological, of several ads over the course of the cam-

paign. In addition, the user could see the broad spectrum of Kerry's advertising appeals all at once. Thus a user viewing an ad in which Kerry attacked Bush had the chance to see positive ads about John Kerry and messages about his own positions on issues over which he attacked Bush. Such balance and incrementalism is rarely possible with television ads, where time buys are spread out over different times and outlets and never run in tandem in ways that allow messages to build upon each other.

Original broadcast ads can also be presented on the Web in enhanced or revised versions. For instance, Bush's ad "Weapons," a May 2004 television release, was converted to "Weapons, Interactive Version" online and included interactive features only available in the Web version (American Museum of the Moving Image 2004).

Web Ads Developed for Fund-Raising

Web ads developed for fund-raising purposes took many forms in 2004. Some were simple banner ads or images that became animated when the user clicked on them to see the message. For instance, one Kerry ad provided an animated video of George Bush portrayed as a king sitting on a pile of money with an audio that proclaimed "Bush is attacking John Kerry with a mountain of money. Your $25 gift now can put us over the top and help topple Bush" (Faler 2004c). Kerry used this form of Web advertising very effectively, raising $80 million from online fund-raising efforts that included advertising (Cone 2004).

Original Web Ads

These ads were not aired or distributed through traditional channels of communication. The Bush campaign is credited with the beginning salvo for this direct distribution of advertising messages on the Web during the 2004 general election. The Bush campaign's first negative attack on Kerry was via Web advertising when he launched an attack questioning Kerry's commitment to eliminating special interest influence by pointing out that Kerry had received more special interest money than any other senator and characterizing the senator as "brought to you by the special interests. Millions from executives at HMOs, telecoms, drug companies . . . " ("Campaigns Turn" 2004; "Cyber Ads" 2004). The ad was sent by e-mail to 6 million Bush supporters. The RNC paid for Web ads on over one thousand Web sites criticizing Kerry's voting record against Iraq reconstruction efforts. Kerry fought back with negative Web ads such as "My First Bush Budget," in which Bush is shown as a schoolchild with budget (math) issues/incompetencies (McCullagh 2004).

In late May, the *Washington Post* estimated that Kerry had placed ads on approximately one hundred sites, including newspaper Web sites such as those of *USA Today* and the *Los Angeles Times*, as well as the sites of liberal publications such as the *Onion* and *Billboard* and the Google search engine itself (Faler 2004c). The Kerry campaign used original Web advertising in a number of ways, but it was particularly effective with postdebate banner advertising campaigns designed to promote Kerry as the winner of the debates. A concentrated campaign was developed for this by the Kerry online advertising team, which posted banner ads on more than fifty sites in the hours immediately after each debate (Witt 2004). These ads generated 130 million ad "impressions" (each ad appearance on a computer screen), and internal campaign research showed that 55% of those who saw the postdebate banner ad after the final debate thought that Kerry had won, compared to 49% of those who had not seen the ads (Bassik 2004–2005).

The Democratic National Convention (DNC), RNC, and independent groups such as America Coming Together and MoveOn also sponsored Web-only ads. Nielsen//NetRatings determined that, in the first four months of 2004, the RNC netted 550 million impressions; Kerry's campaign achieved over 60 million impressions during this same time period (Faler 2004c).

Independent groups often used Web ads that were outrageous and humorous spoofs. MoveOn.org sponsored a contest for which individuals submitted their own ads designed to portray "Bush in 30 Seconds." These ads were then posted on a Web site and made available for viewing. Of course, the group did not broadcast all of the ads on broadcast outlets, but they served as a location for individuals to vent their anger and to depict Bush in many outrageous ways.

Overall, the production of Web advertising by independent groups received some of the greatest attention in 2004. Many were humorous and satirical, others hard-hitting and ruthless in their candidate attacks. The Institute for Politics, Democracy & the Internet at George Washington University analyzed a large group of these Web videos sponsored by independent groups. A well-known example that should be applauded for its equal demeaning of Bush and Kerry was JibJab.com's "This Land Is Your Land." Not only did this one video produce phenomenal Web-site traffic—perhaps as many as 50 million people saw it—but it received additional magnification through replays on numerous news and talk shows (Darr and Barko 2004).

The George Washington University analysis (Darr and Barko 2004) reports the results of Google, Yahoo!, and other search engine queries used to locate many of these independent Web videos and to assess the links to them, and the report lists many of the independent videos produced in 2004 and the goals of their creators. A search of Google and Yahoo! links to many of the independent video sources on October 17, 2004, and analyses of news coverage of the videos concluded that, although many of the more well-known sites such as JibJab got a lot of coverage by the mainstream media, many of these Web ads "fly under the radar" and received little press scrutiny (Darr and Barko 2004: 19).

Many of these independent Web ads involved disturbing distortions hidden below a humorous presentation. The Institute for Politics, Democracy & the Internet has warned: "But along with reinvigorated civic participation there exists a darker and angrier side of the political Internet. . . . Some independently produced Web videos . . . used heavily edited photographs or film from campaign events or news stories, juxtapositioning sometimes graphic and emotional images with news headlines, voting records and political statements. Others were animated, a format that some video producers feel increases the humor of their work and makes their scathing commentary all the more lethal" (Darr and Barko 2004: 5).

Blog Ads

The concept of using political advertisements on blogs was developed in the early 2004 campaign and was used frequently by state and lower-level candidates because of cost savings. Blog ads provided chances to detail lots of issue info and negative info on the opponent (Faler 2004b). Kerry used blog ads for this purpose, as well. Because many blogs have clearly identifiable political leanings, political Web ads can be targeted to left and right by choosing blogs that have definite political leanings: on the left, DailyKos.com, TalkingPointsMemo.com, and Atrios.blogspot.com; on the right, InstaPundit.com, RightWingNews.com, and LittleGreenFootballs.com/weblog/ (Faler 2004b). Many candidates outside the presidential race also adopted blog advertising. For instance, Erskine Bowles used blog ads extensively in his unsuccessful North Carolina Senate race—they were less costly and "reached a more interested audience" (Cone 2004: 4).

Content of Web Political Advertising

The dominant content of the Kerry and DNC ads was fund-raising. This was the main purpose of 78% of the Kerry and DNC Web ads. On the other hand, 57% of the Bush and RNC Web ads stressed recruitment and persuasion (Cornfield 2004). Some examples from the Web ads were provided by the Pew Internet & American Life Project (Cornfield 2004).

Despite the publicity and media coverage about negativity in political Web advertising, a content analysis of 137 political Web ads in 2004 conducted by the Pew Internet & American Life Project found that 56% of the ads were either entirely positive or were comparative with a positive ending about the sponsoring candidate (Cornfield 2004).

Thus, although many of the best-known and best-publicized Web ads were extremely negative in their content, the Bush Web ads were the only ones that were in absolute numbers more negative than positive. However, even the Bush campaign relied most heavily on a positive message, a Laura Bush banner ad that linked to a two-and-a-half-minute video of Laura Bush touting the president's commitment to education by saying he has "been a friend to parents and teachers who want to improve American schools." This ad, which ran on sites targeted at women, such as the *Parents* magazine site (Parents.com), played on about fifty similar sites and on newspaper sites in swing states (Faler 2004c). This one ad accounted for 98% of the Bush Web ad placements (Cornfield 2004).

Effects of Web Political Advertising

How effective are such Web ads in shaping voter attitudes toward the candidates? Very little research tests this issue directly for the 2004 campaign. Earlier research established that political information seeking about politics on the Internet is determined by political trust, the amount of Internet usage, and interest in politics (Kaye and Johnson 2002). Other researchers have provided evidence that mere exposure to the simplest form of Web advertising, a candidate's Web site, can enhance liking for the candidate (Hansen 2000; Hansen and Benoit 2002) and decrease political cynicism (Tedesco and Kaid 2000).

Nisbet and Scheufele (2004) found that exposure to Internet political information in combination with discussions about politics had a positive effect on political efficacy and political participation levels but not on increased factual political knowledge. Internet effects alone were modest.

Studies of the 2000 presidential election campaign advertising messages found that the channel of message communication affected voter responses to candidates. For instance, citizens who watched ads on the Web were likely to vote for Gore while those who viewed the same ads on TV favored Bush (Kaid 2002). Channel of ad exposure also seemed to affect a range of related information-seeking and voting behaviors (Kaid 2003). These studies seem to indicate that even the mere transfer of the same ad from broadcast to Internet can result in a different effect on viewers. This seems to be especially true when citizens also have the chance to engage in other information seeking and acquisition while in the Internet viewing environment.

Kaid and Postelnicu (2005) compared the effects of 2004 presidential ads viewed on television with the same ads when viewed on the Internet with opportunities for additional information seeking about the ads. They found that John Kerry's ads were more likely to enhance his image and learning scores when exposure occurred on the Web with access to additional information sources. Television, however, was more likely to reduce feelings of political cynicism and alienation for young voters.

Channel differences also were apparent for evaluations of the political ads themselves. Interestingly, young voters who saw the Web spots evaluated the spots as significantly less credible than did those who saw the same ads on television (Kaid and Postelnicu 2005). However, voters exposed to the Internet version of the ads found the exposure was very helpful in "sorting out the truth and falsity of the ads."

Another reason for considering the effectiveness of Web advertising is its viral nature. Political Web ads are often passed from one user to another through e-mail and messaging. When the Kerry campaign responded to Bush's initial Web ad attacking his special interests connections, Kerry's response was e-mailed to 300,000 backers who were asked to forward the ad on to ten of their friends ("Cyber Ads" 2004).

Political strategists are suggesting that using humor and satire for Web political advertising is a particularly effective way of taking advantage of the viral nature of Web advertising. Humorous videos, jokes, and banner and interactive ads have been very effective in the Web attack war (Ragusa 2004), and they are quickly sent on to friends and coworkers. In 2004, at least 32 million Web users reported that they exchanged jokes and humorous materials with friends and associates (Rainie, Cornfield, and Horrigan 2005).

News Coverage and Evaluation of Advertising on the Web

During the 2004 campaign, the Web played another interesting role in the spread and evaluation of presidential campaign advertising. Adwatches, which were initially adopted by the mainstream media as a way to evaluate the candidate's televised advertising and to expose and police misrepresentations and deceptive practices (Kaid et al. 1993), were taken up in 2004 by the Internet as well. However, on the Web the adwatches were not the exclusive purview of the mainstream media. Other actors in the political communication process became players in the adwatch game, providing analyses of competing ad claims. Suddenly, adwatches could be found on the sites of independent organizations and educational institutions. For example, Factcheck.org provided such analyses from the Annenberg Public Policy Center and did checks of facts and details of the advertising claims of candidates, parties, and groups. Not to be outdone, parties engaged in their own adwatches. GOP.com critiqued Kerry ads and the ads of independent groups attacking Bush.

Web ads themselves, because they were novel, attracted the attention of journalists both on and off the Web. Adwatches about Web ads in the mainstream also magnified the effects of the ads through free news media coverage (Faler 2004a).

Ads were also frequently discussed on blogs that used their built-in audiences for commentary and rants about ads. A good example was the damage done in the primaries to Howard Dean by analysis of attack ads against Dean by the 527 group Americans for Jobs & Healthcare. The group effectively used its ad analyses to score against Dean (see www.bopnews.com/archives/000288.html.). In yet another adwatch variation, the RNC used an online "fact log," or "flog," to analyze, rebut, and neutralize attacks made against Bush (Anderson 2004).

The Future of Web Ad Wars

This description of the role of political Web advertising in the 2004 campaigns suggests an increasingly important role for political advertising as it takes on new forms and is in turn formed by new technologies. However, the freewheeling days of unregulated Internet advertising in politics may come to an end soon. The FEC may curtail the unrestricted nature of Web political advertising (McCullagh 2005).

As mentioned earlier, the FEC's original interpretation meant that Web political advertising itself, and the prohibition against coordination with parties or candidates, was not subject to the BCRA provisions. A U.S. district judge ruled in September 2004 that Internet advertising should not be exempt from the regulation of political campaigning and should thus be subject to the same regulation as political campaigning in other communication venues as set out specifically in the BCRA: "any broadcast, cable or satellite communication, newspaper, magazine, outdoor advertising facility, mass mailing or telephone bank to the general public, or any other form of general public political advertising."

However, the FEC's initial attempt at rule making for this situation, a draft proposal released in March 2005, did not take a very definite stand against the Internet advertising and did not satisfy many who object to the exclusion of the Web from other campaign regulations. More extensive regulations may be forthcoming before the next major election cycle, or Congress may be persuaded to adopt new and stringent regulations to curb Web advertising or to make it subject to the same rules as other forms of electioneering.

Regardless of whether or how the legal and regulatory environment for political Web advertising is altered, this new form of candidate promotion is sure to thrive and develop into an important force in American elections. Research has already targeted local television news Web sites as high-traffic sites where candidate advertising can thrive (Felchner 2004). Political Web advertising will likely become a greater force in state and local campaigns, where money is often less plentiful and where candidates must fight desperately to compete for media coverage in crowded and demanding political landscapes. While $4.2 million in Internet advertising was spent in the 2004 presidential race, another $3 million went to pay for Internet advertising in federal, state, and local races below the presidential level (TNS 2004). Spending on Internet advertising will likely increase in future elections.

New technologies also seem certain to breed even newer innovative distribution of campaign messages. One already foreseeable trend is the use of "podcasts" (downloadable audio files). Politicians are already looking to their use in future campaigns. With an iPod, the user can subscribe to various podcasts (news and promotional materials), which are added to their iPods via syncing. These podcasts have been labeled as "the latest and greatest of all propaganda tools" ("Mobile Phone" 2005: 1). Using cell phones as well, the podcast technology can deliver immediate messages and also provide immediate feedback by asking users to call or text their reactions back to the source, much like the television show "American Idol" ("Mobile Phone" 2005). The RNC is already engaged in this technology, and 2008 presidential hopeful John Edwards began releasing podcasts in March to keep his candidacy in the limelight—or at least within earshot.

Note

The author would like to thank Monica Postelnicu for her assistance with this research. An earlier version was presented at the Eastern Communication Association Conference, Pittsburgh, April 2005.

References

American Museum of the Moving Image. 2004. *The Living Room Candidate: The Desktop Candidate: Web Ads, 2004.* Available at livingroomcandidate.movingimage.us (accessed April 17, 2005).

Anderson, Nick. 2004. "Web Ads Alter Political Landscape." April 11. Available at www.twincities.com/mid/twincities/news/nation/8398525.htm (accessed April 15, 2004).

Atkin, Charles K., Lawrence Bowen, Oguz B. Nayman, and Kenneth G. Sheinkopf. 1973. "Quality Versus Quantity in Televised Political Ads." *Public Opinion Quarterly* 37: 209–224.

Baker, C. Edwin. 2002. *Media, Markets and Democracy*. New York: Cambridge University Press.

Bassik, Michael. 2004–2005. "What John Kerry Taught Us about Online Advertising." *Campaigns & Elections* (December/January): 79.

Bipartisan Campaign Reform Act of 2002 (BCRA). 2002. 116 Stat. 81.

Bryant, Jennings P., and Dolf H. Zillman. 1985. *Selective Exposure to Communication*. Hillsdale, NJ: Erlbaum.

"Bush, Kerry Don't Spend Much on Online Ads." 2004. *BizReport*. October 4. Available at www.bizreport.com/news/8110/ (accessed April 25, 2004).

"Campaigns Turn to Internet for Political Ads." 2004. *CNN.com*. May 17. Available at www.cnn.com/2004/ALLPPOLITICS/05/17/how.works/ (accessed May 9, 2005).

Chisolm, Kari. 2004. *Politics and Technology: Advertising*. October 13. Available at www .politicsandtechnology.com/advertising/ (accessed April 25, 2005).

Cho, Jaeho, Gil de Zuniga Homero, Hernando Rohas, and Dhavan V. Shah. 2003. "Beyond Access: The Digital Divide and Internet Use and Gratifications." *IT & Society* 1 (4): 46–72.

Cone, Edward. 2004. "Web Politics 2.0." *Ziff-Davis CIO Insight*. November 5. Available at www.cioinsight.com/print_article2/0,2553,a=138678,00.asp (accessed April 25, 2005).

Cornfield, Michael. 2004. "Presidential Campaign Advertising on the Internet." Pew Internet & American Life Project. November 5. Available at www.pewinternet.org/pdfs/PIP_Pres_Online_Ads_Report.pdf (accessed April 27, 2005).

"Cyber Ads." 2004. *Online NewsHour*. Public Broadcasting Service. February 20. Available at www.pbs.org/newshour/bb/media/jan-june04/cyberads_02-30.html (accessed April 25, 2005).

Darr, Carol C., and Julie Barko. 2004. *Under the Radar and Over the Top: Online Political Videos in the 2004 Election*. Washington, DC: Institute for Politics, Democracy & the Internet, George Washington University Graduate School of Political Management.

Faler, Brian. 2004a. "Presidential Ad War Hits the Web." *Washington Post*, March 15: A10.

———. 2004b. "Some Candidates Turn to Blogs to Place Ads." *Washington Post*, April 18: A05.

———. 2004c. "Presidential Ad War Escalates Online." *Washington Post*, May 31. Available at www.bizreport.com/news/7303/ (accessed April 25, 2005).

Felchner, Morgan Elizabeth. 2004. "The Internet Advertising Dilemma." *Campaigns & Elections* (September): 24.

Festinger, Leon. 1957. *A Theory of Cognitive Dissonance*. Stanford, CA: Stanford University Press.

Global Reach. 2004. *Global Internet Statistics*. March. Available at global-reach.biz/globstats/refs.php3 (June 30, 2004).

Hansen, Glenn J. 2000. "Internet Presidential Campaigning: The Influences of Candidate Internet Sites on the 2000 Election." Paper presented at the annual meeting of the National Communication Association, Seattle, November.

Hansen, Glenn J., and William L. Benoit. 2002. "Presidential Campaigning on the Web: The Influence of Candidate World Wide Web sites in the 2000 General Election."

Paper presented at the annual meeting of the National Communication Association, New Orleans, November.

Hindman, Douglas Blanks. 2000. "The Rural–Urban Digital Divide." *Journalism & Mass Communication Quarterly* 77 (3): 549–60.

Jones, Clifford A., and Lynda Lee Kaid. 2004. "After McConnell: Candidate Advertising and Campaign Reform." *Political Communication Report* 14: 1–4. Available at www.ou.edu/policomm/1402_2004_spring/Jones_kaid.htm.

Kaid, Lynda Lee. 2002. "Political Advertising and Information Seeking: Comparing Exposure via Traditional and Internet Channels." *Journal of Advertising* 31 (1): 27–35.

———. 2003. "Effects of Political Information in the 2000 Presidential Campaign: Comparing Traditional Television and Internet Exposure." *American Behavioral Scientist* 46: 677–91.

———. 2004. "Political Advertising." In *The Handbook of Political Communication Research*, edited by Lynda Lee Kaid, 155–202. Mahwah, NJ: Erlbaum.

———. 2005. "Videostyle in the 2004 Political Advertising." In *The 2004 Presidential Campaign: A Communication Perspective*, edited by R. E. Denton Jr. Lanham, MD: Rowman & Littlefield.

Kaid, Lynda Lee, and Daniela V. Dimitrova. 2005. "The Television Advertising Battleground in the 2004 Presidential Election." *Journalism Studies* 6 (3): 165–75.

Kaid, Lynda Lee, Robert H. Gobetz, Jane Garner, Chris M. Leland, and David Scott. 1993. "Television News and Presidential Campaigns: The Legitimization of Television Political Advertising." *Social Science Quarterly* 74 (2): 274–85.

Kaid, Lynda Lee, and Clifford A. Jones. 2004. "The New U.S. Campaign Regulations and Political Advertising." *Journal of Political Marketing* 3 (4): 105–110.

Kaid, Lynda Lee, and Monica Postelnicu. 2005. "Political Advertising and Responses of Young Voters: Comparison of Traditional Television and Internet Messages." *American Behavioral Scientist* 49: 265–78.

Kang, Jerry. 2000. "Cyber-Race." *Harvard Law Review* 113: 1130–1208.

Kaye, Kate. 2004. "Estimated Political Web Ad Expenditures Reveal That Money Is Still Miniscule." *Media Daily News.* February 20. Available at www.aef.com/06/news/data/2004/2516 (April 15, 2005).

Kaye, Barbara K., and Thomas J. Johnson. 2002. "Online and in the Know: Uses and Gratifications of the Web for Political Information." *Journal of Broadcasting and Electronic Media* 46 (1): 54–72.

Krebs, Brian. 2004. "News Web Sites Court Campaign Ads." *Washington Post,* July 13. Available at www.washingtonpost.com/wp-dyn/articles/A26819-2004Jul30.html (May 9, 2005).

Manatt, Dan. 2004. "Web Video." *Campaigns & Elections* (June): 36.

McCullagh, Declan. 2004. "Liberal Net Rules Spawn Political Attack Ads." *CNET News.Com.* May 6. Available at www.news.com.com (accessed April 25, 2005).

———. 2005. "Political Web Ads May Be Curtailed." *CNET News.Com.* February 15. Available at www.news.com.com (accessed April 24, 2005).

"Mobile Phone Podcasts Likely Frontrunners in US Politics." 2005. Wireless IQ. April 25. Available at www.wirelessiq.info.com (accessed April 25, 2005).

Nisbet, Matthew C., and Dietram A. Scheufele. 2004. "Political Talk as a Catalyst for Online Citizenship." *Journalism & Mass Communication Quarterly* (81) 4: 877–96.

Nielsen//NetRatings. 2004a. "Three out of Four Americans Have Access to the Internet, According to Nielsen//NetRatings." March 12. Available at www.nielsen-netratings .com/pr/pr_040318.pdf (accessed April 27, 2005).

———. 2004b. "Web Surfers Are More Politically Active Than General Population, According to Nielsen//NetRatings." March 19. Available at www.nielsen-netratings .com/pr/pr_040319.pdf (accessed May 11, 2005).

Papacharissa, Zizi. 2002. "The Virtual Sphere." *New Media & Society* 4 (1): 9–27.

Poster, Mark. 1997. "Cyberdemocracy: Internet and the Public Sphere." In *Internet Culture*, edited by David Porter, 201–217. New York: Routledge.

Ragusa, Rand. 2004. "Using Humor in Online Attack Ads." *Campaigns & Elections* (August): 32.

Rainie, Lee, Michael Cornfield, and John Horrigan. 2005. *The Internet and Campaign 2004.* Washington, DC: Pew Internet & American Life Project.

Schroeder, Chris. 2004. "Online Ads." *Campaigns & Elections* (February): 38.

Surlin, Stuart H., and Thomas F. Gordon. 1976. "Selective Exposure and Retention of Political Advertising." *Journal of Advertising* 5:32–44.

Tedesco, John C., and Lynda Lee Kaid. 2000. "Candidate Web Sites and Voter Effects: Investigating Uses and Gratifications." Paper presented at the annual meeting of the National Communication Association, Seattle, November.

TNS Media Intelligence/CMR. 2004. "U.S. Political Advertising Spending Reaches $1.45 billion." December 20. Available at www.tnsmicmr.com/news/2004/110104 .html (accessed November 1, 2005).

Tomlinson, James E. 2003. "Organizing an Online Campaign: The Legacy of McCain2000.com." In *The Millennium Election: Communication in the 2000 Campaign*, edited by Lynda Lee Kaid, John C. Tedesco, Dianne G. Bystrom, and Mitchell S. McKinney, 179–188. Lanham, MD: Rowman & Littlefield.

Witt, Louise. 2004. "Kerry Campaign Dumps Cash on Web." *Wired News.* October 15. Available at www.wired.com (accessed May 9, 2005).

6

Self-Referential and Opponent-Based Framing: Candidate E-Mail Strategies in Campaign 2004

Andrew Paul Williams

POLITICAL CAMPAIGNS INCREASINGLY RELY on electronic media in their attempts to communicate with citizens. Essentially, since the 1996 U.S. election cycle, the Internet has become a requisite part of modern campaigning. Candidates are now expected to have a substantive Web presence that includes multimedia, interactive features, and mechanisms for user feedback.

An integral part of this online presence includes the regular distribution of candidate e-mail messages. This chapter provides an overview of the candidate campaign e-mail messages from incumbent Republican President George W. Bush and Democratic challenger Senator John F. Kerry during the 2004 general election cycle and specifically focuses on self-referential and opponent-based issue and attribute framing.

Candidate Use of E-Mail Messages

During the past couple of election cycles, it appears that more candidates are offering subscriptions to e-mail messages. Generally, candidate Web site users are offered an option to sign up to receive e-mail messages from a given candidate. These e-mail messages range in distribution and content from calendar items to endorsements, to polling data, and to occasional issue coverage. Trammell and Williams (2004: 111) note that "each e-mail message is often written as if it is coming straight from the candidate," but in fact the majority of campaign e-mails are from campaign managers, members of the staff, and other political actors.

The limited research on e-mail messaging from political campaigns indicates that candidates have not taken advantage of multiple technological advantages that such controlled electronic messaging offers. For example, in a study of legislators' use of e-mail messaging, Sheffer (2003) found that political actors also believe that e-mail messaging was not being used to its potential, but respondents indicated they were uncertain as to how to effectively integrate e-mail messages with their overall communication strategies.

Trammell and Williams (2004) analyzed the use of campaign e-mail messaging during the 2002 gubernatorial race between incumbent Governor Jeb Bush and his challenger, Bill McBride. Through the use of a quantitative content analysis, their study indicated that these candidates' e-mail message strategies were often incongruent with those of their other Internet communication efforts, such as their Web sites and online news releases. Additionally, they found that both campaigns made little use of multimedia or the interactive capabilities of e-mail messaging (Trammell and Williams 2004).

Stromer-Galley (2003) asserts that e-mail messages may have the effect of encouraging information-seeking for users and increase the dissemination of information on the part of campaigns. An example of such effective message dissemination is provided by Ciolli (2000) of Long Island's *Newsday*, who described Arizona Senator John McCain's efforts during the 2000 election cycle as an example of a candidate who strategically used e-mails as a way of communicating with more than forty-three thousand supporters.

During the 2002 midterm elections, the excessive use of e-mail distribution in California caused a negative backlash in which many citizens criticized this tactic as sending out "spam" and questioned both the legal and ethical issues of mass e-mailing (Nissenbaum 2002). However, in a report from the Center for Information & Research on Civic Learning & Engagement (CIRCLE), Levine (2004) noted that results from a survey of young Americans indicated that respondents enjoyed receiving e-mail updates from campaigns on a weekly basis.

Garret LoPorto, a viral marketing campaign consultant, asserts that, "the Internet makes possible a whole new level of viral marketing—putting out targeted messages to a group of like-minded individuals and creating a snowball effect—for political campaigns" (Richards 2004).

Similarly, Cornfield (2004) notes that e-mails are easily forwarded, have immediate source credibility by information provided in the subject and sender columns, and can be an integral part of viral marketing strategies. He also argues that candidates will find the strategic use of e-mail more effective than Web sites for Internet campaigning, because e-mail messages deliver information directly to the user, while Web sites must be sought out.

An example of the positive impact of the use of e-mail as part of an integrated Internet campaign comes from the United Kingdom in 2000, when the

Tories began to aggressively send e-mail messages and use their party Web site to target votes for key seats in Parliament (Watson 2005).

From a political public relations perspective, campaign e-mails can be viewed as potent forms of controlled media. These tools allow candidates the opportunity to communicate in detail about the campaign and to frame both themselves and their opponents in terms of issues and attributes.

Framing

Framing theory suggests that the media have the power to select not only what is covered, but also how items are covered. One of the clearest, and most frequently cited, definitions of news framing explains that a media frame is the "central organizing idea for news content that supplies a context and suggests what the issue is using selection, emphasis, exclusion, and elaboration" (Tankard et al. 1991: 3). Similarly, Gamson and Modigliani (1987: 143) define framing as "the central organizing idea or story line that provides meaning to an unfolding strip of events."

Entman (1993: 52) states that, "to frame is to select some aspects of a perceived reality and make them more salient in a communicating text." According to Gitlin (1980), "media frames" organize the world both for journalists who report it and, to some important degree, for consumers who rely on their reports.

In an analysis of framing European politics in both print and broadcast news, Semetko and Valkenburg (2000) identified five frames that categorized the media content: (1) conflict frames; (2) human-interest frames; (3) economic consequences frames; (4) morality frames; and (5) responsibility frames.

Scholars have been warned to avoid what is considered to be *ad hoc* framing: "By *ad hoc* we mean frames defined specifically for a single study with little or no attention to explicating either their basic characteristics or theoretical context" (McCombs and Ghanem 2003: 79). However, it is acknowledged that, in building on prior research about the use of frames in political news, scholars may benefit by evaluating both issue-specific and generic frames (De Vreese 1999; De Vreese, Jochen, and Semetko 2001). Essentially, examining emergent frames allows for a more nuanced analysis of given content.

However, Williams and Kaid (2006) argue that all frames—generic or issue-specific—are not created equal, and that media frames can be classified as being either substantive or ambiguous. They characterize the ambiguous news frame as vague and indistinct, providing little to no context or clear data. Conversely, the researchers assert that a substantive news frame is detailed and informative, offering context and detailed information.

Williams and Kaid's argument for the emergence of these two new classifications of media frames differs from Iyengar's classification of frames (1991) as being episodic or thematic. Both categories of frames help to describe how the frames actually function within the context of the given content. While this classification of episodic and thematic frames deals with how the coverage is framed—and distinguishes frames as being either specific or broad in nature—Williams and Kaid's ambiguous and substantive frames (2005) consider what is framed, and distinguish frames as being either essentially empty or full in nature.

This chapter evaluates both candidates' self-referential and opponent-based issue and attribute framing in their official campaign e-mail messages. Self-referential framing affords the candidates the opportunity to shape their messages favorably on issue and attribute content. Opponent-based framing allows the candidates to juxtapose their issue stances and attributes against those of their competitors, emphasizing positive aspects about themselves and the negative about their challengers.

Candidate Use of E-Mail Messages in U.S. Campaign 2004

The chapter reports an evaluation of campaign e-mail messages from the hot phase of the 2004 U.S. presidential race. The e-mails evaluated in this chapter were official messages sent to the author/subscriber from Labor Day weekend through Election Day. The author subscribed on the campaigns' Web sites to receive e-mail messages from both campaigns in Florida, a battleground state.

In total, only seventy-eight campaign e-mail messages from the U.S. presidential candidates were evaluated. The campaign of incumbent Republican President George W. Bush sent twenty-eight messages, whereas challenger Democrat John F. Kerry's camp sent fifty. The small number of e-mail messages evaluated in this chapter represents the universe of such campaign communications, and thus is what an average citizen who subscribed to receive e-mails would have been exposed to from the candidates.

Despite the small number of e-mail messages sent by the Bush and Kerry campaigns, the 2004 race proved to be one in which the Internet advanced the viability of candidates. This was particularly evident with the tremendous success of Howard Dean during the primary phase of the campaign. Dean's ability to raise unprecedented money (largely from small donations) and to mobilize voters proved to be a turning point in electronic campaigning.

Kim and Margolis (2004) argued that campaign e-mails from both political parties and candidates played an important role during the primary phase of election 2004. "Such was surely the case with the Dean campaign, where e-mobilization efforts and e-mailing played vital roles in his early success in the 2004 contest" (Drinkard and Lawrence 2003).

"E-mails also advanced during the 2004 campaign cycle with better graphics and presentation, more interactive features, and a stronger tie to the online campaign. Messages often featured direct links to new website features such as updates on fund-raising efforts or new online advertisements" (Wiese and Gronbeck 2005: 359).

Williams (2005) argued that the most significant advance in Web campaigning in 2004 was the use of viral marketing tactics, including the spreading of e-mail messages:

> This spreading of information by average citizens relates to the issue of whether users are being pushed or pulled to given content. Pulled media is user driven and for individuals (usually supporters) who seek the site or content because of their own interests or predispositions. Pushed media reaches individuals (even nonsupporters) who did not seek out the site or content but are instead drawn to it unwittingly. (Williams 2005: 251)

Williams and Trammell (2005) note that not only did e-mail messages provided political campaigns in the 2004 U.S. presidential race ways to communicate with strategic publics, but also that e-mail messages are powerful political marketing tools that can be forwarded to myriad nonsubscribers. Therefore, candidate e-mails can be considered a form of viral marketing that can overcome selective exposure similar to televised political advertisements. The researchers noted that Bush's e-mail messages typically provided a mechanism to forward them to five other individuals simultaneously, while the Kerry campaign did not take advantage of such a tool and only suggested the forwarding of some of its e-mails.

Framing in Candidate E-Mails in 2004

In their e-mail messages, Bush and Kerry attempted to frame themselves and their opponents in terms of their respective issue stances and attributes. The candidates also sought to use these controlled communications as efforts to frame their opponents—which of course was done in a negative light in general or in juxtaposition to positive aspects of the campaign sending the e-mail messages. Typical issue frames included conflict, economic consequences, political consequences, societal impact/national identity, human interest or human impact, and morality. Attribute frames included qualified or unqualified, trustworthy or untrustworthy, knowledgeable or ignorant, powerful or inept, and powerful/strong or follower/weak.

Self-Referential Framing

Both campaigns' e-mail messages obviously attempted to frame the candidates in the most positive ways possible through the use of self-referential frames that emphasized the strengths of their issues stances and their own positive attributes as leaders.

Bush Campaign Self-Referential Issue Framing

In regard to issues, the Bush campaign e-mail message self-referential framing strategy was largely to focus on Bush as a war president. These messages often focused on societal impact in the forms of the economy and sought to demonstrate Bush's leadership during the post-9/11 age of terror.

For example, in an e-mail to the author on September 17, 2004, from President George W. Bush, the incumbent framed himself in terms of his resolve in the face of conflict, in improving national health care and the economy:

> The choice is between winning the war on terror by defending the homeland, taking the battle to the terrorists and fighting them where they live and train— or retreating to a pre-9/11 worldview that treats acts of terrorism as a law enforcement issue. The choice is between a practical approach that puts doctors and patients in control of health care decisions or a government-run system that would cost more than $1.5 trillion and put bureaucrats in charge. The choice is between an economic agenda that recognizes America's economy is growing, but can do more, or an agenda that raises taxes, increases regulations and stifles our economic recovery.

Similarly, in an e-mail message to the author on October 15, 2005, Bush campaign chairman Marc Racicot relied on an ambiguous self-referential frame and asserted, "The President is right on the issues and is doing the right things to grow our economy and make America safer."

In an e-mail message to the author on September 1, 2004, Arnold Schwarzenegger provided broad perspectives about Bush's economic accomplishments:

> When President Bush took office, our economy was slipping into decline. He cut taxes, unleashed the power of America's free enterprise economy, and now our country is coming back. America has the highest economic growth of any industrialized nation in the world and we are creating new jobs at a rapid pace.

In a more substantive e-mail message to the author on August 31, 2004, Rudolph W. Giuliani provided a focused framing of the president in regard to international conflict: "In order to keep the pressure on al-Qaeda, we must keep George W. Bush in the White House. In order to take the fight to our enemies, we must have the strength of conviction, and support for our Armed Forces."

Bush Campaign Self-Referential Attribute Framing

In terms of image or attribute framing, the Bush camp framed the president as trustworthy and emphasized that he was a strong leader.

For example, in an e-mail message to the author on October 22, 2004, President George H. W. Bush and Barbara Bush explained, "This week, Barbara and I went to the polls and voted early for our son, the President, America's strong, determined, focused and steadfast leader." Similarly, in an e-mail message to the author on September 2, 2004, Laura Bush said: "These are times that require particularly strong and determined leaders. And I'm proud my husband is that kind of leader."

In an e-mail message to the author on October 15, 2005, Bush campaign chairman Marc Racicot emphasized positive attributes of the president with a call to action: "If we want to ensure four more years of clear direction, principled leadership, and a reliance on the people, not the government, to drive our country, we must get out the vote and win."

In an e-mail message to the author on August 31, 2004, Rudolph W. Giuliani framed Bush as a strong leader in relation to the war on terror: "President Bush has been the steady hand we need in these times of uncertainty and danger. . . . He chooses to fight terror in places like Baghdad and Kabul, rather than New York and Kansas. . . . This is a fight that requires strength, determination and resolve."

Kerry Campaign Self-Referential Issue Framing

In regard to issues, the Kerry campaign used self-referential framing of the challenger's issue stances in opposition to Bush and frequently attempted to address very broad issues and alternatives in communication efforts that lacked much substantive detail.

For example, in a lengthy e-mail message to the author on November 1, 2004, John Kerry asserted numerous issues stances in an attempt to differentiate himself from the incumbent:

I believe we begin by giving this country we love a fresh start. . . . I believe we begin by moving our economy, our government, and our society back in line with our best values. I believe we do whatever it takes to lead our troops to success and bring them home safe. And when they do come home, I believe we begin by rebuilding an America with a strong middle class where everyone has the chance to work and the opportunity to get ahead. . . . You can choose between four more years of George Bush's policy to ship jobs overseas and give tax breaks to the companies that do it—or a president who will reward the companies that create and keep good jobs here in the United States of America. Tomorrow you will face a choice between four more years of George Bush's giveaways to the big drug companies and the big HMOs—or a president who will finally make health care a right, and not a privilege, for every American. This election is a choice between four more years of tax giveaways for millionaires along with a higher tax burden for you—or a president who will cut middle-class taxes, raise the minimum wage, and make sure we guarantee women an equal day's pay for an equal day's work.

Tomorrow, America faces a choice between four more years of an energy policy for big oil, of big oil, and by big oil—or a president who finally makes America independent of Mideast oil in ten years. A choice between George Bush's policy that just yesterday showed record profits for oil companies and record gas prices for American consumers. I believe that America should rely on our own ingenuity and innovation, not the Saudi Royal family.

In an e-mail message to the author on October 1, 2004, Kerry senior adviser Joe Lockhart offered the ambiguous statement that Kerry "offered clear plans for Iraq and for fighting terrorism," but did not provide any such details of what the challenger's plans were.

In a similar e-mail message to the author on September 2, 2004, Mary Beth Cahill vaguely asserted, "If you believe America needs to move in a new direction, join with us. John and I offer a better plan that will make us stronger at home and more respected in the world," but again provided no substantive facts to back up this claim.

Kerry Self-Referential Attribute Framing

In terms of self-referential attribute framing, the Kerry camp framed the challenger as trustworthy and emphasized that he was a knowledgeable and strong leader.

For example, in an e-mail message to the author on October 1, 2004, Mary Beth Cahill stressed that Kerry had "strength, conviction, and a steady command of the facts." Likewise, in an e-mail message to the author on October 1, 2004, Joe Lockhart asserted that Kerry had "the strength and conviction that Americans expect in our president." In the final days of the campaign, an e-mail message to the author on October 31, 2004, from Mary Beth Cahill said the election offered "a fresh start with John Kerry."

Opponent-Based Framing

In terms of opponent-based framing, each campaign attempted to juxtapose its candidate against the other by portraying the opponent in negative ways. These e-mail messages were attempts to undermine both the issue stances and the attributes of the opponent and, similar to the self-referential e-mails, ranged from substantive to ambiguous in their use of frames.

Bush Campaign Opponent-Based Issue Framing

In terms of image or attribute framing, the Bush campaign e-mail messages framed the opponent as untrustworthy or unqualified and emphasized the candidate's perceived shortcomings in relation to issue stances.

For example, in an e-mail message to the author on October 21, 2004, Senator Bill Frist argued that Kerry's health plan would have significant negative economic consequences for the nation:

> John Kerry has a $1.5 trillion big government health plan that will put over 80 percent of those covered on Medicaid, will raise taxes an average of $969 per year per family, and will vastly expand the role of government in your health care decisions. . . . His plan would create a federally run reinsurance program which makes the government responsible for 75 percent of health care expenses greater than $30,000. If government has the responsibility of everything over $30,000, they certainly will regulate everything up to that threshold as well. Payments, reimbursements and prices would ultimately be set by government and that turns into government rationing. This plan does nothing to address the underlying root causes of the soaring cost of healthcare today. It simply shifts that cost to the backs of taxpayers—to the tune of an almost $1000 tax increase.

In a succinct e-mail message to the author on October 9, 2004, Ken Mehlman asserted, "John Kerry has a 20-year record of supporting bigger government, higher taxes and higher health care costs," but little factual data was given to support these claims.

Bush Campaign Opponent-Based Attribute Framing

The Bush opponent-based attribute candidate e-mail messages tended to frame Kerry as untrustworthy and inept and played up the attributes of Kerry as a "flip-flopper" and an ultraliberal who was out of touch with mainstream American values.

For example, in an e-mail message to the author on October 7, 2004, President George W. Bush argued:

My opponent continues his pattern of confusing contradictions. After voting for the war, after saying my decision to remove Saddam Hussein from power was the right decision, he now says it was all a mistake. . . . He can't be for getting rid of Saddam Hussein when things look good, and against it when he's falling in the polls. He can't claim terrorists are pouring across the border into Iraq, yet at the same time try to claim that Iraq is somehow a diversion from the war on terror. . . . This is just one example of how my opponent's weak, vacillating views would make for a more dangerous world.

Similarly, in an e-mail message to the author on August 4, 2004, Ken Mehlman framed Kerry as weak or a follower: "From talking tough about the need to remove Saddam Hussein and his weapons of mass destruction in 2001 to declaring himself the antiwar candidate in 2004, Kerry's stance on Iraq has shifted with the political wind."

In an e-mail message to the author on October 14, 2004, that made a more direct attack at Kerry's trustworthiness, Marc Racicot stated, "John Kerry showed how far he's willing to go to deceive the American people about his record when he said 'I've actually passed 56 individual bills that I've personally written.' The fact is that he has only been the lead sponsor of 5 bills and 4 resolutions that have become law."

Sticking with the mainstream, American-values theme, in an e-mail message to the author on November 11, 2004, George W. Bush stated, "There is a mainstream in American politics, and my opponent sits on the far left bank."

Kerry Campaign Opponent-Based Issue Framing

In regard to issues, the Kerry campaign e-mail message opponent-based framing of the president's issue stances focused on numerous perceived failures, particularly in regard to foreign policy, the domestic economy, and international conflict.

In an e-mail message to the author on October 7, 2004, John Kerry stated, "George Bush is the first president since Herbert Hoover to lose jobs on his watch. . . . Wages are falling, medical bills are rising, and families cannot send their kids to college."

Additionally, in an e-mail message to the author on September 15, 2004, John Kerry, said, "George Bush and Dick Cheney have lost over a million jobs, made our health care crisis worse, and turned record budget surpluses into record deficits." In a similar e-mail message to the author on September 9, 2004, Mary Beth Cahill stated, "George Bush can't defend his record of exporting jobs, soaring health care costs, dangerous dependence on Middle East oil and a disastrous foreign policy."

In an e-mail message to the author on August 31, 2004, Mary Beth Cahill asserted that, "The friends of George Bush and Dick Cheney count their tax refunds while the average American counts the days until the next paycheck."

In an e-mail message to the author on September 20, 2004, John Kerry argued that "the president has made a series of catastrophic decisions from the beginning in Iraq. At every fork in the road, he has taken the wrong turn and led us in the wrong direction." However, little factual data were given to back up this claim.

In a substantive e-mail message to the author on October 15, 2004, Joe Lockhart directly attacked Bush's actions in regard to international conflict:

> Even before invading Iraq, the Bush administration knew that a huge facility, called Al Qaqaa, contained nearly 380 tons of deadly explosives. Despite the fact that they knew exactly where this facility was and what was there, they took no action to secure or protect the site. Due to the stunning incompetence of the Bush administration and their incomprehensible failure to plan, these explosives have disappeared.

In a similar vein, an e-mail message to the author on September 24, 2004, from Mary Beth Cahill, broadly argued, "We all know the harsh realities of Iraq. Unfortunately, George Bush has no plan to get us out of Iraq."

Kerry Campaign Opponent-Based Attribute Framing

Overall, the Kerry opponent-based attribute e-mail messages portrayed Bush as inept, an elitist who is not in touch with middle-class Americans, and a failure.

In an e-mail message to the author on October 7, 2004, John Kerry stated, "When it comes to the struggles our families are facing, George Bush just does not get it." Likewise, in an e-mail message to the author on August 31, 2004, Mary Beth Cahill claimed that, "The bottom line is, when it comes to the concerns of the middle class, George Bush just doesn't get it."

In an e-mail message to the author on October 1, 2004, Kerry campaign manager Mary Beth Cahill asserted, "George Bush has a record of failure to defend." Also, in an e-mail message to the author on October 14, 2004, Kerry senior adviser Joe Lockhart broadly asserted that Bush is both out of touch and dishonest: "Bush pretends our problems don't exist, and he won't level with the American people."

Likewise, in an e-mail message to the author on October 15, 2004, Joe Lockhart said, "The Bush administration's incompetence and arrogance has endangered the lives of our troops and the American people."

In a focused e-mail message to the author on September 15, 2004, John Kerry amplified his attacks on the Bush administration's record: "They misled America into war, failed to plan for the peace, and are running up a $200 billion bill at the expense of America's middle class taxpayers."

Similarly, in an e-mail message to the author on September 20, 2004, John Kerry portrayed Bush as dishonest in regard to the Iraq war:

> The first and most fundamental mistake was the president's failure to tell the truth to the American people. He failed to tell the truth about the rationale for going to war. And he failed to tell the truth about the burden this war would impose on our soldiers and our citizens. By one count, the president offered 23 different rationales for this war. If his purpose was to confuse and mislead the American people, he succeeded.

Candidate E-Mail Messages: Evolution and Opportunities

Overall, the use of e-mail messages has become a source of candidate-controlled communication during a political campaign, but these efforts still need much more advancement, in terms of frequency, the use of technological features, and integrated message strategy.

In general, the political campaigns' use of e-mail messaging in the 2004 election cycle was underwhelming. With a low number of messages being disseminated, matters were even worse regarding content. A majority of these communication efforts either were direct requests for donations or calls for support. Many of the campaign e-mails did not even have an issue or attribute of coverage of the respective candidates, and these messages certainly had nothing substantive. It was disappointing that out of the limited number of e-mail messages distributed the majority of these were campaign strategy, horse-race coverage, and calendar items that prevailed over e-mail messages that provided detailed issue and attribute content.

Another significant problem with many campaign e-mail messages was the lack of multimedia offering and incongruence with the look of the candidate Web sites. A lack of an integrated political marketing approach was evident. Just relying on the same banner to create a similar look is not enough. The e-mails would benefit from integrating both elements of style and content from the candidate Web sites. Also, instead of being primarily one-directional and text-based, incorporating the strategic use of hyperlinks—to draw users to campaign homepages and to positive media coverage—and providing more multimedia offerings could enhance e-mail message reinforcement and credibility.

E-mail messages provide campaigns with the unique opportunity to communicate directly with the electorate in a personalized way. The power of e-mails to reinforce supporters, to reach undecided voters as well as opponents, is unprecedented. To benefit from these advantages, campaigns need to disseminate e-mail messages on a regular basis that have substantive, detailed content that is congruent with the campaigns' other Internet-based communications, such as Web sites and online news releases and political advertising.

Additionally, regular dissemination of candidate e-mail messages can provide an opportunity for campaign-controlled media to stay in keeping with mass media coverage of salient issues and attribute coverage. The timely distribution of shorter, focused messages instead of lengthy e-mails could potentially help the campaigns to have more impact in shaping public opinion.

In terms of substantive and ambiguous framing, the evaluation of e-mail messages reported in this chapter indicates that the candidates' reliance on vague shortcuts to information, instead of detailed facts, is similar to what Williams and Kaid (2005) found about mainstream media framing of political events and elections. Whether the content of the e-mail messages is self-referential or opponent-based frames, it is advisable that the campaigns offer clear facts instead of broad statements. This approach could increase the clarity and impact of candidate e-mail messages.

Note

The author would like to thank Kaye D. Trammell and Stephanie Shum for their assistance with this research.

References

Bush, George H. W., and Barbara Bush. October 22, 2004. "We've already voted. Will you vote early?" E-mail message to the author.
Bush, George W. November 1, 2004. "A Clear Choice—Make Sure You Vote." E-mail message to the author.
———. October 7, 2004. "Stand with Us to Victory." E-mail message to the author.
———. September 17, 2004. "Vote Now." E-mail message to the author.
Cahill, Mary Beth. August 31, 2004. "Tonight." E-mail message to the author.
———. September 24, 2004. "He said what? / How you can help." E-mail message to the author.
———. October 1, 2004. "You saw our next president." E-mail message to the author.
———. October 31, 2004. "Volunteer Monday and Tuesday." E-mail message to the author.

Ciolli, Rita. 2000. "Reaching Voters Via the Internet: Candidates Harness Web's Power." *Newsday*, January 17: A06.

Cornfield, Michael. 2004. *Politics Moves Online: Campaigning and the Internet.* New York: Century Foundation.

Davis, Richard. 1999. *The Web of Politics: The Internet's Impact on the American Political System.* New York: Oxford University Press.

De Vreese, Claes H. 1999. "News and European Integration: News Content and Effects in Cross-National Comparative Perspective." *Research Report.* Amsterdam School of Communications Research, University of Amsterdam, Netherlands.

De Vreese, Claes H., Peter Jochen, and Holli A. Semetko. 2001. "Framing Politics at the Launch of the Euro: A Cross-National Comparative Study of Frames in the News." *Political Communication* 18 (2): 107–122.

Drinkard, Jim, and Jill Lawrence. 2003. "Online, Off and Running: Web a New Campaign Front." *USA Today.* July 14. Available at www.usatoday.com/news/politic selections/2003-07-14-online-cover-usat_x.htm (accessed May 15, 2005).

Entman, Robert M. 1993. "Framing: Toward a Clarification of a Fractured Paradigm." *Journal of Communication* 43 (4): 51–58.

Frist, Bill. October 21, 2004. "Sen. Bill Frist on Kerry's Health Plan." E-mail message to the author.

Gamson, William A., and Andre Modigliani. 1987. "The Changing Culture of Affirmative Action." *Research in Political Sociology* 3: 137–77.

Gitlin, Todd. 1980. *The Whole World Is Watching: Mass Media in the Making and Unmaking of the New Left.* Berkeley: University of California Press.

Giuliani, Rudolph W. September 31, 2004. "Strength, Determination and Resolve." E-mail message to the author.

Iyengar, Shanto. 1991. *Is Anyone Responsible?* Chicago: University of Chicago Press.

Kerry, John. September 15, 2004. "Don't let them hide from reality." E-mail message to the author.

———. September 20, 2004. "Iraq." E-mail message to the author.

———. October 7, 2004. "Senator Kerry, we've got your back." E-mail message to the author.

———. November 1, 2004. "A clear choice." E-mail message to the author.

Kim, Joongsik, and Michael Margolis. 2004. "What They Did Online: Campaign E-Mail in the 2004 Presidential Nominating Contest." Paper presented at the 3rd Annual American Political Science Association Pre-Conference on Political Communication, Chicago, September.

Levine, Peter. 2004. "Young People and Political Campaigning on the Internet." *CIRCLE: The Center for Information & Research on Civic Learning & Engagement,* 2004. Available at www.civicyouth.org (accessed May 18, 2005).

Lockhart, Joe. October 1, 2004. "The reviews are in." E-mail message to the author.

———. October 14, 2004. "Three victories." E-mail message to the author.

———. October 15, 2004. "Incompetence." E-mail message to the author.

McCombs, Maxwell, and Salma Ghanem. 2003. "The Convergence of Agenda Setting and Framing." In *Framing Public Life: Perspectives on Media and Our Understanding of the Social World*, edited by Stephen D. Reese, Oscar H. Gandy Jr., and August E. Grant, 67–81. Mahwah, NJ: Erlbaum.

Mehlman, Ken. August 4, 2004. "See for Yourself." E-mail message to the author.

———. September 22, 2004. "The Final 72 Hours." E-mail message to the author.

———. October 9, 2004. "Reviews Are In—President Bush Won Decisive Victory!" E-mail message to the author.

Nissenbaum, Dion. 2002. "Use of Spam in Campaign Spurs Debate." *Mercury News*, April 4. Available at www.mercurynews.com/mld/mercurynews/news/2996334.htm (accessed May 15, 2005).

Racicot, Marc. October 14, 2004. "President Bush Finished Strong—It's Our Turn." E-mail message to the author.

———. October 15, 2004. "Tomorrow Is the Big Day." E-mail message to the author.

Richards, Patti. 2004. "Internet's Snowball Effect Changes Political Campaigns." *Massachusetts Institute of Technology*. 20 October. Available at web.mit.edu/newsoffice/2004 (accessed May 15, 2004).

Sheffer, Mary Lou. 2003. "State Legislators' Perceptions of the Use of E-mail in Constituent Communication." *Journal of Computer Mediated Communication* 8 (4). Available at jcmc.indiana.edu/ (accessed February 3, 2005).

Schwarzenegger, Arnold. September 1, 2004. "Land of Opportunities." E-mail message to the author.

Semetko, Holli A., and Patti M. Valkenburg. 2000. "Framing European Politics: A Content Analysis of Press and Television News." *Journal of Communication* 50 (2): 93–109.

Stromer-Galley, Jennifer. 2003. "Diversity of Political Conversation on the Internet: Users' Perspectives." *Journal of Computer-Mediated Communication* 8 (3).

Tankard, James W., Laura Hendrickson, Jackie Silberman, Kriss Bliss, and Salma Ghanem. 1991. "Media Frames: Approaches to Conceptualization and Measurement." Paper presented at the annual meeting of the Association for Education in Journalism and Mass Communication, Boston, August.

Trammell, Kaye D., and Andrew Paul Williams. 2004. "Beyond Direct Mail: Evaluating Candidate E-Mail Messages in the 2002 Florida Gubernatorial Campaign." *Journal of E-Government* 1 (1): 105–22.

Vlahos, Kelley Beaucar. 2003. "Internet Campaigns Generate Buzz for 2004." June 26. *FOXNews.com*. Available at www.foxnews.com/story/0,2933,90307,00.html (accessed May 15, 2005).

Watson, Roland. 2005. "2001: The E-Mail Campaign Shots Still Lost in Cyberspace." *Times Online*, 17 February. Available at www.timesonline.co.uk/printFriendly/0,,1-18169-1488533-18169,00.html (accessed May 15, 2005).

Wheeler, Brian. 2004. "The Internet and Elections." *BBC NEWS*, 8 December. Available at news.bbc.co.uk/1/hi/uk_politics/4077105.stm (accessed May 15, 2005).

Whitney, William H. 2004. "Digital Politics: Plumbing the Net's Power." *Columbia Journalism Review* (March/April): 9.

Wiese, Danielle R., and Bruce E. Gronbeck. 2005. "Campaign 2004 Developments in Cyber-Politics." In *The 2000 Presidential Campaign: A Communication Perspective*, edited by Robert E. Denton, 217–39. Lanham, MD: Rowman & Littlefield.

Williams, Andrew Paul. 2005. "The Main Frame: Assessing the Role of the Internet in the 2004 U.S. Presidential Contest." In *The 2000 Presidential Campaign: A Communication Perspective*, edited by Robert E. Denton, 241–54. Lanham, MD: Rowman & Littlefield.

Williams, Andrew Paul, and Lynda Lee Kaid. 2006. "Media Framing of the European Parliamentary Elections: A View from the United States." In *Campaigning in Europe–Campaigning for Europe: Political Parties, Campaigns, Mass Media and the European Parliament Elections 2004*, edited by Michaela Maier and Jens Tenscher, 295–304. London: LIT.

Williams, Andrew Paul, and Kaye D. Trammell. 2005. "Candidate Campaign E-Mail Messages in the Presidential Election 2004." *American Behavioral Scientist* 49 (4): 560–74.

7

The Role of Campaign Web Sites in Promoting Candidates and Attracting Campaign Resources

Monica Postelnicu, Justin D. Martin, and Kristen D. Landreville

THE FIRST AMERICAN PRESIDENTIAL CANDIDATES to use the Internet as a campaign tool were Democrat Bill Clinton and Republican Bob Dole in 1996. At the time, political Web sites were modest collections of simple text pages with information about the candidates and their platforms. Since these modest beginnings only ten years ago, the Internet has evolved into a vital and sophisticated channel of communication between politicians and voters, generating a level of excitement and activity among communication scholars unseen since the infusion of television into American life (Tedesco 2004).

Politicians and their consultants were quick to seize the Internet's power of communication with voters in an unmediated, instant, one-to-one, and one-to-many manner. Norris (2001) calculated that well over one thousand political parties around the world had established an online presence. Political pundit and former Clinton adviser Dick Morris (1999: xviii) accurately predicted the enormous role the Internet would play in elections when he remarked in his book *Vote.com* that "The Net will increase, exponentially, our capacity to participate in all levels of government." Similarly, Ralph Nader's campaign Webmaster in 2000, Jonah Baker, declared that the Internet "was our ultimate means of communication with people," highlighting the central role of this new medium in a presidential election (Bimber and Davis 2003: 3).

The public kept pace with the politicians. Americans, youth in particular, are increasingly more likely to access the Internet for political news than either network news broadcasts or print newspapers (Pew 2004). During the 2004 presidential campaign, 75 million Americans used the Internet to obtain news about the election, to discuss political candidates with others, and to directly engage in politics (Pew 2004). In October 2004, a month before the elections, 3.7 million people visited John Kerry's campaign Web site, and 3.2 million visitors went to George Bush's site (ComScore 2004). Bush's Web site, GeorgeWBush.com, attracted about 16 million unique online visitors during the campaign, and JohnKerry.com received about 20 million visits (Pew 2005: 4). Internet users, those who listened to National Public Radio, and people who read weekly news magazines were the American mass media consumers most informed about the 2004 presidential election (Pew 2004). These findings led Stromer-Galley (2004) to remark that, unlike all prior presidential elections, the 2004 campaign for the White House can be earmarked as the first true "electronic election."

What did voters find online during the 2004 presidential campaign? What communication tools were used by the two candidates in their attempt to attract the audience support? What type of content was provided to voters? How did the candidates use their Web sites to promote their image and issue stances? The purpose of this chapter is to answer the above questions and to comprehensively describe the content of two of the most sophisticated American campaign Web sites. This attempt to chronicle campaigning trends of the most intense online political campaign waged to date focuses on how the two opponents used their campaign Web sites for issue and image promotion, fund-raising, and political mobilization.

A random sample of front pages from Bush's and Kerry's campaign Web sites were content analyzed on various levels, such as type of political discourse and tools used to inform and to energize supporters. The analysis presented in this chapter looked at sixty front pages drawn from GeorgeWBush.com and JohnKerry.com equally between October 2003 and October 2004. Examining how Bush and Kerry used online communication over this one-year period spanning the Democratic primaries and the general elections, this chapter concludes that the Internet has become a mandatory tool in political campaigns and an essential channel to attract voters, volunteers, and donors.

Issue Promotion

Promoting messages without the filter or interpretation of journalists and pundits is one of the main benefits of campaign Web sites. In a media environment where the average length of recorded statements directly from the candidates is declining, the ability of the Web to give campaigners an unfettered platform for issue promotion is significant. American voters attending traditional media sources are exposed to less and less information directly from the campaigns and from the political candidates themselves (Bimber and Davis 2003). Some voters have reacted by looking for political information online, as some perceive the Internet offers enhanced engagement and a control of campaign dialogue (Stromer-Galley and Foot 2002).

A survey of voters who browsed a candidate's campaign Web site in the 2000 election showed that learning about a candidate's issue positions was the second most common reason for going online (Bimber and Davis 2003: 115). Similarly, another survey of Dutch voters found that the number one reason visitors accessed political Web sites was to acquire information about the stances of various political parties (Boogers and Voerman 2003). Nixon, Ward, and Gibson (2003) also note that political Web sites in the United States, Australia, Korea, and France primarily serve their audiences by providing stances on issues, information about various political parties, as well as details about candidate personalities. The Internet seems to offer needed change from campaign communication dominated and distorted by mass media to interpersonal and personalized campaigning where candidates and voters alike have control over the message, its context, and its timing.

In 2004, both presidential contenders took advantage of the Internet's power of direct communication with voters and established Web sites that, among other functions, served as campaign manifestos explaining each candidate's position on issues. Both Web sites included an "Issues" section discussing the candidates' views on the economy, health care, terrorism and the Iraq war, foreign policy, education, environment, and several other topics.

Although a Web site has almost no limitation in terms of space and stores a wide variety of messages, both candidates kept their discourse focused and consistently addressed only a few topics each. About half of all home pages in our sample discussed or provided hyperlinks to an average of six issues. President Bush's front pages tended to reference the Iraq war most frequently, followed by terrorism, health care, tax cuts, and job growth. Senator Kerry's top five online issues discussed online were health care, the economy in general, the Iraq war, unemployment, and education.

Each candidate tried to set the agenda by promoting the issues with which they felt most comfortable, and over which they could claim ownership. It is no surprise that President Bush made the Iraq war a central topic of his online plea for reelection and framed it in terms of national security and rightful defense against terrorism. Even the attacks against his Democratic opponent were frequently related to this very topic, although he could have debated Kerry on several other important subjects. Similarly, Senator Kerry followed in the steps of previous Democratic presidential candidates by trying to divert attention to issues such as the economy and the health-care system. He framed the Iraq war as a failure and a problem needing a solution by setting up a Web

site section titled "Iraq Plan for Peace." The Democratic challenger also replied
to the president's discourse on job growth with a section about economy and
jobs, specifically unemployment.

In expressing their issue stances, both candidates exploited the Internet's
specific communication capacity in creative ways. Otherwise dry and dull
text-based Web pages with explanations of the candidates' views were accom-
panied by interactive and multimedia elements making information easier to
read and learn. Throughout the campaign, for instance, the home page of
GeorgeWBush.com displayed an interactive opinion poll about the president's
defense budget. The possible answers to the question "President Bush's defense budget will fulfill which of these goals?" were (1) "Increase pay for our
servicemen and women," (2) "Continue to eliminate inadequate military
housing," (3) "Provide the next generation of weapons to assist our troops in
the field," and (4) "All of the above." The purpose of such a poll was not to test
online visitors on their knowledge of Bush's platform but to promote the president's issue positions among those individuals who would not browse his
Web site beyond the home page.

Another way presidential candidates in 2004 touted their issue positions was
through political advertisements on their Web sites. In roughly the past fifty
years, televised political advertisements have been the candidate-controlled vehicle of choice for presidential candidates in promoting issues and addressing
or attacking political opponents (Kaid and Chanslor 2004). In 2004, for the
first time in a presidential election, both the Bush and Kerry campaigns
merged the forces of televised political advertisements and Internet-based
communication, as both camps made televised spots available on their Web
sites. In addition, each candidate published issue and attack ads that were never
meant to air on television and were produced exclusively for the Internet. Interactive versions of television spots were also an innovation of this election
cycle. The Web version of Bush's spot called "Weapons" featured hyperlinks to
additional information supporting the claims in the ad. After viewing the advertisement, online visitors could click a military airplane, a tank, or a soldier's
armor that appeared in the video clip to learn when and how Senator Kerry
voted against military spending used to develop those weapons.

Humorous attack ads on the Internet as well as political jokes at opponents'
expense were a defining characteristic of this online campaign. The "Flip-Flop
Olympics" on Bush's Web site is a prime example of the use of interactivity to
humorously attack an opponent. Linked from the front page, the Flash game
featured caricatures of Kerry and "judges" Hillary Clinton, Edward Kennedy,
and Howard Dean. Somewhat as in the children's game "Simon Says," the participant was asked to recall Kerry's "for" and "against" statements in the correct order to score high and win a gold medal. With carnival music playing,

the four rounds covered his positions on the No Child Left Behind education policy, owning a sports utility vehicle, the Bush tax cut, and the Iraq war. At the game's end, the participant could sign up to volunteer and e-mail the game to friends and family.

Overall, television ads extended their power to the Internet and became an important tool for issue promotion online as well. The release of a new television spot was promptly announced by a press release posted on the candidate's Web site and by the publication of that spot on the home page. In a few instances, a candidate's Web site even addressed the opponent's advertising, usually in terms similar to televised adwatches—news segments in which journalists or pundits critique the style and substance of political spots.

Image Promotion

Just as important as promoting specific issues, political candidates must create a personal identity that voters feel they can trust, and must move beyond political identities highlighting their achievements and agenda alone. The Internet allows candidates to dedicate an unlimited amount of time and space to this. Showcasing personality and family using traditional media, advertising, and campaign rallies is significantly more expensive and time intensive than inviting Internet users to browse a campaign Web site. Web sites can enhance feelings of personalized communication through reading the candidates' blog, through listening to audio and watching video of candidates giving speeches at rallies, and through galleries containing photographs of the campaign trail.

On the Bush campaign Web site, visitors could view photos stored in "leadership," "grassroots," and "agenda" photo galleries. Bush shaped his image by appearing with different supporting groups in photos in a "coalition" gallery. Kerry's photo gallery featured "top pics," which pictured Kerry with former President Bill Clinton. RSS (really simple syndication) and Atom feeds, which allow Web sites to distribute short headlines, updates, or comments to a wide number of people and allow visitors to track headlines or changes to a Web site, were available for Kerry supporters who wanted to be alerted to the most recent photos.

Both the Bush and Kerry campaigns used their Web sites to appeal to particular voting blocs. From the front page, a visitor could choose from among a dozen or more groups, which would take them to a separate page where the candidate then proclaimed his solidarity with and dedication to a certain demographic. Most of the groups were the same between the two candidates, which included people of faith, particular minority groups, farmers and ranchers, veterans, students, women, and sportsmen. However, Kerry's "communities" included a few demographics that Bush's "coalition" groups did not: scientists and engineers, LGBT (lesbian, gay, bisexual, transgender), Americans with disabilities, Arab Americans, and lawyers, to name a few.

Other attempts to promote and control image involved candidate biographies. Candidate biography hyperlinks were prominently placed next to issue and agenda links on the front pages. On Bush's biographical Web page, besides the written summary of Bush's life, visitors could view "The Pitch," the video biography of Bush shown at the Republican National Convention.

Families of the candidates also played an important image role in the campaigns. The Bush campaign Web site had individual hyperlinks for Laura Bush and Lynne Cheney, as the Kerry campaign Web site did for Teresa Heinz Kerry and Elizabeth Edwards. Laura Bush, in particular, enjoyed popularity among married and older women as a teacher and mother who seemed down to earth. Her section consisted of a brief biography, recent news about the first lady, and the latest photos of her. By contrast, Teresa Heinz Kerry did not always receive the most flattering media coverage. The Kerry campaign Web site tried to portray her as more likable by including a "Meet Teresa" section, which described her as a "philanthropic innovator" and "an environmental visionary."

The daughters of both presidential candidates contributed to their family image. The Bush twins authored their own blog, "Barbara and Jenna's Journal," documenting their experiences on the campaign trail with their "Dad." Kerry's family page focused on his role as a typical father: "And sometimes they [Kerry's daughters] poke fun at him, too. Like the time he came out in the middle of summer wearing a full-piece wetsuit and Hawaiian shorts. But even Alex and Vanessa will admit, you have to love someone who learns to snowboard at 55 and plays his guitar on the campaign bus."

Additionally, both Bush and Kerry sought to create a branded image that could be marketed to voters. "Wstuff," "W Wear," and "Kerry Gear" were the products of this goal, offering buddy icons, screensavers, and wallpapers for the technology buffs, while traditional bumper stickers and T-shirts were offered as well. These promotional materials also raised funds for the campaigns.

The photo galleries, supporting groups, blogs, biographies, promotional materials, and family information can make visitors feel as if they are getting to know the candidate and getting a glimpse into their daily lives, and thus build a sense of trust in the candidate as a person and not just a politician. All of these aspects of the candidate Web site can influence the image formation of the candidate in the visitor's mind and possibly influence the visitor's vote.

Fund-Raising

When candidates began using Web sites to communicate with voters in the mid-1990s, they did not immediately use the Internet for political fund-raising (Banwart 2002). That, however, has changed, and nowhere has the ability of the Internet to generate political and financial capital been more evident than in the 2004 presidential election. Former Vermont Governor Howard Dean, in his failed bid to win the Democratic nomination for president, led a memorable grassroots effort to mobilize supporters and attract financial contributions on-line. "When you looked at him, you were going to think Internet and personal empowerment in the same way you thought Vietnam hero when you looked at John Kerry, or Southern optimism when you looked at John Edwards," explained Dean's campaign manager (Trippi 2004: 100). Once a little-known northeastern governor, Dean used the Internet to generate a flurry of activity, largely among young voters, and led Democratic opponents in fund-raising all the way up to the Iowa Caucus. Dean raised over $20 million online, about 40% of his total receipts. These numbers speak for themselves about the Internet's power to orchestrate mass grassroots communication and to energize voters on a level unparalleled by previous mass media–based campaigns.

Postelection reports confirmed that President Bush and Senator Kerry were equally successful in their efforts to obtain financial support online. The former collected about $14 million, or 5% of his total fund-raising, while the latter raised about $89 million, equivalent to 33% of his total receipts. Much of the money raised online was in small donations, less than $200 (Pew 2005).

Our content analysis showed that fund-raising tools were present on all the home pages of the two presidential contenders throughout the election year, and also in about 20% of the blog posts sampled from the same period. This supports a previous finding that candidates tend to use their Web sites for fund-raising while using blogs for informal interaction and political mobilization (Williams et al. 2005). On average, each home page offered visitors about three opportunities for donation: a short phrase containing the words "donate" or "contribute" displayed as one of the hyperlinks on the side navigation bar; a second more graphical hyperlink, a small icon or a small symbol prominently placed on the top navigation bar, close to popular hyperlinks such as those to the candidates' blogs; and an even more obvious invitation placed somewhere else on the home page, for instance accompanying the main news piece or the story of the day.

Candidates do not, however, benefit mainly from one-way communication online, according to Cornfield (2004), who argues that expansive hyperlinking both from and to candidates' Web sites and blogs creates networking benefits reaching far beyond the impact of still photographs and written commentary on the page. More and more, argues Cornfield, candidates are using blogs not only to provide a political quasidiary, but also to hyperlink to other favorable blogs throughout the country, ones that often make regional or national headlines and draw sizable audiences. According to the *New Scientist* (Appell 2004), one blogger cum fund-raiser who calls himself Atrios managed to raise more than $300,000 for the John Kerry campaign as well as more modest sums for a handful of U.S. congressional campaigns as Democratic sympathizers stumbled upon this juggernaut of a blog.

Periodically during the campaign, fund-raising became the main focus of communication between the candidates and the voters. Entire blog threads were dedicated solely to such efforts, and donation requests would be disguised as news. Dean's action "Raise the Bat"—an online competition of fund-raising between his supporters and those of Wesley Clark, publicized and managed by Dean's campaign through blog posts solely—is an example of such news-style appeals to fund-raising. John Kerry applied the same news-driven fund-raising strategy when he asked online supporters to make a statement on the day he accepted the party nomination, and successfully collected $5.6 million (Cornfield 2004: 2).

With more than $100 million transferred from voters to both campaigns over the Internet, the 2004 presidential campaign was the first one that effectively encouraged voters to donate significant amounts of money online. In 1996, Clinton's Web site obtained only about $10,000, and the 2000 Republican and Democratic candidates raised only a few million each rather than the predicted tens of millions (Bimber and Davis 2003). The success of the 2004 election can be attributed to the development of secure online transactions combined with the widespread adoption of Internet use among the American public, as well as to the demographic characteristics of online users (more affluent, more educated, more politically active).

Voter Mobilization

Apart from collecting important financial resources, 2004 presidential campaign Web sites also served to recruit volunteers and organize them into complex and energetic networks of campaign supporters, confirming the Internet's potential to stimulate civic and political engagement (Nisbet and Scheufele 2004). GeorgeWBush.com and JohnKerry.com became virtual public spaces that united supporters of the two candidates into online communities unbounded by time and space. During this past election, about 13 million Americans, or about 11% of all Internet users, engaged in active political behaviors online such as donating money, volunteering, or looking for political events to attend (Pew 2005: ii).

Both presidential campaign Web sites abounded with opportunities for involvement with the campaign, both online and offline. Almost all home pages (98%) in our sample contained a "get involved" section or a hyperlink to it. Opportunities for involvement ranged from simple actions such as donation or voter registration to more complex engagement such as organizing a party for the candidate or inviting friends and acquaintances to a fund-raiser.

Taking advantage of the Internet's interactive possibilities, each campaign devised original strategies and tools to attract and energize volunteers. Through the Bush Web site, the president's supporters could organize their "personal precinct," a personal action center with tools for recruiting volunteers, sending e-mails to voters and mass media representatives, and organizing parties for their candidate. To keep users of these virtual precincts motivated, the campaign enabled personal statistics so each activist could keep track of how many new people joined the campaign, registered to vote, or participated in an event as a result of his or her efforts.

The Kerry campaign responded with a similar tool called "Kerry Core," which gave supporters a personal Web page on the candidate's Web site and the ability to send e-mails, organize fund-raisers and other events, or contact other volunteers and media representatives. By offering supporters the chance to use such powerful tools in exchange for merely opening a free online account on the candidate's Web site, campaigns made volunteers feel empowered and important, as if they owned part of the campaign.

Giving supporters the chance to become part of the campaign in the privacy of their own home, without direct physical contact with the campaign headquarters, was one of the advancements of the 2004 elections. Online communication allowed people to connect with the candidates and to other voters according to their own schedules, needs, and levels of involvement. Josh Ross, Kerry's director of Internet strategy, captured the benefits of using the Internet as an organizing tool: "This allows people to be self-starters and do their own thing, and they don't necessarily have to wait for instructions from the campaign," he stated (Schlesinger 2004: 26).

Lack of physical contact did not mean lack of communication. On the contrary, the electronic medium facilitated continuous and instant interaction between the campaign staff and supporters. Contact information by mail, phone, fax, and e-mail was prominently displayed on each home page. On average, the front pages of the two candidates' Web sites included about three opportunities for the visitors to contact the campaign, either by traditional methods such as mail or phone or by online channels such as chat. Almost all pages had a hyperlink to a campaign directory, where contact information was available for national and regional campaign staff as well as for other volunteers. Also, about half of the Web pages in our sample solicited communication from visitors; for instance, the moderator of a scheduled chat asked participants to send questions in advance, and a note on Bush's site invited supporters to come up with ideas for what "W" can stand for. Such findings speak perhaps to the ability of political campaigns to diversify their Web content and to offer differing ways of getting involved to various publics.

In some ways, the Internet became the initial medium candidates accessed to communicate with the citizenry in 2004; in July 2004 (Wilgoren 2004), the *New York Times* reported that John Kerry would make his pick for a vice-presidential running mate public by e-mailing the more than 1 million members occupying Kerry's electronic rolls at the time. This marked the first time a U.S. presidential nominee announced his other political half in this way.

The ability to lure support, though, does not seem equal across all political parties and candidates. Gibson, Römmele, and Ward (2003) noted that, in the 2002 German national elections, the quality of Web sites was markedly different between large and small parties. The difference in online campaigning capabilities of these parties was visible. In the United States, the success of political campaigning seems also to be linked to the quality of the online presence. The 2003–2004 online presence of Howard Dean, for example, was as attractive as it was functional and, ultimately, garnered millions of dollars and grassroots support and placed Dean out in front early in the Democratic primary. Web sites for other primary candidates, such as former Ambassador Carol Moseley Braun and U.S. Congressman Dennis Kucinich, did not seem to offer the quality of Dean's Web pages.

The Web and Message Promotion, Fund-Raising, and Voter Mobilization

While additional research is needed to comprehensively describe the role of campaign Web sites in American politics, the 2004 presidential elections proved that the new medium has a spectacular impact in at least three areas of campaign communication: message promotion, fund-raising, and voter mobilization. The Internet's potential for both mass and interpersonal communication promoted direct dialogue between candidates and millions of voters, bypassing mass media gatekeepers. Secure transaction technologies combined with inventive marketing on part of politicians resulted in some of the most memorable and productive fund-raisers ever. Also, interactive tools such as Bush's Action Center and Kerry's Core inspired voters—many who

had never been involved with a political candidate—into active political behavior and enthusiastic participation in the campaign. As one media pundit
put it, "In the history books, the presidential campaign of 2004 may be known
as the one in which the Internet came of age—as fundraiser, scandal breaker,
and vote stimulator" (Taylor 2004:1).

The 2004 campaign indelibly established the Internet as a political communication vehicle; by May 2005, with the presidential campaign of 2004 fad-
ing from recent memory, Americans who previously joined the e-mail rolls of
the Bush campaign were still receiving carefully crafted information about Republican initiatives, legislation proposed by the Bush administration to the
Congress, as well as other matters via electronic mail. Some such e-mails
urged recipients to contact their congressional representatives in order to
demonstrate support for the president's directives on Social Security reform,
the impropriety of Senate filibusters in blocking U.S. judicial nominees, and
the energy policy he was attempting to usher through Congress. Likewise,
even after losing the 2004 presidential election of 2004, John Kerry operatives
still update via e-mail more than 3 million people about Kerry's activities, and
his Web site is still active and offers frequently updated information about the
erstwhile presidential contender.

References

Appell, David. 2004. "U.S. Campaign Trail Takes to the Net." *New Scientist*, August
    21: 24.
Banwart, Mary C. 2002. *Videostyle and Webstyle in 2000: Comparing the Gender Dif-
    ferences of Candidate Presentation in Political Advertising on the Internet.* Doctoral
    dissertation, University of Oklahoma.
Bimber, Bruce, and Richard Davis. 2003. *Campaigning Online: The Internet in the U.S.
    Elections.* New York: Oxford University Press.
Boogers, Marcel, and Gerrit Voerman. 2003. "Surfing Citizens and Floating Voters: Re-
    sults of an Online Survey of Visitors to Political Web Sites during the Dutch 2002
    General Elections." *Information Policy* 8 (1–2): 17.
ComScore Media Metrix. 2004. "25 Million Americans Visited Politics Sites in the
    Final Month of the Presidential Race." November 15. Available at www.comscore
    .com/press/release.asp?press=517 (accessed January 20, 2005).
Cornfield, Michael. 2004. "Internet (sic) Miscellany." *Campaigns and Elections* (Sep-
    tember): 31.
Gibson, Rachel K., Andrea Römmele, and Steven Ward. 2003. "German Parties and In-
    ternet Campaigning in the 2002 Federal Election." *German Politics* 12 (1): 79–108.
Kaid, Lynda Lee, and Mike Chanslor. 2004. "The Effects of Political Advertising on
    Candidate Images." In *Presidential Candidate Images*, edited by Kenneth L. Hacker.
    Lanham, MD: Rowman & Littlefield, 133–50.

Morris, Dick. 1999. *Vote.com: How Big-Money Lobbyists and the Media Are Losing Their Influence, and the Internet Is Giving Power Back to the People.* Los Angeles: Renaissance.

Nisbet, Matthew C., and Dietram A. Scheufele. 2004. "Political Talk as a Catalyst for Online Citizenship." *Journalism & Mass Communication Quarterly* 81 (4): 877–96.

Nixon, Paul, Steven Ward, and Rachel Gibson. 2003. "Conclusions: The Net Change." In *Political Parties and the Internet: Net Gain?* edited by Rachel Gibson, Paul Nixon, and Steven Ward. London: Routledge.

Norris, Pippa. 2001. *The Digital Divide.* Cambridge: Cambridge University Press.

Pew Internet & American Life Project. 2004. "Cable and Internet Loom Large in Fragmented Political News Universe." January 11. Available at www.pewinternet.org (accessed April 25, 2005).

———. 2005. "The Internet and Campaign 2004." March 6. Available at www.pewinternet.org/pdfs/PIP_2004_Campaign.pdf (accessed April 25, 2005).

Schlesinger, Robert. 2004. "Online Strategies Still Hit and Miss for Campaigns." *Campaigns & Elections* (October–November): 26–29.

Stromer-Galley, Jennifer. 2004. "Making the Difference: The Internet as Key Variable in Political Campaigns." Paper presented to the Political Communication division of the National Communication Association, Chicago, November.

Stromer-Galley, Jennifer, and Kirsten A. Foot. 2002. "Citizen Perceptions of Online Interactivity and Implications for Political Campaign Communication." *Journal of Computer-Mediated Communication* 8 (1).

Taylor, Catherine P. 2004. "The Selling of the President—The Online Version. *Adweek,* 22 November.

Tedesco, John C. 2004. "Changing the Channel: Use of the Internet for Communicating about Politics." In *Handbook of Political Communication Research,* edited by Lynda Lee Kaid. London: Erlbaum.

Trippi, Joe. 2004. *The Revolution Will Not Be Televised: Democracy, the Internet, and the Overthrow of Everything.* New York: Regan.

Wilgoren, Jodi. 2004. "Kerry Says Announcement of Pick to Come Via E-mail." *New York Times,* July 3: 11.

Williams, Andrew Paul, Kaye D. Trammell, Monica Postelnicu, Kristen D. Landreville, and Justin D. Martin. 2005. "Blogging and Hyperlinking: Use of the Web to Enhance Viability during the 2004 U.S. Campaign." *Journalism Studies* 6 (2): 177–86.

8

Joy and Sorrow of Interactivity on the Campaign Trail: Blogs in the Primary Campaign of Howard Dean

Jennifer Stromer-Galley and Andrea B. Baker

ON AUGUST 26, 2003, Democratic presidential primary candidate Howard Dean headed to Bryant Park in New York City to deliver the culmination speech of the "Sleepless Summer" campaign tour. In what has now become campaign lore, a supporter had posted to Howard Dean's weblog, Blog for America, and suggested that Dean take the stage holding a red baseball bat. The symbolism would not be lost on the thousands of blog readers and Dean supporters who had been "swinging the bat" to raise funds for Dean. On that energy-filled evening, full of hope and promise of the success of the Dean insurgency campaign, Dean took the stage wielding a red bat, to the thrill and tears of his "Deaniacs."

To hear Joe Trippi, Dean's campaign manager, tell the story, carrying the red baseball bat on stage that summer evening was a result of a citizen-centered, grassroots campaign that harnessed the full power of the Internet. Trippi (2004a) used the fantastic tale of the bat as a symbol of the direct relationship between the citizen-centered weblog and the Dean campaign.

Beneath the surface of the baseball-bat story, a thorough reading of the blog comments from that fateful day suggests a more complicated picture of the relationship between the weblog participants and the Dean campaign. According to those comments, the campaign staff did not read the blog comments and respond to the bat suggestion directly. A blog commenter wrote in at 6 p.m. (three hours before Dean's scheduled speech): "I know this is probably the last thing anyone has time to think about—but any chance of someone getting a real red bat and giving to Dean on stage at NYC, to celebrate the million we're pretty sure to have by then? The crowd would go BERSERK." His suggestion was seconded by another supporter, who wrote: "The red bat in NY on stage tonight is GREAT! Campaign staff—are you listening? This would really work!" The campaign staff did not provide any indication that they were listening. A third supporter took the initiative to call campaign headquarters in Burlington, Vermont. He then wrote in the comments section: "They are going to call Clay [Johnson, campaign staff] who is updating the bat and in touch with the campaign and tell them to GET DEAN A RED BAT!!!!!!!!!!! before he goes on stage in NY. (One of the big plastic ones from the toy store.)" (001247.html.)[1] Campaign staff responded to supporters by taking the phone call seriously and getting a bat into Dean's hands for the campaign event.

As evidenced by supporters' own words, the phone call was the impetus for the red baseball bat event, not the blog; the comments apparently were unread by campaign staff. The question "Are you listening?" was frequently directed to the campaign in the comments section of the blog. This suggests that Dean's decentralized, grassroots campaign used the blogs to promote the campaign and to talk with supporters, but staffers were not as responsive as the citizen-supporters would have liked. However, the campaign did not want to risk alienating supporters who were taken in by the inviting language and personal narratives of the blogs, and by the appearance that they were being integrated into the campaign's inner circle. Hence, the joy of the blogs was the façade of interactivity they produced, which generated spectacular support for Howard Dean. The sorrow was that as the campaign began to crumble in the early primaries, the shallow quality of the interactivity was exposed and supporters expressed feelings of being duped.

This chapter provides a descriptive account of the rise and fall of Howard Dean's Democratic presidential primary campaign, focusing first on the hype generated by the campaign and by the news media's coverage of the campaign's innovative use of a relatively new technology on the Internet, called weblogs. Second, we focused on the messages on the weblog generated by the campaign and on the messages created by the citizen-supporters who wrote in the comments section of the blog. As students of political campaigns, we note that campaigns in past elections have made limited use of the technological features of the Internet to enable communication between the campaign and its supporters (Stromer-Galley 2000). Thus, the innovative use of the weblog in the Dean campaign was an obvious place to investigate: Was there genuine interaction between citizens and campaign staff on the blogs? By genuine interaction, we mean interaction that occurs between citizens, and between citizens and campaign staff, channeled through the technologies of the Internet. Our investigation suggests that the campaign primarily created a façade of interaction, using several devices to cast an appearance of genuine interactivity. These devices, which included parasocial interaction, blurred the boundaries between mass and interpersonal communication, leading to a kind of pseudo-community (Beniger 1987). Appearances deceive, however, and as the campaign faltered, the deception was felt increasingly by supporters of the Dean campaign who wanted the campaign to answer directly to their pleas. When they went unanswered, the frustration and anger were palpable.

The Hype

The campaign generated and received, in turn, a great deal of attention for its technological innovations. Campaigns tend to be conservative in their strategies, adopting tried and true methods of organizing, fund-raising, and attracting supporters. Thus, when a campaign innovates and is apparently successful in that innovation, the press takes notice.

The Campaign

Joe Trippi, Howard Dean's campaign manager, was the brains behind the innovation of harnessing the Internet in the presidential primary campaign. After two decades of work on political campaigns, Trippi began working for dot com start-ups to feed his growing fascination with the Internet and Internet-related technology (Trippi 2004a). He was lured to the Dean campaign in January 2003. His fascination with both technology and politics positioned him well to be the first campaign manager willing to take innovative risks with the Internet during a political campaign. It also helped that the Dean campaign in January was a blip on the radar screen of politics. Dean was polling 1% or 2% in Iowa and New Hampshire. The campaign had only seven staff members and was far behind its competitors in the three critical components of a campaign: staff, money, and supporters. Being so far behind meant the campaign could take risks that the front-runners could not.

Trippi (2004a) explained that the only way for Dean to win the primaries would be to run a different kind of campaign. Trippi reminisced: "our only hope for winning now was to decentralize the campaign, ease control away from the candidate and his handlers in Vermont (myself included), and let the momentum and the decision making come from the people—stop trying to control the river . . . just open the flood gates and see where the current took us" (Trippi 2004a: 82). Trippi gave Dean the credit for suggesting that the campaign decentralize its operations. That Dean was willing to relax control over the direction of the campaign "excited" Trippi: "Like someone whose entire iife has been building to this point, I knew without looking what our only hope would be: the Internet" (82).

One major innovation he instituted was establishing a weblog on the campaign site. The first blog was handcrafted by Matthew Gross, the resident blog creator and manager, in March 2003. It was called the "Dean Call for Action Blog." It allowed campaign staff to post a running commentary about the campaign, but it did not include functionality for readers to comment. For Trippi's birthday in June, the campaign shifted to using MoveableType blogging software, which included a commenting feature.

Trippi heralded the blog as a way to field strategy ideas and mobilize supporters for activities. Trippi claimed the blog was a fundamental part of the campaign's strategy. For example, in a postmortem speech to the Institute for Politics, Democracy & the Internet conference at George Washington University in March 2004, he said that the blog participants served as the eyes and ears of the campaign, watching what was happening and providing critical feedback: "Twelve or 13 or 14 of us working every night can't spot the hole or the mistake we just made, but our supporters could spot us and tell us about it and fix it for us right away" (Trippi 2004b). In an interview with Stanford professor Lawrence Lessig (2003: 70), Trippi said, "the blog has been amazing. We just learn so much and get so many good ideas about how to move forward." Gross told a journalist that the blog was receiving approximately 2,300 comments a day and had collected 160,000 from June to November 2003 (Faler 2003: 12). Trippi reported that he read many of the comments, and at least two of his staff members were reading all of them (Cone 2003). By their account, the blog readers would help Dean win the election; staff just needed to explain how and set parameters for the blog's use.

Trippi's second major innovation was actually created by others. MeetUp.com had been established to help people with shared interests to find each other online and then meet offline. People interested in knitting or in science fiction could get together in a coffee shop in their town to continue the conversation. Trippi noted early in the campaign that "MeetUp for Dean" groups already were popping up across the country, and that more people were signed up to MeetUp for Dean than for other Democratic primary candidates. After much negotiating with the small staff in Vermont, he managed to get a hyperlink added on the Dean for America Web site to MeetUp.com. On the blog and on the Web site in the months that followed, harnessing the organizational power through MeetUp was a central focus for the campaign.

A third innovation that Trippi advanced was using the readers of the blog and visitors to the Web site to help organize for the campaign and to give money to the campaign. The campaign developed several ways for people to work for the campaign. They developed "Get Local" tools designed to help citizens find other supporters and organize events to bring visibility and recruit more supporters. They also used online tools to help raise money for the Dean campaign. They used the blog to announce and drive donations during their major fund-raising pushes. In the upper right-hand corner of the blog, an icon of a bat could be clicked to donate money to the campaign. According to the Center for Responsive Politics (n.d.) Dean raised $51 million in individual campaign contributions, and 61% were from donations of $200 or less. Cone (2003) reported that the average donation was $77 and 25% of the donors were thirty or younger.

The News Media

When the Dean campaign launched its weblog on March 15, 2003, little attention was paid in the mainstream press. After the blog began bringing in million of dollars of donations from online supporters, however, the media took notice. Journalists and pundits found it noteworthy that Dean had raised so much money from an active, supportive community that had formed through the blog area of the Dean campaign Web site. Reporters soon started asking about Howard Dean and his blog. Indeed, from January 1, 2002, to December 2003, Dean's weblogs received more coverage in the *New York Times* and *Washington Post* than other campaign blogs (Park 2004). Reporters portrayed a complex story about an interactive technology that transformed a not so savvy Internet politician into a leading candidate for the Democratic presidential primary.[2]

Headlines in 2003 heralded the Dean campaign as revolutionary. The revolution, as the journalists reported it, came in the novel way the campaign was using the Internet. The August 6 edition of *Front Page Magazine.com* announced "Dean's Internet Revolution" (Morris 2003), and on July 3 in *Salon.com*, Manjoo (2003: 40) wrote, "Meet Howard Dean: physician, former governor from Vermont, and presidential candidate from the great state of Blogland." The weblog, a novelty for political candidates, was featured prominently in coverage about the Dean campaign. It did not hurt that the campaign was able to meet its fund-raising goals, in part with contributions by the people who were reading the Dean weblog. Manjoo announced Dean as the candidate from "Blogland" and found it particularly noteworthy that in less than twenty-four hours the campaign raised $802,803 from its blog.

Newspapers sang Dean's praises after Dean successfully raised 7 million dollars by the July 1 campaign fund-raising filing deadline. The fund-raising demonstrated that the campaign had built a grassroots following with limited on-the-ground resources but with almost limitless online resources. Reston (2003: 11) declared that Dean's use of the Internet "has transformed political campaigns forever," and Cone (2003: 13) said, "Not since the Nixon–Kennedy debates has there been a comparable shift in the art and science of running a campaign."

Journalists focused on the campaign's use of the Internet to organize supporters in ways that had not been tried before. The best example is Dean's direct involvement of the people in an Internet vote asking whether he should cede public financing (Reston 2003). This move was an indicator that the campaign was willing to give up control over important decisions and allow citizen-supporters to guide the workings of the campaign.

The novelty apparent in direct involvement of citizens in the campaign was most visible through the campaign's weblog. The blog was a different format than traditional candidate Web sites. Dean's staff posted several times a day on the blog, unlike on Web sites that may get updated once a day at best. Sometimes staff wrote about strategy; other times they commented on press coverage. In the *Washington Post*, Faler (2003: 10) described the weblogs as campaign journals "all written in a breezy conversational tone that contrasts with the campaign-speak found on more traditional Web sites." The question is whether the blog actually improved interactivity between citizens and candidates. Were citizens and staff talking *with* one another or *at* one another?

The Hope

Why study whether candidates are utilizing the Internet's interactivity capabilities to increase communications with voters? Presumably, interactive communication not only leads to a more informed public, but also opens the doors to a more direct form of democracy where citizens have input into decisions that have an impact on their interests (see, for example, Barber 1984). Since Tim Berners-Lee's 1992 invention of HyperText Markup Language (HTML), which gave birth to the World Wide Web, a significant amount of research has been conducted to determine whether this new communication technology has improved the democratic process. Until Dean, the consensus was that, like radio and television, the Internet offered the possibility of increased communication between citizens and candidates but was unable to deliver much more than hope (for an elaboration of this argument, see Margolis and Resnick 2000).

Interactivity

Much like its predecessors in television and radio, the Internet was initially believed to be the technology that could break through traditional political campaigning. Selnow (1998) wrote convincingly about the potential of the Internet to create a more direct form of democracy. Instead of top-down dissemination of information, the Internet provides the opportunity for politicians and voters to interact with one another. Candidates can speak directly to the voters and bypass the press. The public also has the opportunity to give feedback to the candidates. This enhances the possibility for a more horizontal communication framework as opposed to the top-down strategy of dissemination that campaigns have been using for decades. Scholars hoped that the interactive capabilities would be the key element that set the Internet apart from previous communication technologies (Hacker 1996).

Interactivity can be defined in several ways. McMillan (2002), in a comprehensive literature review of the concept, identified three types of interactivity. These types are human-to-human, human-to-document, and human-to-system. Human-to-human interaction is generally conceptualized as communication between people channeled through a medium (Rafaeli 1988; Rafaeli and Sudweeks 1998; Stromer-Galley 2000), for example, two people who talk on a telephone or who send and receive e-mail. Human-to-document interaction includes parasocial interaction, which is when people develop a sense that they know the celebrities or entertainers presented to them through mass media (Horton and Wohl 1956). Human-to-system interaction is interaction that occurs with the medium (Stromer-Galley 2000; Sundar 2000). Hyperlinking is a good example of this type of interaction. The hyperlink, when activated, triggers a systemic process of requesting, transmitting, and receiving information.

We contend that the Dean campaign primarily used the blog to facilitate parasocial interaction. Parasocial interaction, in Horton and Wohl's terms (1956: 215), is an "illusion of [a] face-to-face relationship." They observed this illusion in studies of television watchers. They noted that audience members developed an intimate bond with television celebrities, such as talk-show hosts. This bond, however, was illusory. Rafaeli (1990: 136) summarizes Horton and Wohl's research as concluding that "For the audience, the result is compliance and engagement in an unhealthy, one-sided, nonreciprocated, and controlled relationship." As we discuss in the next sections, the Dean campaign used tactics that fostered a sense of interaction between the campaign and its supporters through the weblogs. This sense, however, was more indicative of parasocial than genuine interpersonal interaction.

It is important to note that we do not wish to condemn the revolutionary qualities of the Dean campaign. Given the lack of genuine interactivity in previous campaigns, Howard Dean's campaign pushed the envelope of what campaigns do with Internet-channeled communication strategies. Yet it is important to separate the hype from the reality and recognize how the campaign managed to achieve a kind of parasocial relationship. This façade of interaction, while powerful in its ability to generate hype and enthusiasm for the campaign, was revealed during the critical primary days of the campaign, generating much anguish from his supporters.

Blogs

If Dean's campaign created greater awareness of the technology and added "'blog' to the campaign lexicon" (Faler 2003), then we should make it clear what blogs are. In the early days, Dean had to ask his campaign staff to define *blog*. Because of the publicity the Dean campaign generated around blogs, more people started to ask the question: What is a blog? Rainie (2005a) reported that 27% of Internet users read blogs, but 62% still have no idea what a blog is.

Blogs have been around since the late 1990s, but their use has exploded in the past few years. Drezner and Farrell (2004) reported that the number of blogs has dramatically increased from approximately fifty in 1999 to anywhere from 2.4 million to 4.1 million on the Web currently. Rainie (2005b) said 8 million adults reportedly have created blogs. Weblog content can range from a site that contains miscellaneous personal facts about the blog's author to political commentary and analysis of current events.

Howard Dean was not the only candidate to have a weblog in the 2004 primaries, but he was the first. The other candidates followed suit, especially after noting Dean's remarkable success in raising money from his online followers. The structure of the Dean campaign weblog was as follows. Campaign staff would post a message to the blog, generally written in a conversational tone. Over the course of a day, the campaign would post several times to the blog. Below each "post" would be a link to a "comments" section. Clicking on the "comments" would open up a new window where a reader could read what other people had to say about the blog post, and he or she could write a comment, which would appear publicly for others to read. New posts to the blog from campaign staff were ordered chronologically, from the most recent on top to the oldest on the bottom. In contrast, new posts to the comments from citizens were ordered chronologically from oldest at the top to the newest at the bottom.

The weblog posts came from the campaign staff, including Zephyr Teachout, Matthew Gross, Clay Johnson, and Nicco Mele. Comments from the citizen-supporters were unimaginably voluminous. In December, at the height of the Dean campaign's success, the campaign produced 411 posts to the blog, for an average of thirteen posts a day. At the height of a major fund-raising push on the last day of December, for example, twenty-one posts were written by campaign personnel. Those twenty-one posts generated 4,236 comments in a twenty-four hour period, an average of 202 comments per blog post. Such numbers suggest energy, intensity, and commitment from supporters.

The technological interface of the Dean for America weblog structured the interaction that occurred between the campaign staff and the citizen-supporters of the campaign. Although the weblog appeared to invite citizen interaction with the campaign, the structure of the blog created a hierarchy between campaign staff and citizens. Similar to barriers created by television or radio between performer and audience, the blog interface establishes a performer/audience relationship. Granted, audience members can converse with each other on the blog in ways not possible with a mass television audience; however, the audience cannot turn the tables, take over the blog space, and create new posts. The creation of parasocial interaction with this technology is remarkably easy, because there is a kind of exchange on the blog: a staff member posts to the blog, and the citizens comment on the post. Citizens can see each other's comments and so can the staff—if they choose to. Citizens know that the staff can see their comments, creating the foundation of the façade of interaction.

The Reality

Reading through the weblog—from its inception on March 15, 2003, through Howard Dean's post to the blog on February 19, 2004, thanking his supporters after he announced that he would stop campaigning—is a walk through a blow-by-blow history of the campaign. The posts to the blog by campaign staff chronicled the skyrocketing success of the campaign and then its devastating crash.

Posts from the campaign came in many forms. During the height of the campaign, before the Iowa caucuses and the New Hampshire primary, the posts included invitations to get involved and to give money, reviews of Dean's coverage in the press and his standing in the public opinion polls, announcements of Dean's and Trippi's media engagements, "reposts" of speeches from Dean and press releases from the campaign, announcements of endorsements, guest blogs from Dean supporters or campaign staff, announcements of new technology rollouts and innovations in campaign organizing for supporters to investigate, and announcements of "open threads," where supporters could comment on anything they wished. There were occasional posts announcing jobs available in the campaign. Once or twice a month, Howard Dean would post to the blog, as would campaign manager Joe Trippi and, later, Roy Neel.

Comments by readers of the blog fell into a number of categories. Common responses were support for Dean. Support messages could be as short as "Go Dean!" to several paragraphs detailing why the commenter was supporting

Dean. There were messages attacking Dean's primary opponents and their supporters. There also were comments attacking Dean, posting as "trolls" who were trying to incite Dean supporters. Many messages focused on the community that had developed on the blogs, such as praising fellow blog commentators. We observed a significant amount of criticism and praise for media coverage of the candidate, and reprinting of favorable media stories by blog participants. There was a significant volume of "armchair strategizing," that is, comments urging the campaign to adopt particular strategies, such as producing better advertising or offering suggestions for speeches. We looked for but did not find many comments that discussed the issues that Dean was advancing; issue-related posts were rare, especially compared to the number of armchair strategizing posts.

A Façade of Interactivity

In our close reading of the blog posts from the campaign, we observed several strategies to promote a façade of interaction between the campaign and the citizen-supporters. We identified six ways that this façade promoted a sense of interaction without actually moving to genuine interaction between the campaign and the citizens. One way was to repost a comment from a prior blog post into a new post. Another was to tell blog readers that the campaign was reading their comments. A third way was to post comments directly in the blog comment section. A fourth way was to invite readers to the blog to answer a question or test a new technological feature and post reactions in the comments section. These first four strategies are as close as the campaign got to genuine interaction. These strategies were seen more frequently during the early part of the campaign than during the critical weeks around the primaries. The campaign used two other strategies to invoke a parasocial relationship between the campaign and the supporters. The principals of the campaign—Howard Dean, Joe Trippi, and Roy Neel—posted directly to the blogs, inviting a sense of interaction with these celebrities for readers of the blog. Finally, the authors of the blog posts used language that told supporters that it was "their campaign," that attacks on Dean were attacks on the supporters, and used pronouns such as "us" and "we" that invited the supporters into a rhetorically constructed inner circle of the campaign.

Citizen Comments Held Up as Examples

One way interactivity was constructed on the blogs was by reposting comments in new threads, often in the service of urging supporters to do more to get Howard Dean elected. Zephyr Teachout, grassroots coordinator for the campaign, was the campaign staffer who used this strategy most frequently. As an illustration of the strategy, in a post urging supporters to donate money to the campaign, Teachout reprinted a comment by a supporter urging readers of the blog that "if you can reach $250 in donations for this quarter, there is Federal matching. It'll make a HUGE difference to get those funds early in the campaign. Ok, and we're squeezing out another $25 today to help push the bat up to $1M. Can you do the same?" (000506.html). Teachout reprinted comments such as this one that featured support or strategy for the Dean campaign. She used such comments from supporters as testimonials to underscore her commands urging blog readers to do more for the campaign. In this example, she used the supporter's comment and its reference to the "bat" to inform readers that a bat icon on the home page of the Dean for America Web site was a hyperlink to donate money to the campaign. As money came into the campaign, they updated the bat to reflect the increase in the Dean coffers.

As another example, Teachout would ask blog readers questions such as "Why are you sleepless?" in reference to the Sleepless Summer campaign tour in 2003, and "What is your vision for America?" during the campaign's last-ditch effort to win Wisconsin. Teachout reposted several responses in the comments in a new blog summing up what supporters were thinking and wishing for. Her new post after asking supporters why they were sleepless was constructed as a litany of reasons to support Dean and of explanations of activities being conducted to get Dean elected (001233.html). Messages such as Teachout's create a sense that the campaign is engaged in a kind of slow dialogue with supporters, with a few lucky writers getting their comments held up for other readers to see.

"We're Listening"

Early on and at moments of crisis during the campaign, the blog writers from the campaign would tell readers that the campaign was reading blog comments. Kate O'Conner, who toured with Dean on his campaign stops, wrote a post early on telling readers that she had conveyed words of support to Dean from the blog community. In June 2003, Dean's son was arrested for stealing alcohol from a country club. Dean canceled two days of campaigning to fly home to be with his family. O'Conner wrote in her post, "We just arrived back [to Vermont], and I wanted to tell all of you how much your words of support and encouragement mean to the Gov. We had a layover in Detroit and I had a chance to read your comments on the blog. I told the Gov. about them and he really appreciates your kind thoughts" (000469.html). This message indicates that Dean is not reading the blogs, which could signify that blog readers who express themselves to the campaign are not being paid attention to; blog readers are talking to themselves.

O'Conner's explanation, however, that she read the comments and conveyed the sentiments to Dean, redeems the blog comment section from being an echo chamber. Although Dean is not reading them, he knows what supporters are saying because his staff keeps him apprised.

During the major campaign crises, such as the second-place finish in the New Hampshire primary, which was followed by the resignation of Joe Trippi as campaign manager, staffers posted statements that they were "listening" to the comments on the blog. Supporters, who were disillusioned after the great hype that had been building around the campaign in November and December 2003, demanded that the campaign listen to them. The staff, in turn, responded by writing posts such as the following. Joe Rospars, a staffer who posted regularly to the blog, wrote that "There's a lot to discuss tonight" after the loss in New Hampshire, and told readers to "use this thread to speak out— we're listening" (003444.html).

Yet telling the readers of the blog that they are listening is not the same thing as listening and then responding to supporters. One supporter posted a long message on January 24, three days before the New Hampshire primary and after the disappointing third-place finish in the Iowa caucuses. His message was titled "Give us a sign" and expressed his concern that the campaign was not listening to supporters who had what he thought were good suggestions to help the campaign (003358.html). The "sign," in the form of a response to his observations, was never given.

Posting Comments

The campaign staff, on occasion, posted directly in the comments section. Comments were more likely to occur earlier in the campaign than in the immediate weeks leading up to and through the Iowa caucuses and New Hampshire primary. On rare occasion, a set of exchanges would occur between campaign staff and supporters. For example, on June 8, 2003, Howard Dean posted a thank you note to the blog to those who had contributed money and had gotten involved in the campaign. In the comments section, one man complained that the post from Dean was too short and said, "Come on! Give us the plan man, give us something to run with, rally the troops, or at least tell us you are hiring a military advisor" (000640.html). Others labeled this man a "troll" (that is, someone trying to bait Dean supporters) and told him that if he were not a troll to give a "constructive comment." Yet Trippi responded in the comments to him and to others who requested more information about the campaign strategy. He explained the campaign had staff in "Iowa, New Hampshire, and South Carolina currently" and that "Gov. Dean has been on the road 26 days each month this year—the other 4 have been his only days off." Trippi's response to the "troll" gave a sense that the campaign was reading the comments and was willing to explain or clarify positions and answer challenges when they arose.

Such comments from Trippi or others from the campaign were genuinely interactive, but such interactions were rare. For example, Trippi posted a message on July 6 that was a reaction to a pundit surprised at the strength of the Dean campaign. Trippi wrote that the Dean campaign had work to do, but it had a better connection to average Americans than other political candidates who solicit funds from high-donation givers (000627.html). In the comments section, there were several remarks that praised Trippi for his post. They also made suggestions about strategies the campaign should adopt, such as utilizing MeetUps to educate supporters about how the Democratic party works. None of these comments or suggestions received any reply from Trippi.

Feedback on New Technology

In addition to the three strategies to create a sense of interaction between the campaign and the citizen-readers of the blog, campaign staff invited readers to provide feedback on new technology. For example, in October, Teachout announced that the Web team was going on a retreat to evaluate several of the online tools developed to help supporters organize. She wrote: "We'll be talking about where we're headed over the next few months in online organizing tools, with lots of notes and suggestions from blog comments and elsewhere. So help us out on this thread. What are the biggest things we can do to improve the organizing tools on our site, for on and off-line organizing?" (001771.html). These kinds of direct questions invited a great wealth of comments from readers. In a few rare cases, the staff member who posted the thread would respond to questions by supporters, creating genuine interaction between the campaign and supporters.

These four strategies worked to establish a culture of community for those citizens who read and wrote in the comment section. These strategies were more common in the earlier months of the campaign, from March through December 2003. The comments from citizens indicated that they felt that they were part of the campaign, working in solidarity with Howard Dean and his staff to get him elected. The blog comments made references to the campaign being "their campaign," and they developed slogans saying that they "were Dean."

Parasocial Interaction

The campaign also generated a sense of parasocial interaction between the campaign and its supporters by direct messages from the celebrities of the campaign, Howard Dean and Joe Trippi. After Trippi resigned, Roy Neel took the helm as campaign manager and also contributed to the blog. The messages from Dean throughout the campaign were primarily short "thank you" notes that followed major fund-raising drives. He posted once or twice a month, with the exception of May and November 2003, when he posted nothing directly to the blog. The first message from Dean was prefaced by a note from Teachout that "Messages authored by 'Howard Dean' are not written by campaign staff" (000383.html). It is noteworthy that Teachout felt compelled to suggest a level of authenticity to the posts from Dean by assuring readers of the blog that Dean wrote his own notes. Yet Dean's direct posts revealed little about his strategy, his issue positions, or his direct perspective on the campaign. Instead, messages of this sort were filtered through to readers of the blog from his campaign staff.

Messages from Trippi and then from Neel were much more revealing of campaign strategy, and structured not only to thank but also to encourage supporters to do more to help get Dean elected. Trippi posted some comments that were noteworthy in their explanation of the larger campaign strategy. Trippi provided frank details about the campaign's strategy in the early days. In June, for example, he posted to the blog a critical comment about a Drudge Report that the Dean campaign would have an effect on the next Democratic National Committee. That post is not particularly noteworthy. What is, however, is a long comment he contributed halfway down in the comments section where he maps out the campaign's strategy for the coming months. His comment followed a query by a Dean organizer in California asking Trippi to clarify whether the campaign had acquired 1-800 numbers yet. Trippi responded in great detail what the campaign intended to do in the months ahead. He concluded, "We may be a rag tag team of a campaign, volunteers and an extra measure of hope and grit—but we have had a plan for each quarter and exceeded our goals in each of the last two. None of it possible without the strength of people who have given so much of their time and resources to make it all happen—YOU" (000630.html).

The principal leaders for the campaign not only posted about strategy, but also provided rich detail about life on the campaign trail. These narratives created a vision of the daily life of the campaign and invited readers into the "inner circle." A dramatic example came in the wee hours after the Bryant Park capstone speech of the Sleepless Summer Tour. Trippi posted a long reflection on the success of the tour and highlighted his favorite moments. The note read like an end-of-the-journey reflection on the golden moments. Trippi described the Dean campaign staff on the tarmac at LaGuardia airport in New York as they ended the four-day journey. Trippi wrote that as "I tried to find the words to thank everyone for their hard work I choked up a little, and then everyone started to lose it." He described the scene at Bryant Park and the chaos and joy as the event unfolded. He reminisced,

> And I will always remember Howard Dean, the Bat in his hands as the crowd sang take me out to the ball game. He was the one who had come back from every road trip in the early days of the campaign and would say we had to run a decentralized campaign to win—the one who had criss-crossed the country day in and day out with a simple message "you have the power to change our country and our politics." (001273.html)

The posts from the principal leaders revealed the daily workings of the campaign and provided behind-the-scenes tales that invited readers of the blog to experience the campaign *as if they were insiders.*

Finally, the campaign staff who wrote the blog posts utilized language that invited identification and promoted, through their language, a level of intimacy between the campaign staff and the citizens. The posts written by campaign staff were often informal in tone. A post on Halloween from Teachout, for example, had the heading "OOOOOOOO-pen Thread." In the body of the blog, she wrote "C'mon, I can be a little playful on Halloween." She continued, "I just got back from the Castro [in San Francisco] with local Dean organizers—an event well worth spending a few more verbs on, but I'm beat" (002076.html). Her playfulness in the headline, and casual language ("C'mon") are similar to a note someone might write to a friend. Her description of her physical well-being ("I'm beat") gave readers an intimate view of her current state. Writing such as this invites readers into Teachout's world and promotes a sense that readers of the blog hold knowledge about the campaign to which general observers of the campaign are not privy.

Blog posts used the phrase "your campaign" often, especially when the campaign was under attack. In mid-December, a group calling itself "Americans for jobs, health care and progressive values" aired an ad in South Carolina and New Hampshire with an image of Osama bin Laden and a voiceover questioning Dean's experience with foreign affairs. Mark Sundeen, a staff blog writer, announced the ad and wrote the following: "They're not trying to stop Howard Dean. They're trying to stop you—stop you from taking your party back, stop you from taking your country back, and stop you from bringing more Americans back into this process" (002667.html). In a later post, Sundeen wrote, "Last night a secretive group of Democrats attacked your campaign" (002670.html). This phrase "your campaign" is important, because it transfers ownership of the campaign to the citizen-supporters. It underscores a sense that the Dean campaign is less about Howard Dean and more about the grassroots movement.

Unlike other campaigns, where there is a clear division between staff and volunteers, the Dean campaign's rhetoric blurred such a division and constructed weblog participants as being the heart of the campaign. The prevalent rhetoric is of the "grassroots" and its power. Trippi was one of the most vocal advocates of the power of the grassroots. In his posts on the blog, he frequently invoked the grassroots as being a powerful force, larger than the campaign itself. The effect of this was the creation of an intimate bond between supporters and the campaign. In effect, the campaign indeed became the citizens' campaign, attacks on Dean were attacks on them, and they were given privileged, private knowledge about the principals of the campaign and their daily experiences on the campaign trail.

Joys and Sorrows

With Joe Trippi's guidance, Howard Dean decentralized the campaign, thereby opening up greater opportunities for citizens with a little creativity or organizational ability to seemingly *become* the campaign. The comments section of the blog was populated with narratives of Dean supporters who boasted with pride their fund-raising, visibility, and organizational efforts to bring others to the Dean camp.

The campaign was able to propel itself from nearly last in public opinion polls and fund-raising at the beginning of 2003 to leading the pack of candidates at the end of 2003. The insurgency campaign was made possible through the innovations that Trippi developed using the Internet and its related technologies. That insurgency campaign brought people into the political process who had not been active before or in many election cycles. The large number of small donors is one example of this (Center for Responsive Politics n.d.; Cone 2003). That the Dean for America blog was transformed into the Democracy for America blog after Dean quit the campaign is evidence that a ground movement was built and continued long after the official campaign was over. In this way, the positive effect of the Dean campaign's revolutionary tactics was to mobilize and energize a segment of the U.S. populace in fairly novel ways. The novelty was the use of the Internet, rather than traditional campaign tactics, to raise money, identify and create new supporters, and get volunteers working for the campaign.

Yet the façade of interactivity that the campaign created through the tactics described in the prior section led to perceptions on the part of supporters that their opinions and their suggestions mattered. Trippi, Dean, and the other principals of the campaign undoubtedly cared about the supporters and their opinions, but the reality of campaigning is that in the heat of battle only so much attention can be paid to the hundreds of thousands of comments flooding into the campaign from the blogs. Thus, in the crisis days after the losses in Iowa and New Hampshire, supporters began posting comments asking for information from the campaign. For example, one supporter wrote: "HQ???? Your people are begging for information here. . . . We are being asked to contribute (which we are) on a day when much is up in the air concerning money, strategy, etc. Please provide us with information and guidance!" (003449.html). Yet there was no direct answer to these pleas in the blog.

In telling supporters in the early days that the campaign was listening to supporters' comments, an expectation was created that if citizens had feedback or concerns, they would be addressed by campaign staff. One of the issues of contention for some blog participants was the campaign's advertising strategy, especially after the loss in Iowa, and many comments complained about how poorly done and boring Dean's ads were. Several offered suggestions for new ads. When no campaign staff posted a new message or a response in the blogs about the ads, this caused some to ask the campaign to please reply. For example, "T" wrote:

> Dear Governor Dean,
>   I would walk through fire for you.
>   Will you please reassure us that this campaign really does value our insight and contributions by responding to our concerns about lack of a quality media strategy and the best ads? You are right that the campaign will move fast now, and without terrific ads the country will not know you like we do.
>   Thank you for all you do for us.
>   T in S.D.

There were no replies from the campaign in the blog responses to posts and no clear indication that the campaign was even following the blog responses at this time—a period of crisis for supporters of Dean.

The creation of parasocial interaction by the campaign created problems for the campaign when it faltered. In hearing that the Dean campaign was "their campaign," writers to the blog comments section felt a certain entitlement to suggest activities for the campaign that had the potential to work against the interests of a Dean candidacy. For example, in early January, campaign supporters in the comments section began speculating and hoping that Iowa Senator Tom Harkin would endorse Dean. Supporters urged other supporters to e-mail and to call Senator Harkin to urge him to endorse Dean. This suggestion did not come from campaign organizers. Supporters generated such a flood of phone calls that Matthew Gross posted on January 9 a blog thread asking that people stop calling the senator's offices. Titling his message "Phone Calls to Harkin," Gross wrote, "Iowans for Dean director Jeani Murray kindly requests that Dean supporters cease calling Senator Tom Harkin's office" (003034.html). This and similar enthusiasm to contact political leaders, such as union leaders, Bill Bradley, and Al Gore, led on several occasions to the campaign asking supporters to stop. Although there did not appear to be negative political fallout from these citizen-generated activities, the risk was high that such activities could get out of hand and end up being abusive. This, in turn, could have had negative consequences for the image of Howard Dean as well as the future support for his candidacy.

Additional problems for the campaign developed when supporters began suggesting that they knew more about how to run a campaign than the staff hired by the Dean campaign. Such comments increased in frequency when the campaign faltered after Iowa and the "Dean Scream." Several supporters, many who had been with the campaign for months, began posting notes suggesting that their expertise was stronger than that of those who were paid staffers. For example, one of the core citizen-bloggers wrote in the comments section that Matthew Gross and Mark Sundeen needed to create a hyperlink from the Dean Web site to a *Washington Post* video clip about Howard Dean. The supporter continued, "YOU MUST DO THIS. it is excellent. do NOT miss out on an opportunity to help yourselves. LISTEN to us. . . . WE on the blog get it more than YOUR OWN media people" (003349.html). This supporter's comments, one of several of this type, claimed authority over the campaign strategy. In the early days of the campaign, the staff members fostered a perspective that the campaign's supporters were knowledgeable experts who could help the campaign by doing what they thought was appropriate to help get Dean nominated. This strategy proved problematic, however, when the citizen-supporters lost confidence in the campaign staff.

Indeed, supporters, when the campaign faltered during the primaries, began suggesting that they run the campaign *without the campaign*. In other words, some supporters suggested that the campaign staff were not able to run the campaign, that they did not have the good ideas, and therefore that the supporters should, in essence, hijack the campaign. One message on February 1, after the second-place finish in New Hampshire and Trippi's resignation, said, "We really are the campaign. Look at what the campaign has done, and look at what we have done. We started the meetups. . . . If you have an idea for getting the word out, GO FOR IT!! Don't wait for the campaign. We are so strong, it can barely keep up. We are fighting a battle on 2 fronts, while the other campaigns only have 1" (003486.html). This message suggests that the rhetoric that it was *their* campaign has been taken to heart. When the road got tough for the campaign, some supporters believed it was in their best interest to do whatever they felt they should to get Dean elected, regardless of the guidance and mandates from campaign headquarters.

Conclusion

Thus, after a careful reading of the Dean blog posts and citizen comments, it seems that the campaign was interacting *at* citizens rather than interacting *with* citizens. Rather than genuine interaction between the staff and citizens, the weblog was used as a way to relay information to citizens, but was not used as a forum to dialogue with citizens. Granted, at times staff responded directly to citizen comments, but those occasions were rare and generally stopped after a single response from staff. Sustained engagement between campaign staff and the blog participants was minimal. Instead, the staff used strategies that gave the impression that they were involved in the conversations taking place on the blog. Posting citizens' comments on the blog as examples, explicitly stating staff were listening, engaging campaign celebrities, and using empowering language gave the impression that the campaign was truly listening and that the decision-making power was with the people. However, as the campaign moved into the primaries, citizens realized that genuine interaction with the campaign was lacking. When they began pushing the campaign for answers and guidance and demanding responses from the campaign, they received silence in return.

Using the blogs to foster a sense of ownership of the campaign proved to be a double-edged sword. On the one hand, the use of new communication technologies to bring citizens into the process enabled the Dean campaign to surge to the front of the pack. On the other hand, those same people who felt invested in the campaign wanted their hard work and support acknowledged and their suggestions heard and responded to by the campaign staff. The joy of weblogging is that it energized and seemed to invite citizen-supporters *into* the campaign. The sorrow is that weblogging maintained a hierarchical relationship between citizens and the campaign and reinforced that citizen-supporters were not ultimately insiders.

Notes

1. Throughout the paper, where we have directly quoted from the blog comments, we include the HTML file where the comment can be found. The Democracy for America Web site (the former Dean for America site), as of this writing, provides an archive of all posts to the blog during the Dean campaign. The archive can be found at www.blogforamerica.com/archives. The specific HTML file for this direct quote, for example, can be found at www.blogforamerica.com/archives/0012447.html.

2. Interestingly, reporters mused that Dean was not even aware of what weblogs were until his campaign staff urged him to adopt one as part of his campaign strategy. Joe Trippi, Dean's campaign manager, told Reston (2003: 14) that he "never tried to fool anybody into thinking [Dean] was some kind of Internet wizard."

References

Barber, Benjamin R. 1984. *Strong Democracy: Participatory Politics for a New Age.* Berkeley: University of California Press.

Beniger, James R. 1987. "Personalization of Mass Media and the Growth of Pseudo-Community." *Communication Research* 14 (3): 352–71.

Center for Responsive Politics. n.d. "2004 Donor Demographics." *OpenSecrets.org.* Available at www.opensecrets.org/presidential/donordems.asp (accessed May 15, 2005).

Cone, Edward. 2003. "Presidential Marketing: Howard Dean's Blog." *Eweek.* November 18.

Drezner, Daniel W., and Henry Farrell. 2004. "Web of Influence." *Foreign Policy* (November–December): 32–40.

Faler, Brian. 2003. "Add 'Blog' to the Campaign Lexicon." *Washington Post,* November 15, A 04.

Hacker, Kenneth L. 1996. "Missing Links in the Evolution of Electronic Democratization." *Media, Culture & Society* 18 (2): 213–32.

Horton, Donald, and R. Richard Wohl. 1956. "Mass Communication and Para-Social Interaction: Observations on Intimacy at a Distance." *Psychiatry* 19: 215–29.

Lessig, Lawrence. 2003. "Interview with Joe Trippi." *Lessig Blog.* Available at www.lessig.org/blog/archives/001428.shtml.

Manjoo, Farhad. 2003. "Blogland's Man of the People." *Salon.com.* July 3.

Margolis, Michael, and David Resnick. 2000. *Politics as Usual: The Cyberspace "Revolution."* Thousand Oaks, CA: Sage.

McMillan, Sally J. 2002. "Exploring Models of Interactivity from Multiple Research Traditions: Users, Documents, and Systems." In *The Handbook of New Media,* edited by Leah A. Lievrouw and Sonia Livingstone, 163–82. Thousand Oaks, CA: Sage.

Morris, Dick. 2003. "Dean's Internet Revolution." *Frontpagemagazine.com.* August 6. Available at frontpagemag.com/Articles/ReadArticle.asp?ID=9252 (May 15, 2005).

Park, David. 2004. "From Many, a Few: Intellectual Authority and Strategic Positioning in the Coverage of, and Self-Descriptions of, the 'Big Four' Weblogs." Paper presented at the annual meeting of the International Communication Association, New Orleans, May.

Rafaeli, Sheizaf. 1988. "Interactivity: From New Media to Communication." In *Advancing Communication Science: Merging Mass and Interpersonal Processes,* edited by Robert P. Hawkins, John M. Wiemann, and Suzanne Pingree, 110–34. Thousand Oaks: Sage.

———. 1990. "Interacting with Media: Para-social Interaction and Real Interaction." In *Mediation, Information and Communication: Information and Behavior,* Vol. 3, edited by Leah A. Lievrouw. New Brunswick, NJ: Transaction.

Rafaeli, Sheizaf, and Fay Sudweeks. 1998. "Interactivity on the Nets." In *Network & Netplay,* edited by Fay Sudweeks, Margaret McLaughlin, and Sheizaf Rafaeli, 173–90. Cambridge, MA: MIT Press.

Rainie, Lee. 2005a. "Data Memo: The State of Blogging." Pew Internet & American Life Project. Available at www.pewinternet.org/pdfs/PIP_blogging_data.pdf (accessed May 15, 2005).

———. 2005b. "Reports: Technology & Media Use." Pew Internet & American Life Project. Available at www.pewinternet.org/PPF/r/144/report_display.asp (accessed May 15, 2005).

Reston, Maeve. 2003. "A Wired Dean Is Altering the Conduct of Politics." *Pittsburgh Post Gazette,* November 16, A1.

Selnow, Gary W. 1998. *Electronic Whistle-Stops: The Impact of the Internet on American Politics.* Westport, CT: Praeger.

Stromer-Galley, Jennifer. 2000. "On-line Interaction and Why Candidates Avoid It." *Journal of Communication* 5 (4): 111–32.

Sundar, S. Shyam. 2000. "Multimedia Effects on Processing and Perception of Online News: A Study of Picture, Audio, and Video Downloads." *Journalism & Mass Communication Quarterly* 3: 480–99.

Trippi, Joe. 2004a. *The Revolution Will Not Be Televised: Democracy, the Internet, and the Overthrow of Everything.* New York: Regan.

———. 2004b. Remarks to the Institute for Politics, Democracy & the Internet conference, George Washington University, Washington, May 19.

9

The Blogging of the President

Kaye D. Trammell

DURING THE 2004 U.S. PRESIDENTIAL CAMPAIGN, a new online tool was introduced and quickly incorporated into the campaign Web site. Following trends of the Internet, the campaigns of both incumbent Republican President George W. Bush and challenging Democrat Senator John F. Kerry hosted weblogs—or blogs for short—on their official Web sites. While each campaign used the blog in a tactically different way, the strategy of the blog for both candidates was the same: inform people about the campaign and issues of the day. Even so, if that were all the blogs did, then this new technology of "blog" would not be any different than the average Web site, direct mail piece, or advertisement. Yet blogs were heralded as being a special and interactive component—beyond anything that American online campaigns had seen in the past. Just what was so special about blogs that caused such a buzz? This chapter will answer that question by removing the hype and cyperbole about the new tool from the analysis.

In doing so, first this chapter will explore the history of blogs in politics and describe how each campaign used their blogs during the general election cycle of the campaign. While blogs are a facet of online campaigning, overall Web sites are discussed elsewhere in this volume, and so the historical development of campaign Web sites will not be discussed here. Questions such as which tools were used on blogs and analysis of just how revolutionary—or not—those tools were will be reviewed. Finally, this chapter will conclude by discussing the overall impact of blogs on the election and making predictions for the future of blogs in campaigning.

Blogs

Before examining the political blogs studied here, it might be helpful to review other scholarship on blogs. In the past several years, the study of blogs has grown rapidly. The first published studies on blogs provided a lay of the land and compared the media hype to reality in the so-called blogosphere. Several studies by Herring and colleagues offer these initial glances at who is blogging, what they are blogging about, and how they are doing it (Herring, Kouper, Scheidt, and Wright 2004; Herring, Scheidt, Bonus, and Wright 2004). One popular area of such research lies in establishing the motivations of bloggers. For example, Nardi et al. (2004) found the main reasons for blogging to be documenting one's life, providing commentary and opinions, self-expression, communicating ideas, and connecting with others online. Nardi et al. (2004) concluded that blog content and motivations for blogging varied widely, based on the blog. Papacharissi's content analysis of blogs (2004a) to examine the uses and gratifications of writing blogs yielded similar results in that bloggers were primarily motivated by social interaction. Because of this rather personal and "human scale" approach to blogging, many scholars have examined blogs in terms of diary keeping or journaling (Sorapure 2003; Kitzmann 2003).

In looking at the visuals and structure of blogs, researchers have found that bloggers tend to keep the service-provided free templates rather than create looks of their own (Papacharissi 2004a; Scheidt and Wright 2004). That said, bloggers do personalize their sidebar content and offer features, such as "blogrolls," where the blogger links to other self-selected blogs (Scheidt and Wright 2004). Thompson (2004) found that bloggers who do personalize their template look and feel often do so to reflect the topical genre. Apart from the template, bloggers can personalize the site look by adding graphics to individual blog posts. Even so, few bloggers do this.

Blogs in Politics

Considering how quickly technology and fads develop on the Internet, blogs are not as new as some would believe. Blogs in some form or another have been around since the 1990s. Only since the terror attacks on September 11, 2001, did blogs really start to gain mainstream popularity and did the world start to consider their use in the information process (Blood 2002). As such, blogs have provided a personalized approach to presenting news and information. That is, blogs allow people to discuss thematic, big-picture issues in a very episodic and anecdotal way. Trammell (2004a) suggests that this increased personalization of content when discussing politics could allow a po-litical message to fall "under the radar" and not be immediately labeled "po-litical." Rather, Trammell (2004a) suggests that it would just seem someone was telling a story about real experiences.

In regards to politics and blogs, there appear to be two genres of blogs in this category: those run by politicians and those that just talk politics. This chapter will discuss a particular type of the first genre. While American politi-cians appear to be slow to adopt blogs, politicians in the United Kingdom have been blogging for years. Furthermore, British politicians tend to blog while in office—as an effort to reach out to their constituency—whereas the American model appears to be to use the tool to win office and inform voters about the campaign. While this is not the case across the board, the trends do point in this direction. Thus this study will examine how American campaign blogs reach out to prospective voters.

Recent studies have looked at specific elements in these candidate blogs. For example, one study compared the role of the hyperlink in both candidate Web sites and blogs this election cycle (Williams et al. 2005). Williams et al. (2005) found that hyperlinking practices differed on blogs, confirming popular press reports about blogs that blogs link to external resources (sites outside the con-trol of the blogger) at a greater rate than normal Web sites.

Further investigating this concept of interactivity, another study found that campaign blogs promoted interactivity beyond mere technical features such as hyperlinks (Trammell et al. 2006). Trammell et al. (2006) identified that text-based interactivity was present on Bush's and Kerry's campaign blogs, meaning the text fostered a spirit of interactivity by asking readers to do something or get involved. In many instances, the text-based interactivity was combined with more traditional manifestations of interactivity, such as a hy-perlink or providing a means through which the reader could reply (Trammell et al. 2006).

Continuing such examinations of the content on blogs, Trammell (2005) analyzed negative messages on campaign blog posts. This study noted that discussion of the opponent—on both Kerry's and Bush's blogs—was fre-quent and that most opponent mentions were negative. Trammell (2005) suggests that the negative turn to blogs so early in their integration to polit-ical sites is indicative of strategists' perceptions of blog strength as a political message.

While the earlier-discussed inquiries focused on the content of the blogs themselves, other studies have examined the reader of political blogs. Emerg-ing research demonstrates that blogs can influence both media and citizens alike. For example, Drezner and Farrell (2004) suggest that blogs impact the media. Trammell and Britton (2005) studied three famous cases where the popular press proposed that bloggers actually set the media agenda. While blogs can set the media agenda, most blogs react to media reports. A Pew Internet & American Life study, in conjunction with BuzzMetrics, found that political bloggers made an impact on politics, but they often followed the lead of politicians and journalists (BuzzMetrics 2005). Such findings are in line with the intermedia agenda-setting analysis conducted by Trammell, Golan, and Wanta (2005), which found that traditional media set the issue agenda for blogs.

Understanding who uses blogs is also an important area of consideration for this developing campaign communication tool. Studying the "state of blogging," a Pew Internet & American Life Project (2005) report found that the number of people who used blogs as a source of political information increased among those online during the 2004 general election. Johnson and Kaye's blog reader study (2004) noted that people who read blogs rate the medium as the most credible source of information available—even above online newspapers and television broadcasts. Trammell and Kiousis (2005) found an agenda-setting effect occurring as issue salience transferred from the blogger to the reader, as measured in reader feedback elements in political posts.

These studies, considered together, chart a path of information flow. Bloggers get information from media and politicians. While bloggers have successfully impacted the media's agenda, evidence of this remains anecdotal and it appears to be an exception to the norm. People turn to blogs for political information as one of many information sources. As research demonstrates, blog content can be perceived as more influential and credible than traditional media content. Clearly, research suggests that blogs have the potential to play a significant informational and persuasive role in political campaigns. As such, a description of the content of presidential candidate blogs is warranted.

It is evident that much work has been done examining specific content on political blogs since the 2004 election cycle. This chapter will add to this vein of research, but aim to provide a comprehensive descriptive overview of the candidate blogs during the 2004 presidential election. After presenting a description of the types of features offered on the blogs, this chapter will compare the candidate blogs and evaluate the best practices among these blogs. Suggestions for future campaign blogs will be discussed with an eye toward the role of blogs in future campaigns.

This chapter evaluates Bush's and Kerry's blogs and 1,190 blog posts during the 2004 general election. Only blog posts were formally evaluated, using a modified method derived from Banwart's webstyle (2002).Therefore this chapter surveys the features offered (e.g., hyperlinks, blogroll, and comments) throughout the campaign period.

Description of the Blogs

Upon first glance, both blogs appeared very similar. Both blogs used blue as a dominant color in the design. Both had navigation items tying the blog in with the overall Web site at the top. Both used the common blog layout and stamped each individual post with a record of the author, a permanent link to the post, and the date and time the item was uploaded. Anyone familiar with blogs would easily identify this Web content as a blog. As Papacharissi (2004b) points out, both blogs conformed to the in vogue design style of blogs by having the newly updated content (the posts) in the center of the page and sidebars providing links and information down the side, using a multicolumn format. Both blogs adhered to the common blog style by using unique headlines for each post and stamping posts with the date and time the item was uploaded so readers would know how fresh the content was, and for the most part, the blog posts were considerably shorter than other campaign Web content, such as press releases. A reading of the blog posts identifies that the primary purpose of both blogs was to inform various categories of voters—mobilization information for current supporters, facts and figures for undecided voters, issue statements, and a more personal and human portrayal of the candidate and campaign.

That said, these blogs were not carbon copies of one another. There were specific differences between the blogs of Bush and Kerry. Each campaign had a very different approach to getting out the same type of content to prospective readers. This section will discuss the blogstyle of each campaign.

Bush Blogging Style

The Bush blog was formatted in a two-column page layout. Bush's blog was very image-oriented, as the campaign had a logo or other graphic posted next to the various offerings in the sidebar (e.g., volunteer information, featured posts). The only sidebar in Bush's blog was located on the right side of the page. The sidebar contained numerous logos, links, and gateways to other information. The left column was larger and was designed for the blog posts.

In the sidebar on the right, there were three "featured posts." These were archived posts that were chosen by the campaign; the posts had uniform-sized thumbnails to the left and showed the post's title and when it was uploaded to the blog. These featured posts typically contained different message strategies and content—providing something for everyone. On November 2, 2004, the first featured post was an item written on November 1, 2004, called "The First Four Years." This thumbnail image next to this post showed Bush speaking at a rally with a bullhorn. The second featured post was written on October 31,

2004, and titled "Your Halloween Pumpkins"—this was a link to a post that contained several images of pumpkins carved with Bush–Cheney messages on them. The last featured post was an issue post written on October 31, 2004, called "Right War, Right Time, Right Man." Here, it is clear that the campaign targeted people with messages of Bush's credentials ("The First Four Years") and his issue statements ("Right War, Right Time, Right Man"), mixed in with less traditional and more informal content, such as supporter-submitted photos of carved pumpkins at Halloween ("Your Halloween Pumpkins"). This mix of traditional campaign messaging with touches of fun and humor was indicative of the range of content posted to campaign blogs.

The campaign targeted messages based on demographics. For example, on the sidebar there was a link to "State Blogs," where blog users could pick their home state and visit an affiliated blog dedicated to content relevant to their state. Additionally, a "Coalitions" drop-down menu allowed people who were interested in information for groups such as "African Americans," "Democrats," and "Sportsmen" to obtain information targeted directly to their issues.

Another innovative feature about blogs is the use of syndication. RSS or XML syndication allowed users to sign up to receive content when new information was uploaded to the blog. This turns the Web's "pull" technology into a "push" technology where information was pushed directly to subscribers who were interested in it. According to the Pew Internet & American Life Project's state of blogging report (2005), an increasing number of people use syndication to read blogs. The technology is beneficial because users do not have to constantly go to their favorite fifty blogs and see if new content has been added—rather new posts are sent directly to them. Bush offered various types of syndication—users could subscribe to the entire blog, by topic ("Barbara & Jenna," "Morning Reads," "Convention," etc.), or to the special PDA (personal digital assistant) on-the-go version, which would be sent to a digital handheld device (e.g., the Palm Pilot or BlackBerry). This allowed interested parties who may not always remember to visit the blog to still be pushed information from the blog regularly. A final push technology option included the "send to friends" link at the bottom of every post.

Bush's blog had an average of 8.08 posts per day during the fifty-eight-day sample spanning the general election cycle. Overall, there were 496 blog posts in the sample. These posts were short, averaging 294 words per post, and typically contained a "record of the day" (54.6%), meaning the post talked about what was happening that day or recapped an experience/event from the day. Bush's blog posts tended to be very promotional in nature—the blog provided excerpts from speeches given and announced speeches (16.5%), discussed the overall campaign events (20.0%) and Bush–Cheney campaign rallies (32.5%), and mentioned press coverage (32.9%).

For the most part, posts were written by the campaign staff and appeared to be authored from a generic administrative account named "GeorgeWBush .com." The blog did allow other users within the campaign to upload posts, and in these cases the author's name would appear after the "posted by" line at the bottom of each post. When Bush's twin daughters posted to the blog, their posts were labeled to have been posted by "Jenna and Barbara Bush."

There were several trends observed in the content analysis of Bush's posts. Every morning, the blog would feature a "What Is Happening" post that outlined the events of the day, such as speeches, rallies, and media appearances associated with the campaign. Another noted daily element was a review of media articles about the campaign or the candidate.

Other studies have noted the campaign blogs married traditional hyperlink interactivity with text-based interactivity (Trammell et al. 2006). This was a regular occurrence on the blog posts examined here. This September 30, 2004, post titled "Live Debate Response" on Bush's blog is an example of how the text asks the reader to get involved and interact while also providing a traditional means of interactivity through a hyperlink:

> During tonight's debate, you can log on to *DebateFacts.com* [link] to get the facts on Kerry's false claims. Live, during the presidential debate we will *set the record straight* [link] with text and video enabling voters to see how Kerry is playing politics with the most important issues facing our nation. If you're a blogger or have a personal web site, you can *post a Live Debate Feed* [link] on your site, and your readers will be updated on all of Kerry's misstatements, live, and in real-time.

This example illustrates the text-based interactivity present when the blog asks readers to log on to the special site and post a live debate feed on their own personal Web sites. Traditional interactivity is achieved through hyperlinks to these various tools and sites.

Not only did posts seek to engage and interact with blog readers, but they also served as a way to allow blog readers to identify other supporters. Nearly one third (32.2%) of the posts on Bush's blog had photographs or images embedded within the main portion of the post. These pictures were not the typical campaign-produced candidate rally photographs; these were what the campaign called "grassroots" pictures taken by supporters that were submitted to the blog administrators and posted. Supporters would send images of Bush at rallies kissing babies, celebrities speaking at campaign events, and local groups volunteering for the campaign. Additionally, there were photos of the campaign staff and headquarters—allowing blog viewers to get an inside look at the people and process of running a presidential campaign. Photos also served to add humor to blog. For example, one post on October 22, 2004, titled "Standing Up for W in Minnesota" showed a young girl with Pippi Longstocking–type braids in her hair positioned to create a "W" with her braids.

The Kerry Blog

The Kerry blog, on first glance, looked similar to the Bush blog. The dominant color of the blog was blue, and it had accents of red and white, forming the patriotic palette. However, Kerry's blog used a three-column design. On the right side of the page there was a sidebar with various links. Unlike Bush's sidebar, Kerry's sidebar was not graphic heavy and relied more on text than images to communicate. The middle column was designed to hold the blog posts. The left-column sidebar featured blog-specific information, such as the blog archive and links to syndication. At the top of the left sidebar one could find a list of the last five entries on the blog.

The biggest technology difference between the two blogs was that Kerry's blog allowed users to respond to posts through the "comment" feature. While Baker and Stromer-Galley (2004) criticized inattention to blog comments by earlier campaigns using this feature, the comment feature was quite popular on the Kerry blog in that nearly every post had comments, at an average of 198.95 comments per post. Furthering this conversation between the reader and the blog staff, the blog hosted an "Open Thread" almost daily where the campaign blog staff would allow readers to comment off topic in the moderated comment thread. Many of these open thread posts would present a topic for discussion; however, users were allowed to steer the conversation in different directions. In terms of interactivity, this feature and specific use of the open thread blog post presents the most sophisticated engagement tool on the campaign blogs in 2004. Not only did the campaign ask its readers what they thought about specific issues and give readers the impression that they were participating in the strategic planning for the campaign, but also these interactive elements were operationalized through technology. That is, the request to interact and engage was done through interactive features on the site.

The example of the open thread post, where users are able to comment and contribute to the conversation, showed that blogs are capable of McMillan's three types of interactivity (2002). The request from the campaign for users to leave a comment on a particular topic is user-to-user, or what Endres and Warnick (2004) call "campaign-to-user" interactivity. When users click on a hyperlink in order to add a comment, they experience system-to-user interactivity. The process of contributing to the discussion and adding content to the page is a classic manifestation of user-to-document interactivity. The innovative use of the technology to engage prospective voters is a signal that campaign fear of interactivity in Web sites has decreased (Stromer-Galley 2000).

Kerry posted an average of 11.96 posts per day. His posts were longer than Bush's, averaging 394.88 words per post. When some longer posts were teased on the front page of the blog, the readers were given a hyperlink to follow to continue reading the rest of the post. The use of the link to the full post kept the posts on the front page of the blog looking short, creating a document that appeared to have easy-to-read snippets of content.

In regard to the frequency of posting, Kerry's campaign blog did second-by-second reactions to the several debates, posting more than eighty times on the days of debates close to the election (Trammell 2004b). In doing so, the blog offered a rebuttal to what was occurring on screen; however, many of these responses were canned, and several items were posted in duplicate on the blog during the debate (Trammell 2004b). Thus the debate rapid-fire posting seemed more like cut-and-paste posting than thoughtful and relevant additions to what was being said live at the debate.

Posts in Kerry's blog also used text-based interactivity along with traditional manifestations of interactivity. Specifically, many posts asked readers to reach out to other people in face-to-face and interpersonal contexts. For example, a November 2, 2004, post titled "Polls are Open" on Kerry's blog encouraged interactivity and interpersonal contact with other voters and provided a technological feature to encourage voting: "Its 6AM, and polls are now open in Connecticut, Indiana, Kentucky, Maine, New York, Vermont, and Virginia. Go vote, bring your friends to vote, call your friends and remind them to vote or use johnkerry.com to send an *Election Day voting reminder* [link]."

In regard to images within the blog posts, Kerry's campaign used much of the same grassroots photography that was seen on the Bush blog, but at a lesser rate. Only 12.2% of the blog posts analyzed contained a graphic of any sort. In addition to supporter-submitted photos, campaign staff touring with the candidates took photos "on the road" and provided a more intimate look at the campaign than the Bush blog photos did.

2004 Campaign Blogs: Dialogic and Interactive?

Early in the primary season of the 2004 U.S. presidential election, it was said that Americans would choose their next president online. Such a bold statement is the type of cyberbole that this chapter seeks to avoid. Even so, it seems as if campaigns invested heavily in this notion by quickly adopting a technology trend and thereby exponentially increasing the frequency of interactivity with voters.

Bush's blog had strong imagery and offered targeted communication with special reader groups. Kerry's blog posts were longer and more text based and featured fewer hyperlinks; however, the interactivity offered through the comment feature and the open thread posts was unparalleled. While both syndicated their blog posts, Bush's model of allowing subscriptions to single categories of content (instead of an all-or-nothing RSS approach), the "on the go" version, and the "send to a friend" option all signaled advances in personalized content delivery system integration on campaign blogs.

Indeed, it seemed as if one candidate excelled at one aspect of harnessing the technology when the opponent excelled at another aspect. Neither of these two blogs—on their own—was perfect. Neither fully engaged the voter or maximized the experience without room for improvement. However, campaigns have been known to be slow to adopt technology (Stromer-Galley 2000) and this quick adoption of blogs on the campaign Web site is notable (Williams et al. 2005; Trammell et al. 2006). Looked at together, and considered for the inaugural run of American campaign blogging that they are, these blogs represent a true turn toward engaging voters and interacting with them.

Improving Campaign Blogs

In looking at both blogs, it becomes apparent that there are things that campaigns should do and things that they should not when it comes to blogging. Early in the primary season, Garrett (2004) offered a useful list of how campaigns could maximize blog usability and engage voters. Garrett's suggestions stand true today and can be added to with the following suggestions.

Trammell (2004b) found that the candidates themselves rarely wrote posts. Rather, as with many campaign communication pieces, the candidates allowed the official campaign voice to speak. However, with blogs being so frequently updated, with short messages, it seems disappointing that there were not more candidate-authored posts. Future campaigns should attempt more often to post an item written by the candidate reflecting on the day or the campaign. These posts need not be long—indeed, a short, fifty-word post would certainly be enough if done regularly. One of the benefits of a blog is that the reader can get to know the blogger—just as Bush's blog used informality and humor to take the edge off the "campaign mouthpiece," posts written by the candidate can also contribute to humanizing the candidate.

Blogs are known for providing links, yet candidates deployed a linking strategy at a very different rate (Williams et al. 2005). Even though Stromer-Galley (2000) suggests campaigns are wary of giving up control over content and sending Web site visitors to external sites, these sites are said to offer source credibility when linked to (Trammell 2004b). Therefore, future campaign blogs should better utilize the link. In this vein, Bush's blog post composition style was superior to Kerry's in that Bush's posts linked to source material such as media articles or reports upon reference. By contrast, Kerry's posts would quote the facts and cite the source but not offer a hyperlink to it or anything through which one could fact check or further explore the context. In addition to the growth needed in campaign hyperlinking on blogs within the posts, campaigns should embrace the many blog supporters who create blogs on their own and cover the campaign. These non–campaign affiliated independent sources are certainly biased in that they support the campaign, but linking to their blogs in a blogroll on the sidebar would bolster the interactive capabilities on the blog in that users could explore other sources when evaluating campaign messages.

The Kerry idea to respond to the debate—point by point—as it occurred live is an excellent example of how the blog can be used in conjunction with traditional campaign events. This encourages invested supporters to be online and in the comments section while the debate is going on. In essence, one can have a virtual debate party with thousands of other debate watchers around the nation. However, the method of execution was not well thought out. Anyone reading more than five of the campaign-dubbed, rapid-fire blog posts during the debate would discern that these posts were nothing more than copied and pasted talking points prepared before the debate and triggered by the topic discussed live. In fact, reading these posts after the debate was confusing, as there was no context. This rapid-fire posting during live events should be retained, but the posts should be refined. Campaigns should provide context first (e.g., "My opponent just said, ' . . . '"), then jump into the rebuttal. By composing the posts this way, they can be used by others in the future to understand a candidate's stance or ideas. The focus for the rapid-fire posting should be quality, not quantity.

Both candidates syndicated their content, and future blogging campaigns should continue to do this. Some may only want posts about a particular issue, so creating a subject-based syndication category would increase user control over content and could be received well. Additionally, the use of "send this post to a friend" at the bottom of each post increases the viral potential of the posts (Trammell et al. 2006).

Multimedia is a must for campaign blogs. Audio posts, videos, and photographs should be embedded regularly into campaign blog posts. Both candidates posted the newest television ads on their blogs and used photos within posts at varying levels of success. Bush's blog posted photos frequently, but the "behind the scenes" photos from traveling campaign staff posted on Kerry's blog were more compelling. Everyone knows what a political rally looks like; not everyone knows what a campaign staffer looks like at 3 a.m. after working all night for the candidate. Bush's blog did show photos of the campaign headquarters, but these photos were group shots of a room of people and rather impersonal. Future campaign blogs should use images at the rate Bush did, continue to show supporters and showcase grassroots photography, and better depict the experience of working for the campaign through more intimate photos.

This analysis of blogs in the 2004 U.S. presidential election is not without limitations. Positioned somewhere between a qualitative description and quantitative analysis, this chapter only analyzes the campaign-posted content and pays relatively little attention to the content available through the hyperlinks or the blog reader feedback posted in the interactive features such as comments. Future studies should investigate the interactive features and should conduct experiments with users to test the influence of blog posts based on the presence of such features.

A blog alone is not going to win an election. This chapter was not meant to even suggest that. However, a blog strategically deployed in conjunction with other campaign message strategies can be beneficial. By providing facts and issue statements and showing a more human side to the campaign, undecided voters and invested supporters alike can benefit from a campaign blog.

The word "blog" may be a fad that will phase itself out before the next election. But the idea that campaigns must continue to engage, interact, and personalize content delivery for prospective voters will never go away. To date, blogs have offered the best means of achieving these goals, and campaigns have made strong strides forward in harnessing this evolving technology and integrating it into the campaign.

References

Baker, Andrea, and Jennifer Stromer-Galley. 2004. "The Joys and Sorrows of Interactivity on the Campaign Trail: Blogs in the Primary Campaign of Howard Dean." Paper presented to the Political Communication Division, National Communication Association, Chicago, November.

Banwart, Mary C. 2002. *Videostyle and Webstyle in 2000: Comparing the Gender Differences of Candidate Presentations in Political Advertising and on the Internet.* Doctoral dissertation, University of Oklahoma, Norman.

Blood, Rebecca. 2002. *The Weblog Handbook: Practical Advice on Creating and Maintaining Your Blog.* Cambridge, MA: Perseus.

BuzzMetrics. 2005. "Innovative Study Suggests Where Blogs Fit into National Politics." Available at www.buzzmetrics.com/about/pc_news_Pew_BZM_BlogStudy.htm (accessed May 8, 2005).

Drezner, Daniel W., and Henry Farrell. 2004. "The Power and Politics of Blogs." Paper presented at the annual meeting of the American Political Science Association, Chicago, August.

Endres, Danielle, and Barbara Warnick. 2004. "Text-Based Interactivity in Candidate Campaign Web Sites: A Case Study from the 2002 Elections." *Western Journal of Communication* 68 (3): 322–42.

Garrett, Jesse. 2004. "User Experience Analysis: Presidential Campaign Sites." Report prepared for Adaptive Path.

Herring, Susan C., Inna Kouper, Lois Ann Scheidt, and Elijah L. Wright. 2004. "Women and Children Last: The Discursive Construction of Weblogs." In *Into the Blogosphere: Rhetoric, Community, and Culture of Weblogs*, edited by Laura Gurak, Smiljana Antonijevic, Laurie Johnson, Clancy Ratcliff, and Jessica Reyman. Available at blog.lib.umn.edu.blogosphere.

Herring, Susan C., Lois Ann Scheidt, Sabrina Bonus, and Elijah Wright. 2004. "Bridging the Gap: A Genre Analysis of Weblogs." *Proceedings of the Thirty-Seventh Hawaii International Conference on System Sciences* (HICSS-37). Los Alamitos: IEEE Press.

Johnson, Thomas J., and Barbara K. Kaye. 2004. "Wag the Blog: How Reliance on Traditional Media and the Internet Influence Credibility Perceptions of Weblogs among Blog Users." *Journalism & Mass Communication Quarterly* 81 (3): 622–42.

Kitzmann, Andreas. 2003. "That Different Place: Documenting the Self within Online Environments." *Biography: An Interdisciplinary Quarterly* 26: 48–65.

McMillan, Sally J. 2002. "Exploring Models of Interactivity from Multiple Research Traditions: Users, Documents, and Systems." In *Handbook of New Media*, edited by Leah Lievrouw and Sonia Livingston, 162–82. London: Sage.

Nardi, Bonnie, Diane J. Schiano, Michelle Gumbrecht, and Luke Swartz. 2004. "Why We Blog." *Communications of the ACM* 47 (12): 41–46.

Papacharissi, Zizi. 2004a. "The Blogger Revolution: Audiences as Media Producers." Paper presented to the Communication and Technology Division, International Communication Association, New Orleans, May.

———. 2004b. "Campaigning Online: The American Presidency Meets the Internet." Paper presented at the annual meeting of the Association of Internet Researchers, Brighton, England.

Pew Internet & American Life Project. 2005. "The State of Blogging." Available at www.pewinternet.org/PPF/r/144/report_display.asp (accessed February 10, 2005).

Scheidt, Lois Ann, and Elijah L. Wright. 2004. "Common Visual Design Elements of Weblogs." In *Into the Blogosphere: Rhetoric, Community, and Culture of Weblogs*, edited by Laura Gurak, Smiljana Antonijevic, Laurie Johnson, Clancy Ratliff, and Jessica Reyman. Available at blog.lib.umn.edu/blogosphere/.

Sorapure, Madeleine. 2003. "Screening Moments, Scrolling Lives: Diary Writing on the Web." *Biography: An Interdisciplinary Quarterly* 26: 1–23.

Thompson, Gary. 2004. "Visual Factors in Constructing Authenticity in Weblogs." Paper presented in the Communication and Technology Division, International Communication Association, New Orleans, May.

Stromer-Galley, Jennifer. 2000. "On-line Interaction and Why Candidates Avoid It." *Journal of Communication* 50: 111–32.

Trammell, Kaye D. 2004a. *Celebrity Blogs: Investigation in the Persuasive Nature of Two-Way Communication Regarding Politics*. Doctoral dissertation, University of Florida.

———. 2004b. "Year of the Blog: Webstyle Analysis of the 2004 Presidential Candidate Blog Posts." Paper presented at the annual meeting of the National Communication Association, Chicago, November.

——— . 2005. "Negative Messages on Campaign Blog Posts." Paper presented at the annual meeting of the National Communication Association, Boston, November.

Trammell, Kaye D., and Joshua Britton. 2005. "Gatewatching: The Impact of Blog Content on the Mainstream Media." Paper presented at the annual meeting of the Association of Internet Researchers, Chicago, October.

Trammell, Kaye D., Guy Golan, and Wayne Wanta. 2005. "Intermedia Agenda Setting in Television, Advertising, and Blogs during the 2004 Election." Paper presented at the annual meeting of the Association for Education in Journalism and Mass Communication, San Antonio, August.

Trammell, Kaye D., and Spiro Kiousis. 2005. "Agenda-Setting and Blogs: Issue and Attribute Salience Influence on Celebrity Web Sites." Paper presented at the annual meeting of the Association for Education in Journalism and Mass Communication, San Antonio, August.

Trammell, Kaye D., Andrew Paul Williams, Monica Postelnicu, and Kristen D. Landreville. 2006. "Evolution of Online Campaigning: Increasing Interactivity in Candidate Web Sites and Blogs through Text and Technical Features." *Mass Communication & Society* 9 (1): 21–44.

Williams, Andrew Paul, Kaye Trammell, Monica Postelnicu, Kristen Landreville, and Justin Martin. 2005. "Blogging and Hyperlinking: Use of the Web to Enhance Viability during 2004 U.S. Campaign." *Journalism Studies* 6 (2): 177–86.

10

The Age of Reasons: Motives for Using Different Components of the Internet for Political Information

Barbara K. Kaye and Thomas J. Johnson

THE EMERGENCE OF THE INTERNET has reinvigorated flagging interest in the uses and gratifications theory. The basic foundation of the theory, that the audience is active and goal directed, is ideally suited to studying the Internet because it features interactive applications, such as e-mail, bulletin boards, chat rooms, and weblogs, that require members to be active users (Kaye and Medoff 2001). Internet users actively search out information through clicking on links or employing search engines. These actions assume Internet users are goal directed and are aware of their needs, which they are actively attempting to satisfy (Lin and Jeffres 1998).

Most uses and gratifications research has investigated only the World Wide Web or has treated the Internet as one entity, ignoring the possibility that different components of the Internet may gratify different needs. Other research has isolated a component of the Internet, such as e-mail or bulletin boards, and examined what needs it gratifies. These projects do not allow a systematic look at the various needs served by each Internet component.

This chapter examines the gratifications of four Internet components: World Wide Web, weblogs, bulletin boards/electronic mailing lists, and chat forums/ instant messaging. While political Web sites often contain interactive components such as polls, bulletin boards, or chat, users typically receive information but do not contribute to site content or communicate with each other. Weblogs, diary-style Web sites offering news and opinions listed chronologically on the site as well as discussions by their hosts and audience, combine features of Web sites and bulletin boards. Like political sites on the Web, weblogs provide content that is frequently updated and can be assessed at any time. But like bulletin boards, blogs allow readers to comment on the news, and readers can be creators (or at least contributors) to content by adding their opinion to the news of the day or posting news to the blog. Bulletin boards/electronic mailing lists also do not allow for instantaneous communication, but participants are expected to be both sources and receivers of information. Finally, chat forums and instant messaging are Internet components where users "converse" with each other in real time (Kaye and Medoff 2001). Because these four components of the Internet differ on their level of synchronicity (the ability to communicate in real time) and their levels of interactivity, they are likely to serve different needs. Indeed, studies by the authors of Web, chat, and bulletin board use in the 2000 presidential election (Kaye and Johnson 2004a) and weblog use in general (Kaye 2005a, b) suggest that indeed the different components gratify different needs and that different variables explain motives for accessing the four Internet components.

This chapter reports on a survey of politically interested Internet users online during the two weeks before and the two weeks after the 2004 presidential election to examine their motives for using the Web, weblogs, electronic mailing lists/bulletin boards, and chat rooms/instant messaging for political information. This chapter also investigates whether users of these Internet components differ in terms of demographic and political characteristics.

Uses and Gratifications and the Internet

Uses and gratifications researchers assume that audience members actively search out certain media and media content to satisfy particular needs. The uses and gratifications approach assumes, then, that people are able to know and to explain their reasons for using the media and that they identify the media as means to gratify their needs (McLeod and Becker 1981; Palmgreen 1984). The uses and gratifications approach marked a dramatic change from earlier effects research, which assumed that the audience was largely passive. Uses and gratifications research examines what people do with the media, not what the media do to people.

While the uses and gratifications approach has been used extensively to study traditional media, such as newspapers and television (Lin 1996; McLeod and Becker 1981; Palmgreen 1984), increasingly, scholars are extending the theory to examining the Internet because it embodies the notion of an active audience (Ruggiero 2000). Interactivity separates the Internet from traditional, non-online media (Bowman and Willis 2003; Gunter 2003; Stovall 2004). While newspaper activity is largely limited to flipping the pages looking for interesting articles, and television activity is largely restricted to using the remote to switch on the set and browse through the channels, Web surfers can engage in a number of activities, from sending e-mail to buying sneakers and from downloading music to creating their own Web pages. Similarly, while the audience has little influence on the content of traditional media and has to wait until the paper is delivered or a certain television show comes on, the Internet allows greater control of content (Bowman and Willis 2003; Bucy 2004; Stovall 2004). Audience members can go to Internet sites to search out information whenever they wish. They can also respond to content by e-mailing the editor or reporter, commenting on the news, or contacting other people through bulletin boards and chat rooms. Moreover, the Web allows people to create their own pages as well as to contribute news to weblogs and other sites. The Internet, therefore, allows the audience to be message creators as well as receivers (Gunter 2003).

Interactivity and the Internet

Researchers have identified two major types of interactivity: content and interpersonal interactivity (Bucy 2004). Content interactivity refers to features of the Internet that allow users to have control over the delivery, selection, and presentation of online news. This involves the audience member interacting with the technology, such as clicking on a story, downloading audio and video files, or taking part in an online poll. Audience members typically engage in content interactivity when they are searching out information on Web sites. Interpersonal interactivity refers to person-to-person communications both in real time (such as instant messaging and chat) and by posting to bulletin boards or e-mailing and awaiting responses. Weblogs involve a blending of content and interpersonal interactivity. People can simply visit a blog and read news or opinion, or they can comment on the news as well as post their own items.

If individuals are motivated to search out information for specific content and others enjoy the Internet because it allows them to communicate, presumably more interactive components (such as chat and instant messaging) will be used for communication while less interactive ones (such as political Web sites) will be employed for other needs, such as information seeking, guidance, or entertainment (Stafford, Stafford, and Schkade 2004). Studies of Internet components find mixed support for this assumption.

World Wide Web

The Web is largely a one-way form of communication that seems functionally similar to television, where users sit in front of a screen and view content

(Kaye and Medoff 2001). Because of the functional similarities, studies suggest the Web and television serve similar needs, such as entertainment, escape, and social interaction (Charney and Greenberg 2001; Ferguson and Perse 2000; Kaye 1998; Lin 2002; Korgaonkar and Wolin 1999; Papacharissi and Rubin 2000). Similarly, a study comparing online and offline news found that they served similar needs (Lin, Salwen, and Abdulla 2005).

Other research has pointed out that the interactive functions of the Web make it functionally unlike traditional media (Johnson and Kaye 2003). Indeed, studies have identified unique gratifications served by the Web (Charney and Greenberg 2001; LaRose, Mastro, and Eastin 2001), including convenience (Johnson and Kaye 2003; Korgaonkar and Wolin 1999; Papacharissi and Rubin 2000), checking on the accuracy of traditional media accounts, and voicing opinion (Kaye 2005a; 2005b). Further, researchers have discovered certain types of Web site content may gratify certain needs. For example, researchers who have examined Web use for political information found that Web users went online for guidance and for information seeking/surveillance reasons. Entertainment and social connection emerged as weaker motivations for Web use (Kaye and Johnson 2002; 2004a).

Weblogs

When blogs, diary-style sites in which news and opinions are posted and where interaction between blogger and readers is encouraged, began in 1999, the fifty or so blogs that could be found hardly registered a blip on the online radar screen (Amis 2002; Greenspan 2003; Levy 2002). By the end of 2004, however, an estimated 8 million individuals had created a blog and about 27% of Internet users had accessed one (Rainie 2005; "State of the News Media" 2005). Blogs, then, combine both one-way and two-way forms of communication, as readers can simply visit the site and read the posts or can pass on their own news analysis as well as provide links to their own information.

Few researchers have examined uses and gratifications of bloggers. Casual observations by journalists and other political observers have yielded several explanations for why weblogs have gained popularity, and these reasons may be linked to motivations for going online. Several observers have noted that blogs foster a sense of community among their users. Bloggers typically voice their perspectives on issues, which may attract individuals to a particular blog in the first place because they feel a sense of belonging with a group of like-minded individuals (Katz 2002; Seipp 2002; Thompson 2003). Users also find blogs a convenient place to find important information that has been collected from media throughout the world, limiting the amount of time one needs to hunt for news and information from a variety of sites (Blood 2003; Hiler 2000).

Perhaps the biggest reason for the growth of blogs is that users harbor a healthy dislike and distrust of the mainstream media, which they contend are dominated by a liberal elite (Hamdy and Mobarak 2004; Seipp 2002). Bloggers consider themselves viable alternatives to corporate-controlled liberal journalists and contend they offer a different and superior product (Blood 2003; Johnson and Kaye 2004; Lennon 2003). First, bloggers castigate journalists for ignoring certain stories, and they take pride in pointing out errors made by the traditional press (Kurtz 2002; Smolkin 2004). While journalists must adhere to standards of fairness and objectivity, bloggers can present their experiences and opinions about the news (Fallows and Rainie 2004; Grossman et al. 2004), creating a more personal, insightful view about events than the bland facts served up by traditional media (Papacharissi 2004; Reynolds 2004). Indeed, when Kaye (2005a) examined reasons for using blogs, actively searching out information and comparing blog accounts with those found in traditional media proved the main reasons for going online, followed by convenience.

Other important reasons for going online include personal fulfillment (because it is entertaining, exciting, and involving and provides topics for conversation), surveillance (to learn personal qualities and stances of politicians and gather unbiased viewpoints), social monitoring (to find out what others are thinking and learn about others' opinions), and expression/affiliation (to make opinions known and to be in contact with like-minded people) (Kaye 2005a). Further, when Kaye (2005b) analyzed open-ended responses to reasons people visit Web sites, several of the motivations identified in the earlier study emerged, such as personal fulfillment, affiliation, and expression, as well as information seeking. However, the main reason people visited weblogs appeared to be characteristics of blogs they perceived as missing from traditional media, such as depth of information, commentary and analysis, timely and up-to-date information, and admitted bias of bloggers.

Bulletin Boards/Electronic Mailing Lists

Both bulletin boards and e-mail existed before the Web. Bulletin boards were an important way for people to share information during the first Gulf War, and they proved a major attraction of early Internet service providers such as Prodigy and Compuserv (Ogan 1993). Because bulletin boards allow people both to post information as well as read the opinions of others, studies discovered that electronic bulletin board use in general (James, Wotring, and Forrest 1995) and for political purposes (Kaye and Johnson 2004b) served information/learning and socialization needs. Similarly, Garramone, Harris, and Anderson (1986) discovered that political bulletin board users mentioned informational needs as the major reason they visited bulletin boards, but those who posted and received messages listed personal identity needs, such as comparing one's ideas to others, learning what others are thinking, and gaining support for one's views.

Chat Rooms

Chat rooms and instant messaging have received little attention from scholars, perhaps because they are perceived as places singles meet to try to find dates or ways teenagers can talk about their prom dates without tying up the phone lines. However, Web sites are increasingly providing chat elements to allow users to discuss social and political topics, and sites are using chats like electronic press conferences where users can question public figures. Not surprisingly, then, chat may serve both social and informational needs. Fuentes (2000) claims that chat rooms serve as a means for like-minded individuals to discuss issues of interest, suggesting they serve social needs. Similarly, Peris et al. (2002) found that those who visit chat rooms seek friendship and social networks, and have a desire to communicate with others.

The anonymity of chat rooms may allow people to express their views more honestly and more completely than even face-to-face communications. People can become other people in chat rooms; a feeble eighty-nine-year-old man can pretend to be a bronzed twenty-four-year-old bodybuilder. Therefore, chats can satisfy personal identity needs. Similarly, while Atkin et al. (2005) did not specifically explore gratifications for using chat rooms, they did find that those who relied heavily on chat were more likely to be involved in their community, which also suggests that chat serves social needs. However, Kaye and Johnson (2004a) found that politically oriented chat rooms primarily served guidance and informational needs and to a lesser extent entertainment and social utility needs. Kaye and Johnson (2004a) speculated that chatters may form strong bonds online. Therefore, when users engage in political discussions in chat rooms, they are likely to trust and rely on information they receive from their online friends.

Demographic and Political Characteristics of Internet Users

Early studies of the Internet suggested that the typical user hardly represented a snapshot of the average American. Those who went online were primarily young, wealthy, well-educated, and conservative males (Stempel and Hargrove 1996); however, as more people went online, the Internet audience became more mainstream. While Internet users are increasingly looking like the American population as a whole, a digital divide still exists. Users are still predominantly young, well educated, and wealthy (Horrigan, Garrett, and Resnick 2004; Rainie and Horrigan 2005; Salwen, Garrison, and Driscoll 2005). Also men are more likely to go online than women for political news and information (Rainie and Horrigan 2005; Salwen, Garrison, and Driscoll 2005). Several studies have suggested that liberals and conservatives are equally likely to go online (Horrigan, Garrett, and Resnick 2004; Kohut 2004), and the percentage of online news users who voted for Bush mirrored the voting population as a whole (Rainie and Horrigan 2005). However, Kerry voters were more likely to visit issue-oriented and political organization Web sites than Bush supporters, and the Internet was more important in helping Kerry voters decide for whom to vote (Rainie and Horrigan 2005).

While the Web audience is becoming more mainstream, the audience for weblogs resembles that of the early days of the Internet, as blog readers are predominantly highly educated young white males (Kaye and Johnson 2004a; Rainie 2005). But studies disagree on whether users of the Web and weblogs differ politically. Several studies claim that conservatives dominate the blogosphere; for instance, blog users overwhelmingly supported U.S. involvement in the Iraq war (Kaye and Johnson 2004b; Rainie, Fox, and Fallows 2003; Seipp 2002). However, Rainie (2005) suggests those who voted for Kerry slightly outnumbered Bush supporters among blog users in the 2004 presidential campaign.

Because instant messaging use has exploded in recent years, fewer people are visiting chat rooms and online discussion groups (Madden and Rainie 2003). However, the audiences for these Internet components are similar. Users are young, with instant messaging in particular gaining popularity among teenagers, while online discussion groups and chat are visited by young adults. Because users are considerably younger than the general Internet population, they also tend to be less wealthy and less educated (Madden and Rainie 2003; Tsang and Zhou 2005). While instant messaging is not typically linked to political discussions, Kerry voters were more likely to participate in online discussion groups and chat than Bush voters in the 2004 presidential election (Rainie and Horrigan 2005).

Project Goals

Since prior research has yet to fully explore the various characteristics of online users for political information, this chapter aims to explore the demographic and political characteristics of individuals who rely heavily on the Web, weblogs, bulletin boards/electronic mailing lists, and chat rooms/instant messaging for political information. Additionally, this research explores the primary motives for using the Web, weblogs, bulletin boards/electronic mailing lists, and chat rooms/instant messaging for political information by those who rely heavily on these Internet components. An online survey was created to assess politically interested Internet users' motives and gratifications for online political information. Politically interested Internet users were informed of the survey URL through announcements directed to media and politically oriented newsgroups, Web sites, weblogs, electronic mailing lists, and chat rooms representing a cross-section of political ideologies. This convenience sample of politically interested Internet users yielded 1,366 completed surveys. Survey questions covered a range of topics, including reasons for using the Web, weblogs, bulletin boards, and chat rooms; reliance on the Internet for political information; political characteristics; and demographics. Detailed operationalizations of survey variables and data analysis are available in the appendix.

Political and Demographic Characteristics of Heavy Users

Overall, there were several marked differences among individuals who rely heavily on the various Internet components. Examination of the political characteristics reveals that a higher percentage (45.9%) of those who rely heavily on bulletin boards/lists are registered with the Democratic Party than are those who rely on other components. Those who rely on weblogs are least likely to be Democrats (30.0%). Although a greater percentage of those who rely on chat are registered as Democrats (38.1%) than Republicans (35.6%), the percentage of Republicans is the same as those who rely heavily on blogs (35.2%). Heavy blog users are also more likely to be independents (17.6%) than are heavy users of the other components. Moreover, a larger percentage (27.0%) of heavy users of weblogs claim weaker ties to their party of choice than those who rely on the Web (19.4%), bulletin boards/lists (18.5%), and chat rooms/instant messaging (15.3%) (table 10.1).

Heavy users of the various components also differ in political ideology. The greatest percentage (44.1%) of those who rely heavily on weblogs consider themselves very conservative/conservative, while the greatest percentage (49.7%) of those who rely on bulletin boards/mailing lists judge themselves as very liberal/liberal. Additionally, weblogs attract a greater percentage of moderates (24.4%) than do the other Internet components (table 10.1).

Even though the average age of heavy Internet users is relatively the same (m = 43.3 years) for all the Internet components, other demographic differences do emerge. A much higher percentage of males than females (67.3% to

32.7%) rely heavily on weblogs. This ratio represents the largest discrepancy between male and female users among all the components, even though males are more likely to be heavy users of all Internet components. Weblog users were the group most likely to have earned a graduate degree, while chat room/instant messaging users were the least likely to have done graduate work. Furthermore, those who rely heavily on the Web for political information report a much higher annual income ($67,500) than those who rely most heavily on chat rooms/instant messaging ($51,600) (table 10.1).

TABLE 10.1
Profile of High-Reliance Internet Users

	Web *(n = 771)*	*Weblog* *(n = 861)*	*Bulletin Board/* *Mailing List* *(n = 476)*	*Chat Rooms/* *Instant Message* *(n = 120)*
Gender				
Male	59.5%	67.3%	55.4%	57.6%
Female	40.5%	32.7%	44.6%	42.4%
Age (average)	43.8	42.6	44.0	42.7
Education				
High School Grad or less	2.7%	2.2%	3.8%	3.3%
Some College/ Degree	62.5%	60.2%	65.2%	70.0%
Graduate Degree	30.8%	33.7%	27.8%	23.3%
Income (average)	$67,553.00	$66,020.00	$59,151.00	$51,632.00
Political Party				
Republican	32.6%	35.2%	22.6%	35.6%
Democrat	38.6%	30.0%	45.9%	38.1%
Independent	12.3%	17.6%	12.9%	11.0%
Other	16.5%	17.2%	18.6%	15.3%
Strength of Party Ties				
Strong Supporter	54.0%	45.9%	56.0%	58.4%
Moderate Supporter	26.6%	27.1%	25.5%	26.3%
Weak Supporter	19.4%	27.0%	18.5%	15.3%
Political Ideology				
Very Conservative/ Conservative	39.1%	44.1%	32.4%	39.5%
Moderate	21.1%	24.4%	17.9%	17.6%
Very Liberal/Liberal	39.7%	31.5%	49.7%	42.9%

Motivations for Using Components of the Internet

Political Web Sites

Heavy users of politically oriented Web sites tend to seek political information from the Web to gratify convenience and information-seeking needs. The two dominant reasons, mentioned by just over nine out of ten heavy Web users, for using political Web sites are to "access information at any time" and because "information is easy to obtain." The next three reasons given by this group of users are related to information seeking: "to find specific information," "to find information not available in the traditional media," and "to keep up with the main issues of the day." The remaining five reasons are also related to information seeking. Only one reason, "to see how the candidates stand on various issues," is unique to the Web—no other Internet resource is used primarily to seek out candidate information (table 10.2).

Weblogs

Weblogs are considered a cross between Web sites, bulletin boards, and chat rooms. Bloggers encourage input and dialogue from their followers, and they often challenge the veracity of traditional media. Given the nature of weblogs, it is not surprising that the strongest two motivations for accessing these sites are "for information that I can't get from traditional media" and to "check on the accuracy of traditional media." Those who rely heavily on weblogs tend to do so because they do not trust or like traditional media, and for information they cannot find in the mainstream press. Similar to politically oriented Web sites, weblogs are also used because they are convenient, for information seeking, to get a wide variety of viewpoints, and for information to use in arguments with others. However, unlike heavy Web users' perceptions of Web content, those who frequently visit blogs do so because they find them entertaining (table 10.2).

Bulletin Boards/Electronic Mailing Lists

Similarly to weblogs, two of the five primary reasons for using bulletin boards/electronic mailing lists reflect a negative attitude toward traditional media. Heavy bulletin board/list users seek information that is not available from traditional media sources, and they like to check on the accuracy of traditional media reports. These users also connect to bulletin boards/lists because it is convenient to do so. However, unlike heavy users of Web sites and blogs, bulletin board users seek "contact with like-minded individuals" and enjoy participating in discussion and expressing their opinions, which reflects the interactive nature of bulletin boards (table 10.2).

TABLE 10.2
Motivations for Using the Internet for Political Information

	Count	Percentage
Web (High Reliance = 771)		
1. to access political information at any time	686	89.0
2. information is easy to obtain	685	88.8
3. to find specific political information that I'm looking for	669	86.7
4. for information I can't get from traditional media	640	83.0
5. to keep up with the main issues of the day	628	81.4
6. to check on the accuracy of traditional media	600	77.8
7. to see how the candidates stand on various issues	579	75.1
8. to find out about issues affecting people like myself	555	71.9
9. to use as ammunition in arguments with others	551	71.5
10. to get a wide variety of viewpoints	513	66.5
Weblogs (High Reliance = 861)		
1. for information I can't get from traditional media	806	93.6
2. to check on the accuracy of traditional media	771	89.5
3. to keep up with the main issues of the day	770	89.4
4. to access political information at any time	739	85.8
5. information is easy to obtain	734	85.2
6. because it is entertaining	705	81.9
7. to find out about issues affecting people like myself	674	78.2
8. to get a wide variety of viewpoints	669	77.7
9. to find specific political information that I'm looking for	632	73.4
10. to use as ammunition in arguments with others	617	71.7
Bulletin Boards/Electronic Mailing Lists (High Reliance = 476)		
1. for information I can't get from traditional media	289	60.7
2. to be in contact with like-minded people	279	58.6
3. information is easy to obtain	253	53.1
4. to let my opinions be known	251	52.7
5. to check on the accuracy of traditional media	231	48.5
6. to find out about issues affecting people like myself	227	47.7
7. to keep up with the main issues of the day	217	45.6
8. to get a wide variety of viewpoints	214	45.0
9. because it is entertaining	211	44.3
10. to give me something to talk about with others	211	44.3
Chat Rooms/Instant Messaging (High Reliance = 120)		
1. to be in contact with like-minded people	76	63.3
2. to let my opinions be known	73	60.8
3. because it is entertaining	68	56.7
4. for information I can't get from traditional media	65	54.2
5. to get a wide variety of viewpoints	62	51.7
6. to find specific political information that I'm looking for	59	49.2
7. to give me something to talk about with others	58	48.3
8. to feel politically involved	56	46.7
9. to enjoy the excitement of an election race	54	45.0
10. information is easy to obtain	50	41.7
11. to check on the accuracy of traditional media	50	41.7

Chat Rooms/Instant Messaging

Those who rely heavily on chat rooms/instant messaging for political information do so primarily for interpersonal reasons. The top two motivations for participating in online discussion are "to be in contact with like-minded individuals" and "to let my opinions be known." Chat rooms serve interpersonal gratifications much as bulletin boards/mailing lists do. Further, as with weblogs, users find chat rooms/instant messaging entertaining. Like those who rely on the other Internet components, chatters seek information that is not available through traditional media, and they seek a wide variety of viewpoints.

Two reasons emerged for chatting online/instant messaging that did not appear as motives for using the Web, weblogs, and bulletin boards/mailing lists. Engaging in online chat and instant messaging gives users a sense of feeling politically involved. Presumably, ongoing live discussion promotes a sense of involvement through establishing contact with other users. Participating in live political discussion also heightens the excitement of an election race (table 10.2).

Understanding Politically Interested Internet Users and Their Motives

This chapter reports on the primary reasons Internet users go online for political information. More specifically, this research focuses on the motivations that drive heavy Web, weblog, bulletin board/electronic mailing list, and chat room/instant messaging users to these particular online venues.

This chapter first examined political and demographic characteristics of those who are heavy users of each Internet component. It has revealed that Web, weblog, bulletin board/list, and chat room/instant messaging users differ from each other on several key measures. The responses indicate that heavy bulletin board/list users are more likely to be registered with the Democratic Party, but weblog users are more likely to be Republicans and independents. Party affiliation of heavy users of each Internet component closely mirrors their political ideology. A greater percentage of weblog users hold conservative views, and bulletin board users tend to be more liberal-minded. Heavy users of chat rooms and the Web are more evenly divided between Democrat and Republican and between liberal and conservative, but chat users lean more toward the left and Web users lean more toward the right of the political spectrum. Weblog users also stand out from heavy users of the other Internet components as having weaker party ties. These political characteristics are consistent with the findings of other studies that those who turn to weblogs do so not because they distrust and dislike the government, but because they distrust and dislike the media. Indeed, while weblog users do not necessarily have strong party ties, the largely conservative blog users do support the president and his policies (Kaye and Johnson, 2004b). However, because users distrust traditional media, which they perceive as dominated by a liberal elite, they follow bloggers who frequently bash the media, monitor them for inaccuracies or biased information, and gleefully point out their mistakes on their blogs (Seipp 2002). Additionally, this chapter reports that heavy weblog users are more likely to be highly educated, high-income males, which is consistent with other studies that also found that this group of individuals tend to be more conservative and more likely to be Republican (Kaye and Johnson 2004b; Rainie, Fox, and Fallows 2003; Seipp 2002).

On the other hand, bulletin board/electronic mailings lists and chat rooms/instant messaging, which early on provided an outlet for the politically discontented to challenge the government, tend to attract progressive liberals who strongly support the Democratic Party. These liberals oppose Bush and his policies, and are therefore more likely to berate the government than the media. Men and women are more evenly likely to use these two Internet components, but users tend to be a bit less educated and earn less money than their weblog counterparts. Again, these findings are consistent with other studies, which also found that bulletin board and chat/instant messaging users are less educated, less wealthy individuals who were more likely to support John Kerry in the 2004 presidential election (Madden and Rainie 2003; Rainie and Horrigan 2005; Tsang and Zhou 2005).

The Web, which was once seen as an alternative to traditional media that was used by politically disaffected individuals, is the most mainstream of the four Internet components under study. Web users tend to be more evenly balanced between Democrats and Republicans and conservatives and liberals, but they report stronger party ties, and they still tend to be highly educated, wealthy males, as indicated by this research and by other researchers (Horrigan, Garrett, and Resnick 2004; Kohut 2004; Rainie and Horrigan 2005; Salwen, Garrison, and Driscoll 2005).

In addition to political and demographic characteristics, this chapter has also reported the primary motivations for using each of the four Internet components. Because the Internet allows greater control of content (Bowman and Willis 2003; Bucy 2004; Stovall 2004), researchers have identified interactivity as the characteristic that separates the Internet from traditional, non-online media (Bowman and Willis 2003; Gunter 2003; Stovall 2004). Studies have identified two types of interactivity: content and communication (Bucy 2004). Content interactivity refers to features of the Internet that allow users to have control over the delivery, selection, and presentation of online news.

Users most often engage in content interactivity when they are searching out information on more one-way forms of communication such as the Web. Interpersonal interactivity refers to person-to-person communications both in real-time (such as instant messaging and chat) and by posting to bulletin boards or e-mail and awaiting responses. Weblogs involve a blending of content and interpersonal interactivity. People can simply visit a blog and read news or opinion, or they can comment on the news as well as post their own items. Past studies suggest, then, that those who use more one-way sources such as the Web are motivated more by informational needs, and those who rely on interactive elements such as bulletin boards and chat rooms use them to gratify communication needs (Stafford, Stafford, and Schkade 2004). Indeed, our results largely support these claims.

If individuals are motivated to search out information for specific content and others enjoy the Internet because it allows them to communicate, presumably more interactive components of the Internet (such as chat and instant messaging) would be used for communication, while less interactive ones (such as the political Web sites) would be employed for other needs, such as information seeking or guidance.

The Web is largely a one-way form of communication that consists of millions of pages of information put online by a site creator for users to read at their convenience. Although some Web sites contain interactive features such as polls, online ordering, or the ability to choose the color and style of an item of clothing or a vehicle, users are not required to interact with most sites beyond simply accessing the materials. Given the purpose of the Web and that information can be obtained at the click of a button, it is not surprising that heavy users tend to connect to politically oriented Web sites for convenience and for information-seeking purposes. These findings are similar to other research that also found that information seeking and convenience drive users to the Web (Johnson and Kaye 2003; Kaye and Johnson 2002; 2004a; Korgaonkar and Wolin 1999; Papacharissi and Rubin 2000).

Weblogs are unique in that they allow users to be as actively or passively engaged as they wish, and they provide analysis and critique of news events that may not be available in traditional media. Additionally, because bloggers view themselves as alternatives to traditional media, they also provide an outlet for rallying against the media. Given the nature of these sites, heavy users are primarily attracted to blogs for information they cannot get from traditional media and to check the accuracy of media accounts, which indicates distrust and dislike for traditional media. Journalists and other researchers have also observed this antimedia sentiment that seems to be prevalent among weblog users (Blood 2003; Hiler 2000; Kaye 2005a, b; Kurtz 2002; Smolkin 2004). But while others (Katz 2002; Kaye 2005a, b; Seipp 2002; Thompson 2003) claim that weblogs foster a sense of community, this project's heavy weblog users do not tend to seek a community of like-minded individuals, but rather look for a wide variety of opinions. This finding is in line with studies of Internet use in the 2004 campaign, which found that users did not tend to go to the Web simply to visit sites that supported their own views, but sought out a variety of opinions.

Bulletin boards and chat are more interactive elements of the Web, with chat involving conversing with others in real time. Not surprisingly, then, they both are more likely to serve interpersonal communication/socialization needs than the Web or weblogs.

Heavy users of electronic bulletin boards/mailing lists tend to access this component for reasons very similar to why heavy users access weblogs: for information not found in traditional media and to check the accuracy of traditional media. But a main reason people visit bulletin boards/lists is to contact like-minded individuals. These users tend to enjoy the interactive nature of bulletin boards/lists and are motivated to gratify social interaction needs. Although other studies have not reported that bulletin board users harbor negative opinions toward traditional media, they too have found that users are strongly attracted to interactive Internet components for personal identity, social networking, and information seeking needs (James, Wotring, and Forrest 1995; Kaye and Johnson 2004a; Garramone, Harris, and Anderson 1986).

Chat rooms, which by their very nature promote interactivity coupled with self-expression, are primarily used for reasons of social connection and self-expression. Heavy users of chat, however, have also discovered that chat rooms gratify their needs for information, for a wide variety of viewpoints, and as with the other components, for finding information that is not available through the traditional media. These findings are very similar to those of other studies that have also found that chat rooms serve primarily information and social needs (Fuentes 2000; Peris et al. 2002).

Overall, when heavy users of each of the components are examined, this project finds that the Web primarily serves convenience and information needs. Weblogs are used for seeking out information that users perceive cannot be obtained from traditional media and to check the accuracy of traditional media accounts due to users' pervasive distrust and dislike of traditional media. Electronic bulletin boards/lists gratify social networking and information needs, and to a lesser extent, they are used as an alternative to traditional media. Chat rooms (perhaps the most interactive source) are most strongly used for social interaction purposes and for a wide variety of information and opinion.

Project Limitations and Future Research Possibilities

This report of the motivations for using politically oriented Web sites, weblogs, bulletin boards/lists, and chat rooms/instant messaging specifically focused on heavy users of these components. A survey was posted online and targeted to politically interested Internet users. Even though more than two-thirds of the U.S. population regularly goes online ("State of the News Media" 2005), it is difficult to isolate users who do so for political information rather than more general uses. Although generating a random sample, where all Internet users have equal chance of being selected, is ideal, this project employed a convenience sample in which politically interested users were solicited through an announcement sent to politically oriented Web sites, weblogs, bulletin boards/lists, and chat rooms. In situations where random probability sampling is not possible (such as with the Internet), non–probability sampling is acceptable (Babbie 1990), and it is commonly used when posting an online survey. Careful uses of this type of purposive sampling generate results that may be representative of a specific subset of Internet users, but may not be representative of the larger population (Babbie 1990). Nevertheless, this chapter does provide insight into the motivations that propel heavy Internet users to Web sites, weblogs, bulletin boards/lists, and chat rooms/instant messaging. But perhaps in the future there will be some way to generate e-mail addresses of online users and randomly select users to complete the survey. Employing a random procedure may uncover different reasons for using the various Internet components.

Future research could also correlate levels of use with political and demographic characteristics, and factor analysis may also uncover different motivations for using the various Internet components. Uses and gratifications research is vital for expanding the understanding of what motivates online users to connect to the Web, weblogs, and other online venues.

Appendix: Methodological Notes

This project investigates the motivations for using the Web, weblogs, bulletin boards/lists, and chat rooms/instant messaging for political information through a survey that was posted online from October 19 to November 16, 2004, the two weeks before and the two weeks after the 2004 presidential election.

Reasons for using the Web, weblogs, bulletin boards, and chat rooms: Motivations for using the Internet (Web, weblogs, bulletin boards/electronic mailing lists, chat rooms) for political information were determined via a list of twenty-two statements derived from past uses and gratifications studies (Kaye 1998; Kaye and Johnson 2002; McLeod and Becker 1981). Respondents were asked to mark their level of agreement with the reasons for accessing each of the four Internet components. Responses ranged from (1) strongly disagree to (5) strongly agree.

Reliance on the Internet: Reliance on the Internet was assessed by asking respondents whether they "heavily rely," "rely," "sometimes rely," "rarely rely," and "don't rely" on political Web sites, weblogs, bulletin boards/lists, and chat/instant messaging as sources of political information.

Political characteristics: Respondents were asked with which political party they were registered and how strongly they are affiliated with their party of choice (0–10 scale, ranging from no party ties to very strong ties). They were also asked to mark their political ideology (very liberal, liberal, neutral, conservative, very conservative).

Demographics: This project also includes four demographic measures: gender, age, education, and income. Respondents were asked to indicate whether they are male or female and what was their age as of their last birthday. Respondents marked the highest grade completed from the following list: "less than high school," "high school graduate," "some college," "four year college degree," "master's degree," "Ph.D. degree," and "other," and they estimated their 2004 income.

Data analysis: The purpose of this project is to assess why heavy Internet users turn to the Web, weblogs, bulletin boards/lists, and chat rooms/instant messaging for political information. First, the responses to the reliance variable for each of the Internet components were recoded into two separate categories. Those who "relied" or "heavily relied" on a component were classified as high reliance, and those who marked "sometimes rely on," "rarely rely on," and "don't rely on at all" were classified as low reliance. Second, frequencies were run on the political and demographic characteristics of those who rely heavily on the Web, weblogs, bulletin board/mailing lists, and chat rooms/instant messaging. Next, each of the twenty-two reasons for using each of the four Internet components was recoded into one of two categories. Motives marked "strongly agree" or "agree" were recoded into "strong reason," and those marked "neutral," "disagree," and "strongly disagree" were coded as "weak reason." Lastly, measures for reliance on each of the four Internet components and each of the use motivations were cross-tabulated. The top ten reasons reported by heavy users for accessing each Internet component were then counted.

References

Amis, Dave. 2002. "Web Logs: Online Navel Gazing." *Internet Freedom*, September 21. Available at www.netfreedom.org (accessed January 7, 1998).

Atkin, David J., Leo W. Jeffres, Kimberly Neuendorf, Bryan Lange, and Paul Skalski. 2005. "Why They Chat: Predicting Adoption and Use of Chat Rooms." In *Online News and the Public,* edited by Michael B. Salwen, Bruce Garrison, and Paul D. Driscoll, 303–22. Mahwah, NJ: Erlbaum.

Babbie, Earl R. 1990. *Survey Research Methods.* Belmont, CA: Wadsworth.

Blood, Rebecca. 2003. "Weblogs and Journalism: Do They Connect?" *Nieman Reports* (Fall): 61–63.

Bowman, Shayne, and Chris Willis. 2003. *We Media: How Audiences Are Shaping the Future of News and Information.* Reston, VA: Media Center at the American Press Institute.

Bucy, Erik P. 2004. "Second Generation Net News: Interactivity and Information Accessibility in the Online Environment." *International Journal on Media Management* 6: 102–113.

Charney, Tamar, and Bradley S. Greenberg. 2001. "Uses and Gratifications of the Internet." In *Communication Technology and Society: Audience Adoption and Uses of the New Media,* edited by Carolyn A. Lin and David J. Atkin, 379–407. Cresskill, NJ: Hampton.

Cornfield, Michael, Lee Rainie, and John B Horrigan. 2003. "Untuned Keyboards: Online Campaigners, Citizens and Portals in the 2002 Elections." Pew Research Center. Available at www.pewinternet.org/reports (accessed March 21, 2003).

Fallows, Deborah, and Lee Rainie. 2004. "The Internet as Unique News Source: Millions Go Online for News and Images Not Covered in the Mainstream Press." Pew Research Center. Available at www.pewinternet.org/ (accessed July 8, 2004).

Ferguson, Douglas A, and Elizabeth M. Perse. 2000. "The World Wide Web as a Functional Alternative to Television." *Journal of Broadcasting and Electronic Media* 44: 155–74.

Fuentes, Annette. 2000. "Won't You Be My Neighbor?" *American Demographics* 22: 60–62.

Garramone, Gina, Allen Harris, and Ronald Anderson. 1986. "Uses of Political Bulletin Boards." *Journal of Broadcasting and Electronic Media* 30: 325–39.

Greenspan, Robyn. 2003. "Blogging by the Numbers." *CyberAtlas.* Available at internetnews.com/stats/article/php/2238831 (accessed July 24, 2003).

Grossman, Lev, Anita Hamilton, Marianne M. Buechner, and Leslie Whitaker. 2004. "Meet Joe Blog." *Time.* Available at www.time.com/archive (accessed June 21, 2004).

Gunter, Barrie. 2003. *News and the Net.* Mahwah, NJ: Erlbaum.

Hamdy, Naila, and Radwa Mobarak. 2004. "Iraq War Ushers in Web-Based Era." In *Global Media Goes to War: Role of News and Entertainment Media during the 2003 Iraq War,* edited by Ralph D. Berenger, 245–54. Spokane, WA: Marquette.

Hiler, John. 2000. "Blogger's Digest." *MicroContent News.* October 13. Available at www.microcontentnews.com/articles/digests.htm (accessed June 8, 2003).

Horrigan, John, Kelly Garrett, and Paul Resnick. 2004. "The Internet and Democratic Debate: Wired Americans Hear More Points of View about Candidates and Key Issues Than Other Citizens." Pew Research Center. Available at www.pewinternet.org/reports (accessed October 27, 2004).

James, Michael L., C. Edward Wotring, and Edward J. Forrest. 1995. "An Exploratory Study of the Perceived Benefits of Electronic Bulletin Board Use and the Impact on

Other Communication Activities." *Journal of Broadcasting and Electronic Media* 39: 30–50.

Johnson, Thomas J., and Barbara K. Kaye. 2003. "Around the World Wide Web in 80 Ways: How Motives for Going Online Are Linked to Internet Activities among Politically Interested Internet Users." *Social Science Computer Review* 21: 304–25.

———. 2004. "Wag the Blog: How Reliance on Traditional Media and the Internet Influence Credibility Perceptions of Weblogs among Blog Users." *Journalism & Mass Communication Quarterly* 81 (3): 622–42.

Katz, Jon. 2002. "Here Come the Weblogs." In *We've Got Blog,* edited by J. Rodzvilla, 17–24. Cambridge MA: Perseus.

Kaye, Barbara K. 1998. "Uses and Gratifications of the World Wide Web: From Couch Potato to Web Potato." *New Jersey Journal of Communication* 6: 21–40.

———. 2005a. "It's a Blog, Blog, Blog, Blog World: Users and Uses of Weblogs." *Atlantic Journal of Communication* 13 (2): 73–95.

———. 2005b. "Web Site Story: An Exploratory Study of Why Weblog Users Say They Use Weblogs." Paper submitted to the Association for Education in Journalism & Mass Communication, San Antonio, Texas.

Kaye, Barbara K., and Thomas J. Johnson. 2002. "Online and in the Know: Uses and Gratifications of the Web for Political Information." *Journal of Broadcasting and Electronic Media* 46: 54–71.

———. 2004a. "A Web for All Reasons: Uses and Gratifications of Internet Components for Political Information." *Telematics and Informatics* 21: 197–223.

———. 2004b. "Weblogs as a Source of Information about the 2003 Iraq War." In *Global Media Goes to War: Role of News and Entertainment Media during the 2003 Iraq War,* edited by Ralph D. Berenger, 291–301. Spokane, WA: Marquette.

Kaye, Barbara K., and Norman J. Medoff. 2001. *The World Wide Web: A Mass Communication Perspective.* Mountain View, CA: Mayfield.

Korgaonkar, Pradeep, and Lori Wolin. 1999. "A Multivariate Analysis of Web Usage." *Journal of Advertising Research* 39: 53–68.

Kohut, Andrew. 2004. "Cable and Internet Loom Large in Fragmented Political News Universe: Perceptions of Partisan Bias Seen as Growing, Especially by Democrats." Pew Research Center. Available at www.pewinternet.org/reports (accessed January 1, 2004).

Kurtz, Howard. 2002. "How Weblogs Keep the Media Honest." *Washington Post.* Available at www.washingtonpost.com (accessed July 31, 2002).

Lennon, Sheila. 2003. "Blogging Journalists Invite Outsiders' Reporting." *Nieman Reports* (Fall): 76–79.

Levy, Stephen. 2002. "Living in the Blog-osphere." *Newsweek,* August 26, 42–45.

LaRose, Robert, Dana Mastro, and Matt Eastin. 2001. "Understanding Internet Usage: A Social Cognitive Approach to Uses and Gratifications." *Social Science Computer Review* 19: 395–413.

Lin, Carolyn A. 1996. "Looking Back: The Contribution of Blumer and Katz's Uses of Mass Communication to Communication Research." *Journal of Broadcasting and Electronic Media* 49: 574–81.

———. 2002. "Perceived Gratifications of Online Media Services among Potential Users." *Telematics and Informatics* 19: 3–19.

Lin, Carolyn A, and Leo Jeffres. 1998. "Predicting Adoption of Multimedia Cable Service." *Journalism Quarterly* 75: 251–75.

Lin, Carolyn A., Michael B. Salwen, and Rasha A. Abdulla. 2005. "Uses and Gratifications of Online and Offline News: New Wine in an Old Bottle?" In *Online News and the Public*, edited by Michael B. Salwen, Bruce Garrison, and Paul D. Driscoll, 221–36. Mahwah, NJ: Erlbaum.

McLeod, Jack M., and Lee B. Becker. 1981. "The Uses and Gratifications Approach." In *Handbook of Political Communication*, edited by Dan D. Nimmo and Keith R. Sanders, 67–99. Beverly Hills, CA: Sage.

Madden, Mary, and Lee Rainie. 2003. "America's Online Pursuits: The Changing Picture of Who's Online and What They Do." Pew Research Center. Available at www .pewinternet.org (accessed April 15, 2005).

Ogan, Christine. 1993. "Listserver Communication during the Gulf War: What Kind of Medium Is the Electronic Bulletin Board?" *Journal of Broadcasting and Electronic Media* 37: 177–96.

Palmgreen, Philip. 1984. "Uses and Gratifications: A Theoretical Perspective." In *Communication Yearbook 8*, edited by Robert N. Bostrom, 20–55. Beverly Hills, CA: Sage.

Papacharissi, Zizi. 2004. "The Blogger Revolution? Audiences as Media Producers." Paper presented at the annual meeting of the International Communication Association, New Orleans, May.

Papacharissi, Zizi, and Alan M. Rubin. 2000. "Predictors of Internet Use." *Journal of Broadcasting and Electronic Media* 44: 175–96.

Peris, Rosa Anna, Miguel A. Gimeno, Daniel Pinazo, Generos Ortet, Virginia Carrero, M. Sanchiz, and I. Ibáñez. 2002. "Online Chat Rooms: Virtual Spaces of Interaction for Socially Oriented People." *Cyberpsychology & Behavior* 5: 43–51.

Rainie, Lee. 2005. "The State of Blogging." Pew Internet & American Life Project. Pew Research Center. Available at www.pewinternet.org/ (accessed February 1, 2005).

Rainie, Lee, Susannah Fox, and Deborah Fallows. 2004. "The Internet and the Iraq War." Pew Research Center. Available at www.pewinternet.org (accessed December 12, 2004).

Rainie, Lee, and John Horrigan. 2005. "A Decade of Adoption: How the Internet Has Woven Itself into American Life." Pew Research Center. Available at www.pewinternet .org/reports (accessed January 25, 2005).

Reynolds, Glenn H. 2004. "The Blogs of War." *National Interest* 75: 59–64.

Ruggiero, Thomas. 2000. "Uses and Gratifications Theory in the 21st Century." *Mass Communication & Society* 3: 3–37.

Salwen, Michael B., Bruce Garrison, and Paul D. Driscoll. 2005. "The Baseline Survey Projects: Exploring Questions." In *Online News and the Public*, edited by Michael B. Salwen, Bruce Garrison, and Paul D. Driscoll, 121–45. Mahwah, NJ: Erlbaum.

Seipp, Catherine. 2002. "Online Uprising." *American Journalism Review* 24: 42–47.

Smolkin, Rachel. 2004. "The Expanding Blogosphere." *American Journalism Review* 26: 38–43.

Stafford, Thomas F., Mark R. Stafford, and Lawrence L. Schkade. 2004. "Determining Uses and Gratifications for the Internet." *Decision Sciences* 35: 259–88.

"The State of the News Media: An Annual Report on American Journalism." 2005. *Journalism.org.* Available at www.stateofthemedia.org/2005/narrative_online_audience.asp?cat=3&media=3 (accessed March 15, 2005).

Stempel, Guido H., III, and Thomas Hargrove. 1996. "Mass Media Audiences in a Changing Media Environment." *Journalism & Mass Communication Quarterly* 73: 549–58.

Stovall, James G. 2004. *Web Journalism.* Boston, MA: Allyn and Bacon.

Thompson, Gary. 2003. "Weblogs, Warblogs, the Public Sphere, and Bubbles." *Transformations* 7: 1–12.

Tsang, Alex S. L., and Nan Zhou. 2005. "Newsgroup Participants as Opinion Leaders and Seekers in Online and Offline Communication Environments." *Journal of Business Research* 58: 1186–94.

11

Discrediting Teresa:
Wounded by Whispers on the Web

Ashli Quesinberry Stokes

Teresa Sends Jobs Offshore? Check your Heinz 57 labels!
Teresa Heinz Funds Hamas?

—Bogus e-mails from an Internet whispering campaign, election 2004

TWO DAYS AFTER THE 2004 NEW HAMPSHIRE PRIMARY, a political free-for-all began on Yahoo!'s H. J. Heinz Co. online investor message board over Teresa Heinz Kerry. At 10:42 a.m., colonel_kurts asked in a post, "Will HNZ give raise if Kerry wins?" What began with speculation about Heinz Kerry's financial ties to the company quickly spiraled into a widespread online attack. As the rumors zipped around the Web, the Heinz Company was repeatedly forced to comment to the media that purchasing Heinz ketchup did not enhance the fortunes of Heinz Kerry or mean that the company was funding the presidential campaign of John Kerry (Lindeman 2004). Indeed, to diffuse the persistent rumor, the Heinz Company monitored media daily, sent informational letters to 350 journalists in response to media commentary it felt was misleading, and posted a statement on its Web site stating that the company's political action committee contributed equally to the Bush and Kerry campaigns (Lindeman 2004). Meanwhile, savvy entrepreneurs profited from the sales of "W" brand ketchup, with its pitch, "You don't support Democrats. Why should your ketchup?" A few posts on an investor message board had culminated in a full-scale offensive against the "ketchup lady" and her husband.

If the rumors questioned the Heinz Company's political affiliations, they fueled growing negative sentiment about Heinz Kerry. In opinion polls,

Teresa's popularity with voters was sliding; by the time she spoke at the Democratic Convention in July, 61% of respondents to an America Online poll said that she would hurt Kerry's chances of winning the election (Hume 2004). As the campaign progressed, Teresa continued to go from being seen as the campaign's greatest strength to being seen as its greatest liability (Tierney 2004: 1). The Internet played a clear role in crafting this perception among voters. In reality, Teresa had little remaining connection to the H. J. Heinz Company, no Heinz family members had been involved in company management for years, family-related holdings had dropped below 4%, and even the Heinz Company's foundation was separate from the Heinz family endowments. Online rumors, however, helped to fuel suspicion that Heinz Kerry's financial and professional status would make her an unacceptable first lady (Lindeman 2004). In addition to claiming that ketchup sales fueled her fortunes, bogus e-mail messages circulating the Web painted a dubious picture of her ability to successfully meet the role's expectations. Messages claimed she had given millions to groups such as the "Barrio Warriors," a radical Hispanic group that wanted to return all of Arizona, California, New Mexico, and Texas to Mexico (Factcheck.org 2004). Other widely circulated attacks argued that she supported Communists, located Heinz factories overseas, and made millions off of this cheap labor. While a few of these attacks were tenuously rooted in truth, most of the quickly spreading rumors, including her status as "ketchup heiress," were patently false.

The truth *was*, however, that these spurious attacks did help to unite audiences against a Kerry presidency. The malicious speculation spread through the Internet whispering campaigns helped to polarize the candidates and rally supporters in favor of Bush. This chapter suggests that these online attacks gave political supporters innovative weapons to discredit a candidate. Their ability to galvanize negative sentiment against a candidate through polarizing rhetoric extended beyond the capability of typical mainstream media characterization. Indeed, to unite against the possibility of a Kerry presidency, the online attacks surpassed traditional election speculation about a candidate's wife to making Heinz Kerry symbolize all that would be unacceptable in a Kerry victory.

Analysis of Heinz Kerry's treatment in the message board whispering campaign reveals how the Internet can play a pivotal role in presidential elections. Although the 1996 and 2000 presidential elections gave voters the opportunity to visit each candidate's Web site, the increased reach and sophistication of the medium has made organizing supporters, reaching activists in key states, keeping voters connected, raising contributions, and spreading the word about issues and candidates a great deal easier in recent elections. It has also enhanced negative campaigning capabilities. The same characteristics that make the Internet such a powerful positive tool in an election also showcase its power in discrediting opponents. As Goldstein (2003: 1) notes, "The speed and reach of the Internet dramatically increases the velocity and reach of a rumor." A well-placed negative message or a widely disseminated attack on an opponent can go a long way in shaping voter perception, as explication of the "ketchup campaign" will reveal.

To unpack the relationship between the Web, a presidential candidate's wife, and election success, this chapter first explains why a potential first lady's positive reputation can be essential in garnering a win for her husband. It then details how Internet whispering campaigns, as variants of blogging techniques, play a new role in shaping these perceptions. With this framework in place, the essay illustrates how message board users employed polarizing rhetoric to attack Heinz Kerry. The implications of these types of negative online campaigning techniques for the future of presidential election campaigns will then be explored.

Potential First Ladies and Polarizing Strategies Online

The Rhetorical Role of a Presidential Candidate's Wife

Internet whispering campaigns primarily about a candidate's wife, rather than just the candidate himself, can play an important role in an election by helping form voter opinion. Americans may not vote for first ladies, but the performance of candidate wives during an election can increase the appeal of a candidate. Today, 54% of Americans consider the wives when deciding how to cast their vote, a much higher number than in previous years ("Online NewsHour" 2004: 3). These highly visible women can "enhance their husband's image in a mass media culture" by broadening the campaign's reach, by helping their husbands deal with the stresses of the campaign, and by creating a fuller picture of the candidate in question (Borelli 2001: 399). Performing these duties is not easy. Americans do not take the question of who might be first lady lightly, and contenders are closely scrutinized for their suitability for the role. Even before the primaries, numerous media discuss the pros and cons of each candidate's wife. As Goodman (2004: 11) notes, "It's now easier to be a candidate than a candidate's wife. Easier to be judged for yourself than to have every move you make, every breath you take, calibrated for its effect on your husband."

Through their scrutiny, the mainstream news media, including newspapers and broadcast, play a key role in helping determine who voters think will best serve as first lady. Indeed, as the campaign heated up, the glowing media commentary about Laura Bush, in sharp contrast to the increasingly negative portrayal of Heinz Kerry, began to influence voters. The media's ongoing use of a traditional first lady frame means that candidate wives who are deemed "non-traditional" can garner negative media attention. Generally, the media tend to frame more traditional, non–politically active first ladies well, and voters can in turn view these candidate wives more positively. That is, the media frames, or makes more salient, certain aspects of events, people, or issues, helping to form public opinion (Entman 1993; Williams 2004). The preponderance of negative coverage resulting from the media's "politically active" first lady frame suggests that the media and public do not feel comfortable when first ladies move beyond traditional activities (Scharrer and Bissell 2000: 79). As Hess (1996: 6) observes, "the farther we get away from the traditional role, the person loses the protective coating that both the public and the press provide them."

Heinz Kerry's exotic upbringing outside the United States, her awards for extensive work in environmental policy and philanthropy, and her forthright persona all made her sit far outside the traditional frame. As a result, the media's "nontraditional" characterization of Teresa helped result in negative sentiment among voters. By July 2004, the number of those who viewed Heinz Kerry unfavorably had increased from 19% to 31%. By August, four in ten viewed Heinz Kerry favorably, three in ten had an unfavorable opinion, and 27% had not yet decided how they felt about her, according to CNN–USA Today–Gallup polling (Pickler 2004: 2). Meanwhile, Laura Bush enjoyed the highest favorable ratings of any modern first lady (Pickler 2004).

Polarizing Strategies Online

In 2004, blogs and their variants, including Internet whispering campaigns, helped solidify the media's negative characterization of Teresa among voters. Blogs, a contraction for *weblogs*, are new features of the political landscape that allow users to post links to other Web sites, comment on previous users' posts, and discuss mainstream political news and strategy, all in an interactive online format. These forums build on mainstream media because they offer the user the opportunity to reflect, speculate, and criticize typical campaign discourse. As they are a mix of news, rumors, and inside information, they can rally supporters by eschewing some of the objectivity standards of traditional journalism. Blogs' ability to allow users to pick and choose stories from the elite media to influence other users' views of the world has resulted in their being labeled participatory journalism, or journalism from the edges (Lasica 2003). Bloggers thus challenge traditional journalism by selecting, reporting, analyzing, and disseminating news and information, a task typically reserved for the news media (Lasica 2003). Blogs also build on mainstream media by the way users interact with the information offered in the blog forums. Although some do not go beyond gossip and bickering, blogs and their variants can potentially build powerful grassroots support because voters typically regulated outside the formal election system get a chance to hawk or discredit candidates and beliefs with unbridled passion and energy (Weiss 2003; Ustinova 2004).

This ability to focus on particular stories and candidates, spotlight what they consider to be undercovered stories, or forward unproven claims can reveal blogs' negative campaigning potential in elections. Their open forums leave them vulnerable to misinformation that can be quickly spread throughout the Web and offline. Internet whispering campaigns such as the ketchup campaign represent this type of blogging gone awry. Rather than using the Web as a medium to inform and motivate voters by offering them detailed and accurate information about a candidate, these variants operate by spreading negative claims and faulty information to attack the opposing side. Internet whispering campaigns thus build on a classic promotional strategy to discredit an opponent. In the 1930s, companies would hire people to go out in public and secretly spread some rumor or talk about a promotion. A famous example involved a rival of Chesterfield cigarettes that paid men along the Atlantic seaboard to tell store clerks that Chesterfield cigarettes contained a contagious disease in their tobacco. As McLaren (2005: 1) points out, "Such campaigns were, all too often, extremely effective."

Today, the practice is becoming so important online that a marketing conference was held to explore the role of viral, buzz, blogs, word of mouth, evangelism, grassroots, and message boards in connecting with audiences (Robideau 2005). Whether in marketing or political applications, all of these methods center on implanting an idea or message into a Web user's ear, and they frequently work through the sense that the user is getting special or unique information. There is some concern about the general practice. Parents worry about "buzzploitation" by Internet marketers whispering inappropriate information into their children's ears, while political campaign managers worry about the type of damaging information that can spread through these rumors (Robideau 2005).

Although Internet whispering campaigns can be extremely effective in promoting a product, service, or candidate, they can severely damage reputations. Numerous corporations, for example, have been prey for the Internet campaign rumor mill. The Tommy Hilfiger Company, for example, had to battle persistent Internet rumors that its founder had appeared on the Oprah Winfrey show remarking that he regretted that minority customers were buying his clothes (Goldstein 2003). Starbucks was victim of an Internet rumor that called for consumers to boycott the coffee giant because it had closed all its stores in Israel, when the truth was that it had just ended a business arrangement in that country. In politics, the same holds true. Cyber smears damaged

Howard Dean through the constant replaying of the "Dean Scream"; John Kerry, by accusing him of having an affair, à la Bill Clinton, with a White House intern; and President Bush, by adding to Michael Moore's accusation that the president had unsavory ties to Saudi families involved in the September 11 attacks. It is tempting to write off such rumors as unimportant to a campaign's outcome. After all, the lack of credible sources and the "passed along" nature of the information would seem to be trivial in assessing a candidate's character or suitability for the role. On the contrary, the power of these campaigns resides in whisperers' abilities to add to circulating themes presented by the media and use them as weapons in their arsenal of interactive, gatekeeper-free, information sharing.

In the ketchup campaign, Bush supporters dominated the Heinz Company message board for months. They increased unity by building on the media's suggestion that Teresa did not quite fit the mold of an appropriate first lady. Teresa became the negative symbol of what a Kerry presidency would represent. She served as a polarizing device, which unifies through the "creation and/or intensification of fundamental divisions and differences within a group of people" (Jasinski 2001: 436). Typically, polarizing rhetoric unites one segment of people within a larger collective, so its use in the message boards appealed to investors through largely financially based attacks (Jasinski 2001). Attacking her unified supporters by suggesting how she was different from or inferior to them. Although there are several common characteristics of polarizing rhetoric, in the campaign about Teresa, two main strategies predominated: first, posts stressed the "threat" that she posed to the institution of first lady; second, posts employed antithetical, disjunctive, and divisional arguments to illustrate how Teresa was inappropriate for the role. Like other Internet whispering campaigns, the ketchup campaign built on the foundation laid by the news media's coverage of Teresa. Using that reporting as a basis for attacks, users rallied supporters in favor of Bush by pointing out how Heinz Kerry's wealth gave her too much financial influence. Her professional career was attacked for its potential for involving the Kerry administration in unacceptable activism. Posters also went to great lengths to demonstrate how her personality was not suited for the role of first lady.

The Ketchup Campaign's Attack on Heinz Kerry

Attacking Heinz Kerry's Power and Influence

The message boards' focus on Teresa's potential influence as first lady is not surprising. Historically, first ladies are expected to not attract much attention on the presidential stage. Tradition dictates that they act behind the scenes lest they be accused of being power hungry Lady Macbeths ("Online NewsHour" 2004: 2). Yet although expected to be indirect, first ladies can still possess a considerable amount of influence. Watson (1997), for example, argues that the first lady has more power and influence than most senior advisers, cabinet members, and the vice president. Traditional expectations society has about the role of first ladies mean, however, that they have to wield power and influence carefully. Although voters are gradually beginning to accept that first ladies can have professional aspirations and education, traditional legacy still limits them (Wekkin 2000: 603). As she had told the media that she would like to continue in her role as chairwoman of the Heinz Endowments should Kerry be elected, Heinz Kerry would be closely evaluated for her fittingness to exercise the power associated with the institution. Her active role in the Heinz Endowments, as well as ongoing suspicions that she was running the Heinz Company, became grounds for attack. As potential first lady, head of a foundation, and supposed overseer of the Heinz Company business, Teresa was perceived as a clear threat because she would be positioned to wield her influence in the Kerry administration. As a reporter noted, "she'd be wielding two things that are frightening to people—power and money—and that will make people suspicious" (Wilhelm 2004: 7).

In the press, reporters had speculated that Teresa's financial connections and professional aspirations would make her different. They wondered, for example, "what if the country's first lady was also leader of one of the nation's wealthiest foundations?" (Wilhelm 2004: 7). On the Heinz message board, the media discussion of Teresa's wealth and power turned into accusations that her money would give her too much direct influence over the financial concerns of Americans. She was painted as a threat to job security, as posters maintained that she would not protect them against the specter of outsourcing, a hot topic in the election. For example, one said, "If she [Teresa] really would be concerned about job outsourcing she could make her voice heard. Corporations do listen to large shareholders."[1] This post began to divide Heinz Kerry from typical Americans. She was portrayed as being more interested in her own wealth than in helping protect American financial stability. Since Teresa was protected, the writer suggests, why would she feel the need to protect others? This concern about her disinterest in American economic problems was developed further in a following post: "If Kerry is elected, will he and his wife close all those foreign factories and bring all those jobs back to America? Of course they won't. They're making millions off that cheap labor." Instead of helping Americans, the Kerrys are shown as outsiders unconcerned about others because of their wealth. In addition to casting Heinz Kerry as the antithesis of what Americans needed to increase their financial security, these particular lines of attack reveal the power of a whispering campaign to generate suspicion regardless of the veracity of the claim. Although dissenting users posted evidence that Heinz Kerry did not own foreign factories, the users persisted that she profited from her relationship to the Heinz Company and that this connection would be bad for Americans.

Closely related to the attacks on Heinz Kerry's financial influence were ones that accused her of creating conflicts of interest because of her relationship to the Heinz Company. These posts polarized her against Bush supporters through disjunctive, either/or arguments. That is, Heinz Kerry's ties to the Heinz Company, no matter how tenuous, meant that she would inappropriately involve the company in the Kerry administration. The posts built on the mainstream press's assertion that while nothing may be amiss, "perceptions of conflicts of interest will be there and be exploited" (Wilhelm 2004: 1). One post began: "Think of the conflict of interest a President would have who's [sic] wife owns business interests in all of these countries." Another post also directly implied that Teresa's association with Heinz would cause problems for Americans during the Kerry administration: "Think of the conflict of interest a President might have, if the nation has a conflict with any of the countries containing his wife's factories or business interests. How many potential jobs are lost to these locations? Pass it on!!!" In other words, it was not possible that Teresa could be connected to the Heinz Company and appropriately serve as first lady. Her association alone was used as evidence that she would interfere with Kerry's ability to make good decisions.

Other posts were more indirect in insinuating problems arising from Teresa's alleged conflict of interest and showed the speculative nature of Internet whispering campaigns. Concern ranged from her exact role in the Heinz operations to whether or not the company supported the Kerry campaign. One hinted: "Is Teresa still involved in the company? If so Nov. 2 is very relevant, no?" Another continued to argue she was involved: "One more note, if Heinz isn't involved in the Kerry campaign, why do the Kerry for president pins have the Heinz logo on them? They need permission from the Heinz Corporation to use the Heinz logo." Another argued that *any* involvement Teresa had with Heinz Company was problematic: "Even though she may not have anything to do with Heinz, she was stupid enough to carry the Heinz name throughout the years. Guilt by association." In all, then, Teresa's financial status gave her too much influence as a potential first lady. On the boards, it was not possible for a potential first lady to be financially independent and be acceptable. In disjunctive terms, she could not be both. *Either* she was a financially secure career woman *or* she was a traditional first lady.

Another large area of attack concerned Teresa's ability to influence her husband's public policy decisions as first lady. This time Teresa's *professional* status in the Heinz Endowments became the basis of a disjunctive threat. If elected, Heinz Kerry would continue to make policy, although now she would move beyond the Heinz Endowments to actively pushing her agenda in the White House. In mainstream media interviews, Heinz Kerry repeatedly said that she would not want a policy-making job in the Kerry administration. When asked, "Is there room in the White House for your social agenda?" she answered, "I don't have a social agenda." Then, when the interviewer pressed, "And how about an arts and cultural agenda? " she said, "I wouldn't use the word agenda. It sounds like I'm going to make policy. I will continue to deal with my work [with the Heinz Endowments]" (Cole 2004: 257). In another interview, she continued this theme: "I don't do policy for him. He has his professionals for that" ("Online NewsHour" 2004: 7). Clearly, Heinz Kerry tried to downplay her interest in policy.

Neither the mainstream press nor the message boards accepted her answer. In the press, her work with the foundations and interest in the environment still resulted in her framing as a potential policy maker. One journalist worried, "It's one thing to have a first lady advocate, and another thing entirely if she's throwing chips in the pile" (Wilhelm 2004: 8). In discussing her potentially active role in philanthropy and work on the environment, another article in the *Seattle Times* read, "The result would be an unprecedented role for a first lady. In addition to her White House duties, she would also be a leader of foundations awarding grants to environmental groups that often seek to influence policies by lobbying Congress and government agencies" (Bernton 2004: 1). The reporter's use of "unprecedented" and implication that she would be helping to influence policies edged Heinz Kerry toward being an unacceptable activist type of first lady.

Without the objectivity standards that kept the newspaper coverage somewhat neutral, the message board posts went beyond hinting that Heinz Kerry would influence policy to casting her as a powerful activist enemy. Posters used name calling and ridicule to fuel the suspicion that Heinz Kerry would exercise inappropriate activism as first lady: "Unfortunately Teresa is more concerned in her ultra liberal agendas which she supports with huge donations, from moneys she receives from Heinz. I am sure her former deceased husband, from whom she inherited her fortune, is turning over in his grave to see how his money is spent and on whom."

Painted as the opposite of Bush supporters, Teresa was not just liberal, she was "ultra" liberal; indeed, she even denigrated her husband's memory through her activist agendas.

The posts became more vitriolic in associating Teresa with unacceptable causes and activism. One poster said: "Mr. Heinz would turn over in his grave and even vomit out the maggots if he knew that his daughter was a communist.

Buy Hunt's!" Another posted, "I'm also encouraging everyone I know to boycott HNZ until they GET THE LAWYERS MOBILIZED against this woman and her filthy use of a once great company's name to support every left wing cause known to man." The messages built on history in this thread of attack. Although first ladies have a long tradition of social advocacy, particularly in the areas of women's and children's issues, more "activist" forays have been met with disapproval. Eleanor Roosevelt was attacked for "acting unladylike and ignoring her housekeeping and other wifely duties," while Hillary Clinton was called a "bitch" and "congenital liar" for her activities in health-care reform and the Whitewater controversy (Bostdorff 1998).

What differed here, however, was the level of negative attack that could be forwarded; that is, posters could create strongly negative associations about Teresa's influence at will. Thus, when posters closed out this thread with calls to "Boycott Heinz products and quit financing these leftist insurgents in the US" and "quit financing ketchup-Kerry," the image of Teresa's influence on a Kerry presidency was the antithesis of a traditional, behind-the-scenes spouse working for women and children. Instead, Heinz Kerry appeared as a threat to the sacred institution of first lady. This threat became more significant when posters turned away from issues of policy, influence, and activism to attacking Heinz Kerry's personality.

Attacking Heinz Kerry's Personality

Voter expectations about a first lady are affected by the complicated relationship between gender and presidential power. As a public figure, the first lady is a political actor, but as the wife of a president, she risks making her husband appear weak should she appear to compromise his authority or decision making by acting too strong publicly (Borelli 2001; Gould 1999; Jamieson 1995). As a result, first ladies must balance the demands of being perceived as dependent and independent (Bostdorff 1998). Dependent first ladies demonstrate to voters that a president has control within his own family (Bostdorff 1998). Too much independence, however, and a first lady will be criticized.

Two themes surfaced in the posts revolving around the inability for Teresa to subordinate herself to her husband. Her independence and outspokenness, as portrayed by the media, became a particular target for attack on the chat boards. There, even the qualities that might be appreciated in today's progressive women became evidence of Teresa's unsuitability. Her independence became domination and control over her husband. Her outspokenness became evidence of her uncontrollable character. As a result, Kerry's overall credibility was further questioned. The message boards crafted a damaging question through their attacks. How could a president lead effectively if he needed to constantly be "reining in" his wife?

Historically, presidents should appear masculine and strong in order to be perceived as strong leaders. On the message boards, Kerry's leadership ability was attacked through comments that questioned his ability to control the country if he was being "controlled" by Teresa. Heinz Kerry's financial and emotional independence thus surfaced as the basis for an attack against Kerry's authority:

> Every American needs to see this list of companies that the Democratic Presidential nominee's wife owns and controls. Do you find it bothersome that she would have control over him (bucks talk) and he could sell out our entire country??? John Kerry's Wife: do you find it strange that Kerry's wife is never with him? Do you find it strange that you never hear anything about her? This may be why! As time goes on, we're just getting to know the possible future First Lady of the United States of America and it is quite interesting.

These types of comments aligned Kerry with other presidential candidates who appeared to be managing a "strong willed" wife, such as Howard Dean. The post suggested that Kerry did not have enough authority over his wife's comments. As a result, his ability to portray the masculinity and strength expected of presidents was weakened (Powers 2004: 2448).

Once again, however, users built from this original line of attack to more outrageous accusations. The suspicion that Teresa was too independent led to speculation that she was simply out of control. For example, an odd thread began that Teresa was a drunk. Although any drinking problems were difficult to document, Teresa was painted as a reckless alcoholic who would embarrass her husband (and America) if elected. This thread began with a single comment: "She is a drunken disgrace." Immediately, posts ran with this line of attack. One wrote: "If a few years ago John Warner had run for President, while he was married to Liz Taylor, we would have had the same type first lady as if Kerry had won. The only way to appreciate a drunk is to be as drunk as they are. Three cheers and a half gallon for Liz and Teresa." Although one poster complained that the attacks against Teresa were unfair and she would have loved to see Teresa in the White House, a post immediately attacked back: "I too would have liked to see her in the White House. Would have been fun to see Kerry making his state of the union speech and she busts in all shit-faced and starts calling people morons, peons, low lifes and such. Then she pukes in the corner and goes off to the cellar to sleep it off." As this post illustrated, members of the forum built on the perceptions fostered by the press that Teresa was independent to engage in wild speculation about her. Teresa's independence resulted in unfounded attacks on her character.

Meanwhile, in the press, Heinz Kerry's undisciplined speaking style enhanced the perception that the she was too independent. While a good deal of her early responses were reported by the press with a mixture of amusement and consternation, as the election wore on and became more heated, Teresa's style was evaluated more negatively. The press began to move away from discussing Heinz Kerry's outspokenness as merely different to suggesting that she was domineering and difficult to manage, unacceptable qualities for first ladies. Teresa's outspokenness about everything, from the title "first lady" to her thoughts on the merits of Botox, to her position on prenuptial agreements, signified a dominant, unpredictable candidate wife rather than a principled first lady. Through attacks on his wife's outspoken and unpredictable, and therefore also uncontrollable, behavior, Kerry was subtly attacked for lacking authority over his wife's comments. For example, a reporter wrote, "As an alpha female—she's a billionaire who runs the billion-dollar-plus Heinz foundations—Heinz Kerry seems to slip her leash, if indeed she has one, with some regularity" (Voboril 2004: 2).

On the message boards, these reports of outspoken unpredictability became fodder for blistering attacks. Without the gatekeeping function of the press, Teresa's speaking style suggested all that was wrong about her serving as first lady. One user wrote, for example, "And as for Teresa, she is a fruitcake and can't control her mouth." The infamous "shove it" incident became particular evidence for Teresa's unsuitability. Heinz Kerry, after being pursued with biased questions by a conservative member of the press, finally snapped and told the reporter to "shove it." Although the media had a field day with Teresa's inability to remain cool in the face of the reporter's question, many stories did put her comment in the context that the reporter had repeatedly pestered her. On the boards, however, Teresa's behavior proved her unsuitability for the first lady role and demonstrated the type of outbursts we could expect should Kerry be elected. One member hypothesized: "Let's say Kerry wins the election. Can't you see the headlines when Teresa tells the Prime Minister of some country to 'SHOVE IT!' because she disagrees with a comment the PM makes?" This comment continued to suggest that Teresa was the opposite of everything Americans expected in a first lady. She did not value control, respect, poise, or other typical "feminine" qualities expected in the role. Other users confirmed this accusation by posting, "the 'ketchup lady' is just full of it, but not with class." Clearly, fairly neutral media framing of Heinz Kerry as unpredictable and forthright became much more damning when incorporated into the ketchup campaign. Coupled with the various techniques that worked to make Heinz Kerry seem like a power-hungry activist with too much influence, the posts further rallied the investor forum against the prospect of a Kerry presidency.

Wounded by Whispers

In her speech at the Democratic National Convention in July 2004, Teresa Heinz Kerry introduced herself by remarking, "My name is Teresa Heinz Kerry and by now it should come as no surprise that I have something to say" (Heinz Kerry 2004). By October, Teresa had largely fallen silent, though talk about her had not. In assessing the ketchup campaign's success in using polarizing rhetoric to discredit and silence Teresa, rallying Bush supporters, and serving as a model to unify voters in future elections, several observations stand out. The types of attacks lobbied on the H. J. Heinz Company investor message board both echo traditional negative campaign tactics as well as differ from them. The possible role of Internet whispering campaigns in future elections deserves attention as well.

Although located in a Web-based form, the ketchup campaign has its place in the long-running tradition of the media's expressing interest in potential first ladies. While it is tempting to wonder why the media make such a fuss over the suitability of a candidate's wife, the first lady's status as a cherished institution in American society means that all those who may fill the role will be closely scrutinized. Potential first ladies have a mold they must fit, and if they do not, they become ammunition in the polarization arsenal of political campaigns. Ulysses Grant's wife was ridiculed for having a crossed eye, Rachel Jackson was attacked because the divorce she thought had been granted was not yet official when she married Andrew Jackson, and Abigail Adams fell into the "too strong" trap because she was too political and thus reflected poorly on her husband's masculinity (Ryan 2004). Teresa's strong philanthropic background and blunt speaking style made her, too, break the acceptable first lady mold. She was characterized by all media as too nontraditional. As a result, the treatment of Heinz Kerry shows that nontraditional women "may succeed in their careers, [they] may succeed in changing the world, but they're less likely to succeed in revolutionizing the White House" ("Online News-Hour" 2004: 5). For those seeking to prevent Teresa from having the chance, their focus on her, as well as their particular attacking strategy, were therefore typical political choices.

Polarization strategies, in other words, also have a long history in negative political campaigning. Their purpose in Internet whispering campaigns or any other media is to unify supporters by presenting an opposite, unacceptable image. Through the strategy, the unity among one group is intensified by pitting it against its rival camp. Elections, indeed all of politics, thus provide many occasions for the employment of this strategy. Polarization, for example, attacking all Democrats as "bleeding heart liberals" or all Republicans as "wealthy hawks," can motivate supporters and unify them by linking one faction or person in a group to its most extreme elements. Heinz Kerry, as a result of many interests, professional associations, and philanthropic causes, functioned as this extreme that the message board users could rally behind.

Yet, while the ketchup campaign thus reveals some similarities to previous negative campaign tactics, there are several differences that make these Internet attacks risky to ignore for both communication scholars and campaign strategists. When employing polarization rhetoric, advocates seek dramatic confrontations to amplify division, a task made much easier through the use of an Internet whispering campaign (see Jasinski 2001: 436). In the past, candidates using the polarization strategy would have staffers plant hecklers and protesters in their venues for the purposes of exploitation. The candidates could then argumentatively shut down these "props" during a rally. The use of Internet whispering campaigns means that supporters do not physically need to "plant" opponents to carry out this strategy successfully. They can increase division simply by dominating an online forum and drowning out opponents. As a result, the Web can provide a formidable way to unify supporters because there are literally thousands of opportunities to confront opponents.

Similarly, the lack of a gatekeeper in whispering campaigns serves as a key advantage in unifying supporters. Like other Web communities, users of an online forum can further indoctrinate supporters because they do not necessarily have to report the other side of the argument. Posters can amplify the media's information to support only their positions. Unification can grow through sheer message saturation. One of the primary strengths of these campaigns, then, is that they allow negative sentiment to build unfettered. As a professional journalist notes of whisperers, "They're able to toss stuff out that a reporter on a daily newspaper couldn't. They express opinions loudly and with fervor" (Smolkin 2004: 9). However, the same one-sided nature of these forums does make them somewhat limited as a persuasive tool. These campaigns fortify the already supportive. Rather than causing large numbers of voters to distrust or dislike an opponent, they speak to the already convinced, or at least the already sympathetic. The types of messages exchanged through a whispering campaign might further solidify a belief in a particular worldview, but their attacking nature, often based in unfounded accusations, is unlikely to move a user to a new opinion. As we saw in this case, members of the forum overwhelmingly supported one side and suppressed differing viewpoints. Members may have been energized by the message exchange, but they were already clearly attached to Bush.

Nevertheless, Internet whispering campaigns provide several considerations for political strategists. First, if future campaigns wish to tap into these online worlds, they must realize that planting a rumor with a specific public is crucial. In the ketchup campaign, rumors bounced around and spread throughout the

Heinz investor message board. As users were already interested in financial issues, starting an exchange about Teresa's relationship to financial matters was in keeping with the nature of the forum. Online users are already "activated" publics and perhaps provide a new way for political activists to reach voters, provided they tailor their message to a particular forum. However, campaign managers need to be aware of the difficulties in stopping an Internet whispering campaign once it begins. On the Heinz message boards, for example, users aligned with Kerry posted links to Web sites that dispelled the rumors that were circulating. Rather than quieting the negative commentary, however, these posts usually refueled a particular debate. Users would continue to protest that the offered information was inaccurate, and the attacks would continue. Indeed, the H. J. Heinz Company tried for months to correct the belief that the Kerrys unethically profited from their relationship to the company. Regardless, the rumors persisted on the boards that the couple benefited. Thus for future elections, to keep rumors from spreading and adhering in Web communities, campaign staffers may find that acting quickly to squash the rumor is the best strategy in containing it. After all, Internet whispering campaigns can put the burden on the target of the rumor by helping to force them to clarify or correct an accusation. In doing so, however, the perception that one even needs to address the rumor might add to its credence among voters.

Ultimately, when thinking about the future of political campaigning, recognizing the changing nature of the media network that Internet whispering campaigns help represent is crucial. Instead of being dominated by the mainstream press, bloggers and whisperers influence reporters as much as they are influenced by them. These voters may not have traditional power, but they do have enough influence to get ideas noticed or to force traditional journalism to pay attention (Smolkin 2004). *The Washington Times*, for example, had to correct its printing of the ketchup campaign rumors. Therefore, while blogs and Internet whispering campaigns may still be considered supplemental in disseminating information in elections, they must not be overlooked. Although the types of information found in their forums cannot substitute, for example, for the more neutral role of newspapers or provide candidates with specific types of access, such as broadcast, their types of content offer voters different takes on the daily diet of political information. As Lasica (2003: 71) notes, "Weblogs should not be considered in isolation but as part of an emerging new media ecosystem—a network of ideas. . . . These communities also produce participatory journalism . . . which the mainstream media feed upon, developing them as a pool of tips, sources and story ideas. The relationship is symbiotic." In terms of political communication, however, all of this interactivity between the types of media can solidify perception about a particular opponent. In the ketchup campaign, the variety of media converged to craft a widely held opinion among voters. Press discussion of Heinz Kerry's "unsuitable" qualities bled into the blog world and then resurfaced back in the mainstream media as the campaign progressed. All condemned her. In the end, the variety of media sources helped seal the fate of Teresa Heinz Kerry's quest to serve as the next first lady. Her status as the 2004 election's collective media punching bag allowed her to continue to do the types of philanthropic work the Internet whispering campaign worked hard to discredit.

Note

1. All examples of message-board text are taken from the Yahoo! Finance message board in 2004. Messages can be located by searching finance.messages.yahoo.com.

References

Bernton, Hal. 2004. "Heinz Kerry a Major Funder of Environmental Groups, Causes." *Seattle Times*, September 30. Available at seattletimes.newssource.com (accessed October 5, 2004).

Borelli, Maryanne. 2001. "Competing Conceptions of the First Ladyship: Public Responses to Betty Ford's *60 Minutes* Interview." *Presidential Studies Quarterly* 31: 397–414.

Bostdorff, Denise. 1998. "Hillary Rodham Clinton and Elizabeth Dole as Running 'Mates' in the 1996 Campaign: Parallels in the Rhetorical Constraints of First Ladies and Vice Presidents." In *The 1996 Presidential Campaign: A Communication Perspective*, edited by Robert E. Denton. Westport, CT: Praeger.

Cole, Kenneth. October 2004. "Teresa Heinz Kerry." *Vogue*, 256–58.

Entman, Robert M. 1993. "Framing: Toward Clarification of a Fractured Paradigm." *Journal of Communication* 43: 51–58.

Factcheck.org. 2004. "Internet 'Whispering Campaigns' Falsely Accuse Teresa Heinz Kerry." August 4. Available at www.factcheck.org (accessed April 20, 2005).

Goldstein, Michael. 2003. "Companies Fight Web Smears." *New York Daily News*, September 15. Available at www.nydailynews.com (accessed March 30, 2005).

Goodman, Ellen. 2004. "Wives Face the Acid Test." *Boston Globe*, July 25. Available at www.boston.com/news/globe (accessed September 1, 2004).

Gould, Lewis L. 1999. *Lady Bird Johnson, Our Environmental First Lady*. Lawrence: University Press of Kansas.

Guerra, Carlos. 2003. "Is the United States Entering the Age of the Cyber Campaign?" *San Antonio News Express*, 26 August. Available at www2.mysanantonio.com/aboutus/expressnews (accessed April 20, 2005).

Heinz Kerry, Teresa. 2004. Remarks at the Democratic National Convention, July 27, Boston.

Hess, Stephen. 1996. "The Role of the First Lady." *Think Tank*. Available at www.pbs.org/thinktank (accessed January 12, 2005).

Hume, Brit. 2004. Fox Special Report with Brit Hume. Fox News.com. July 28 (accessed January 15, 2005).

Jamieson, Kathleen Hall. 1995. *Beyond the Double Bind: Women in Leadership.* New York: Oxford University Press.

Jasinski, James. 2001. *Sourcebook on Rhetoric: Key Concepts in Contemporary Rhetorical Studies.* Thousand Oaks, CA: Sage.

Lasica, Joseph D. 2003. "Blogs and Journalism Need Each Other." *Nieman Reports* 57 (3): 70–75.

Lindeman, Teresa F. 2004. "Heinz Ketchup Tabled by GOP: Republicans Relish Condiment Alternative." *Pittsburgh Post Gazette*, August 28. Available at www.post-gazette.com (accessed April 20, 2005).

Martel, Ned. 2004. "First Ladies, Second Place." *Financial Times*, January 24, 26.

McLaren, Carrie. 2005. "Undercover Selling: 1930s Whispering Campaigns." *Stay Free! Magazine.* Available at www.stayfreemagazine.org (accessed April 20, 2005).

"Online NewsHour." 2004. "The First Lady: Public Expectations, Private Lives." October 25. Available at www.pbs.org/newshour/vote2004 (accessed January 12, 2005).

Pickler, Nedra. 2004. "Voters Split as Last Debate Nears." *Advertiser*, October 13. Available at www.johnkerry.com (accessed December 30, 2004).

Powers, William. 2004. "Thank You, Mother Teresa." *National Journal*, July 31, 2448.

Robideau, Brad. 2005. "Word of Mouth Marketing Association's Code of Ethics Neglects Parental Involvement." *Marketwire.* Available at www.marketwire.com (accessed March 30, 2005).

Ryan, Joan. 2004. "Laura or Teresa? Who Cares?" *San Francisco Chronicle*, October 3. Available at www.sfchron.com (accessed January 22, 2005).

Scharrer, Erica, and Kim Bissell. 2000. "Overcoming Traditional Boundaries: The Role of Political Activity in Media Coverage of First Ladies." *Women & Politics* 21: 55–83.

Smolkin, Rachel. 2004. "The Expanding Blogosphere." *American Journalism Review* 26 (3): 38–44.

Tierney, John. 2004. "Is America Ready for Teresa Heinz Kerry?" *New York Times*, May 14. Available at www.nytimes.com (January 12, 2005).

Ustinova, Anastasia. 2004. "Political Blogs Catching on as Web Fundraising, Commentary Rise." *Chicago Tribune*, July 27. Available at www.chicagotribune.com (accessed April 20, 2005).

Voboril, Mary. 2004. "Teresa Heinz Kerry Makes Her Mark." *Newsday.com.* July 26. Available at www.newsday.com (accessed December 30, 2004).

Watson, Robert P. 1997. "The First Lady Reconsidered: Presidential Partner and Political Institution." *Presidential Studies Quarterly* 27: 805–19.

Weiss, Joanna. 2003. "'Blogs' Shake Political Discourse." *Boston Globe*, July 23. Available at www.boston.com/news/globe (accessed April 20, 2005).

Wekkin, Gary. 2000. "Role Constraints and First Ladies." *Social Science Journal* 37: 601–10.

Wilhelm, Ian. 2004. "Heinz Funds Face Political Pickle." *Chronicle of Philanthropy*, April 29, 7–12.

Williams, Andrew P. 2004. *Media Narcissism and Self-reflexive Reporting: Metacommunication in Televised News Broadcasts and Web Coverage of Operation Iraqi Freedom.* Doctoral dissertation, University of Florida, Gainesville.

12

Web Interactivity and Young Adult Political Efficacy

John C. Tedesco

T HE EMERGENCE OF THE INTERNET fueled debate between political optimists and political skeptics. Optimists hoped the Internet would mobilize previously disengaged or disenfranchised citizens, while skeptics argued that the Internet would do little more than reinforce the media power structure already in place (Tedesco 2004). According to Norris (2000: 121), "on the one hand, mobilization theories claim that 'virtual democracy' promises a cornucopia of empowerment in a digital world," while "reinforcement theories suggest that use of the Net will strengthen, not radically transform, the existing patterns of social inequality and political participation." While some scholars fear the Internet will fragment, isolate, polarize, and shred our political collective (e.g., Neuman 2001), others hope the Internet will bypass or circumvent the current print and broadcast communication structure (e.g., Rheingold 1995).

Optimists herald the Internet as a "master medium" (Selnow 1998) for its interactive potential to defy the controlled, largely one-directional flow of political media (Hacker 1996; Margolis, Resnick, and Tu 1997; Rheingold 1995). The Internet offers

(a) inherent interactivity;
(b) potential for lateral and horizontal communication;
(c) point-to-point and non-hierarchical modes of communication;
(d) low costs to users (once a user is set up);
(e) rapidity as a communication medium;
(f) lack of national or other boundaries; and

(g) freedom from the intrusion and monitoring of government. (Barber, Matt-son, and Peterson 1997: 8)

Beyond these structural characteristics, Sparks (2001) added anonymity of so-cial actors as an Internet advantage because of its ability to shield discrimi-nating characteristics such as age, sex, or race that could diminish or exclude political voice. Nevertheless, most political communication studies completed prior to the 2004 presidential election indicate that the Internet has rarely ac-complished its interactive, discursive potential.

However, research from the Pew Internet & American Life Project offers new hope for the role of the Internet in American politics. According to Pew, the 2004 election represents a "breakout year" for the Internet as 75 million Americans used the Web to participate in politics (Pew 2005). Furthermore, "there was an increase of more than 50% between 2000 and 2004 in the num-ber of registered voters who cited the Internet as one of their primary sources of news about the presidential campaign" (Pew 2005: i). Additional encourag-ing results from Pew include:

> 42% growth from 2000 to 2004 in the number of people using the internet to re-search candidates' issues positions; 82% growth in the number researching can-didates' voting records; 50% growth in the number taking online polls; a dou-bling of the number discussing politics in chat rooms and other online forums; and a doubling of those making campaign contributions online. (iv)

Clearly, the Internet is becoming a more significant medium for Americans who seek to learn about candidates and issues and to participate in campaigns.

Young Adults, Engagement, and the Internet

According to a Pew Research Center survey (Pew 2004), eighteen to twenty-nine year olds are the most likely of any age demographic to use the Internet for political purposes. Nearly a quarter (24%) of young adults surveyed indi-cate that they use the Internet for at least one campaign activity from among getting candidate issue information, sending or receiving campaign e-mails, getting information on local activities, visiting Web sites of political groups, visiting candidate Web sites, and engaging in chats, discussions, or blogs.

Despite large percentages of disinterested young citizens largely disengaged from politics, the percentage of young adults indicating they turn to the In-ternet for information nearly doubled between 2000 and 2004 (Pew 2004). According to Pew, the percentage of young adults that say they regularly learn something from network evening news decreased from 39% to 23% between 2000 and 2004. During this same time period, the Internet jumped from 13%

to 20% as a source for regular learning among young adults. While the Internet is gaining as a campaign information source for all Americans, its growth is most pronounced among young adults.

Although more young adults are turning to the Internet to learn about politics, their patterned disengagement from political life has been a source of great concern for researchers, civic institutions, and granting agencies. In *The Vanishing Voter*, Patterson (2002) indicates the downward trend in voting during the past several decades is the largest decline in the nation's history. Perhaps more troubling for America's democracy are data indicating that participation rates among our youngest eligible voters have declined more rapidly than participation rates among the general population during the past thirty years. Since earning the franchise to vote in the 1972, and up until campaign 2000, eighteen to twenty-one year olds have voted in steadily declining numbers in each presidential election (Jamieson, Shin, and Day 2002). According to Delli Carpini (2000: 341–42), when compared to their older cohorts from previous generations, our current young adults are

(1) less trusting of their fellow citizens, (2) less interested in politics or public affairs, (3) less likely to feel a sense of identity, pride, or obligation associated with American citizenship, (4) less knowledgeable about the substance or processes of politics, (5) less likely to read a newspaper or watch the news, (6) less likely to register to vote, (7) less likely to participate in politics beyond voting, (8) less likely to participate in community organizations designed to address public problems through collective action or the formal policy process, and (9) less likely to connect individual efforts to help solve problems with more traditional, collective forms of civic engagement.

Nevertheless, election turnout data show a 9% increase in young adult voter turnout when comparing 2000 and 2004 presidential election voting rates. However, until young adult political engagement figures increase steadily over time and reveal that the 2004 turnout results were not context specific, there is reason to examine ways to generate more interest and a higher level of political efficacy among our youngest eligible voters. As young adults increasingly turn to the Internet for political information, it is appropriate to question whether the Web can stimulate political engagement or increase political efficacy.

Young Adult Political Efficacy

There is good reason to believe that engagement and efficacy are strongly related. Young adults regularly cite lack of knowledge about the candidates or political issues as a reason for not voting (see Kaid, McKinney, and Tedesco 2000). The 2000 National Association of Secretaries of State (NASS) survey shows that inefficacy among young voters—or a sense that their vote does not matter and politicians do not value their opinions—serves as a primary predictor of nonvoting. The NASS survey also shows that political ignorance—the lack of knowledge about political candidates or political processes—also serves as a predictor of young adult disengagement (NASS 2000). Clearly, young adults perceive the Internet as helping with political ignorance, as 44% of young people age eighteen to twenty-nine indicate they regularly or sometimes learn about politics from the Internet (Pew 2004). If the Internet can help with political learning, can it also aid in combating political inefficacy?

Political efficacy measures have long been a part of the National Election Studies (NES) and an important variable for assessing political attitudes. Political efficacy was conceptualized more than fifty years ago as the perception that citizens feel capable or empowered to influence the political process (Campbell, Gurin, and Miller 1954). Traditionally, efficacy is considered to have two highly related aspects, internal efficacy and external efficacy (e.g. Acock, Clark, and Stewart 1985; Finkel 1985; McPherson, Welch, and Clark 1977). Niemi, Craig, and Mattei (1991: 1407) associate external efficacy with "beliefs about the responsiveness of governmental authorities and institutions to citizens' demands" and internal efficacy with more individual beliefs and "competence to understand, and to participate effectively in, politics." For example, the NES survey assesses external efficacy through the statements "public officials don't care much what people like me think," "people like me don't have any say about what the government does," and "sometimes politics and government seem so complicated that a person like me can't really understand what's going on." In 1988, NES added new questions to measure internal efficacy through the statements "I feel that I have a pretty good understanding of the important political issues facing our country," "I consider myself well-qualified to participate in politics," "I think that I am better informed about politics and government than most people," and "I feel that I could do as good a job in public office as most other people" (Niemi, Craig, and Mattei 1991). While research shows that some of these items are complex, in that they measure degrees of both internal and external efficacy, they are robust predictors of political efficacy when grouped together. These dimensions have been adapted from the NES study and are applied here to determine the relationship between Internet features and political efficacy.

Web Interactivity

The inherent interactive potential of the Internet distinguishes it from most other mass forms of political communication (Barber, Mattson, and Peterson

1997; Hacker 1996; Tedesco 2004). Much of the hope that the Internet could transform political engagement, ripen young adult dialogue and deliberation, and jolt political participation rested in the expectation that the Internet's interactivity would unbind the hierarchical, noninteractive communication flow typified by print and broadcast media. However, research shows that most political Web sites did not take full advantage of the interactive opportunities (Barber, Mattson, and Peterson 1997; Congress Online 2002; Owen, Davis, and Strickler 1999). In fact, Stromer-Galley's research (2000) shows that candidates purposefully avoid interactive designs out of the fear of losing control over Web site content.

There has been much dialogue and debate on what constitutes Web interactivity (see Bucy 2004; Hacker 1996; Kiousis 2001; Stromer-Galley 2004; Sundar, Kalyanaraman, and Brown 2003). McMillan and Hwang (2002) provide a thorough review of the ways scholars have defined interactivity based on processes, features, and user perceptions. In her work, McMillan (2002) makes a basic distinction between user-to-system and user-to-user forms of interaction. Virtually all political Web sites now have user-to-system interaction, which is characterized by users interacting with the site through hyperlinks, quizzes, and polls, downloading campaign promotional material, and the like. Few political sites provide user-to-user interaction or interactive aspects characterized by chat rooms, blog posts, instant messaging, feedback forums, and even e-mail. When these interactive elements do exist on political sites, any interactive messages displayed on the public Web site pass through a strict gatekeeping process.

In a functional perspective, interactivity is accomplished through dialogic processes of two-way information exchange (Sundar, Kalyanaraman, and Brown 2003). This is also referred to as interactivity-as-process, or the interaction between people (Stromer-Galley 2004). In this project, the functional perspective is adopted such that interactivity should constitute the potential for two-way exchange of information. To date, research exploring interactivity effects of political Web sites has evaluated interactivity in terms of its influence on perceptions of the site or evaluations of the candidates hosting the sites (Bucy 2004; Stromer-Galley and Foot 2002). Nisbet and Scheufele (2004) found that Internet political information, when combined with discussion, increased political efficacy. Web exposure alone did not have a marked influence on political efficacy. Additional research shows that exposure to candidate Web sites has resulted in increased positive evaluations for the candidate (Hansen and Benoit 2002) and decreased levels of political cynicism (Tedesco and Kaid 2000). These studies have provided an important step in our understanding of basic interactivity effects, but broader studies of interactivity effects on political efficacy and political information are needed.

Clearly, when compared to candidate and media voices, the public voice is least represented in our political dialogue (Kaid, McKinney, and Tedesco 2000). Although media report public opinion commonly in the form of political polls, "polls are personified by the reporter, the candidate, the campaign staff, or the academic researcher, who interpret with brief comments the results of hundreds or thousands of people polled" (DeRosa and Tedesco 1999: 66–67). Opportunities for public dialogue with candidates or campaigns are rare in our political system. Hacker (2000) wrote that interactive opportunities should foster learning about political process and political issues due to the active construction of messages. It seems intuitive that opportunities to communicate about politics and invitations to voice opinions in blogs or chats, or to join a threaded discussion, should show young people that someone cares about their opinions. Thus, it was expected that use of interactive functions would also increase efficacy.

A Web-based experiment was designed to shed light on some of the issues discussed in this review of interactivity, interest, and efficacy. More specifically, this chapter aims to address two main questions: (1) What, if any, effect does Web condition (interactive/noninteractive) have on levels of internal or external political efficacy among young adults, and (2) Is there a difference in the way participants from the two conditions evaluate their information levels and ability to participate in politics?

Exploring Web Interactivity Effects

In order to explore the question of Web interactivity effects on political efficacy and political interest, a between-subjects experiment was designed. During the 2004 presidential campaign, students had the opportunity to participate in a thirty- to forty-five-minute research project. Participants were assigned to one of two forms of an interactive condition (interactive/noninteractive). In both conditions, students began by completing short online pretest questionnaires containing measures of political efficacy, basic demographic questions, feeling thermometer evaluations of Bush and Kerry, questions about typical media usage, various questions about political interest and perceptions of political knowledge, and questions about vote preference and voter registration status. Specific experimental controls and questionnaire items appear in the chapter's appendix.

Web Interactivity Effects

The first question in this research project was designed to assess whether interactivity differences between the two conditions resulted in any significant

TABLE 12.1
Pre- and Post-test Changes for Internal and External Efficacy

	Noninteractive Condition		Interactive Condition	
	Pre-test	Post-test	Pre-test	Post-test
Internal Efficacy	3.28	3.39[b]	3.06[a]	2.95[a,b]
External Efficacy	3.32	3.37	3.17	3.09[a]

[a] Between-group statistical significance. For example, the difference between internal efficacy (3.28) in the noninteractive condition pre-test compared with internal efficacy in the interactive condition (3.06) is statistically significant.
[b] Within group statistical significance. For example, the difference between internal efficacy in the pre- and post-test for the noninteractive condition is statistically significant.

changes in either internal or external political efficacy. In order to assess internal and external efficacy, the eight external efficacy items and three internal efficacy items were summed to give each participant separate pre- and post-test internal and external efficacy scores. Table 12.1 shows the mean scores for pre- and post-test internal and external efficacy. The first thing to point out is that there was a statistically significant difference between conditions (3.06–interactive; 3.28–noninteractive) in the pre-test internal efficacy scores, $t(259) = 2.58$, $p < .01$. In this case, lower scores on the five-point scale represent stronger feelings of internal and external efficacy. Internal efficacy scores were significantly better for the interactive condition, even before the experiment started. This finding indicates that the groups were not equal on internal efficacy at the beginning of the study. Nevertheless, the change scores also tell an interesting story.

Table 12.1 shows that exposure to the interactive condition resulted in significantly stronger feelings of internal efficacy. The internal efficacy change from 3.06 to 2.95 in the interactive condition is statistically significant, $t(133) = 2.73$, $p \leq .01$. Interestingly, the reverse was the case for the noninteractive condition. Participants in the noninteractive condition reported significantly lower levels of internal efficacy in the post-test, 3.28 to 3.39 $t(121) = 1.98$, $p \leq .05$. Furthermore, post-test external efficacy scores were significantly different between the interactive (3.09) and noninteractive (3.37) conditions in the post-test, $t(255) = 3.45$, $p \leq .001$. Since there was no difference in these scores during the pre-test, the data suggest that the external efficacy scores were significantly changed as a result of the different exposure groups. In this case, the interactive condition resulted in stronger feelings of external efficacy. Thus, interactive Web sites increased both internal and external efficacy for participants in the study. Interestingly, the noninteractive exposure condition had the reverse effect on internal efficacy, with participants reporting lower levels of internal efficacy after reading information on these sites.

TABLE 12.2
Information Outcome Differences between Noninteractive and
Interactive Web Conditions

Information Outcomes	Noninteractive	Interactive
Informed enough to help others with voting	3.50	3.99*
Candidate and issue familiarity important	4.05	4.23**

* T-test comparison of means significant at the level of p ≤ .001
** T-test comparison of means significant at the level of p ≤ .01

The second question concerned whether participants in the two different conditions would report any differences in information outcomes. In this case, two statements were used to identify various aspects of information outcomes: "People who are not familiar with the candidates and issues should not vote in the upcoming election" and "If a friend asked me about the presidential election I feel I would have enough information to help my friend figure out who to vote for." Participants were asked to indicate their level of agreement with each statement using a 5-point scale ranging from strongly agree to strongly disagree. Table 12.2 shows the information outcome differences between the interactive and noninteractive Web conditions.

As table 12.2 shows, the outcome scores were significantly higher for each variable in the interactive condition. Participants who completed the interactive condition indicated higher levels of qualifications to help others decide for whom to vote $t(259) = -4.22$, $p \leq .001$ and a stronger feeling that candidate and issue information is important to voting $t(259) = -3.38$, $p \leq .05$. While the outcome scores can be considered favorable for both conditions, it is noteworthy that the interactive condition resulted in significantly higher scores for both of the dimensions explored here. Results indicate that interactivity increases favorable information outcomes.

Implications of Web Interactivity

Since the Internet is a primary source of campaign information for young adults, it is important for researchers to explore not only Web site content but also effects of that content on issues of information and understanding, internal and external efficacy, and political engagement. By all measures, political engagement of young adults continues to be low, despite an upturn in turnout for the 2004 presidential election (Levine and Lopez 2002). The Web is unlike the dominant print and broadcast media because it offers the opportunity for interactivity. While the instances of interactivity have remained relatively low on campaign sites, there are now widespread examples of political organizations or politically minded groups that host a large range of interactive Web site features. Since interactivity distinguishes the Web from other forms of communication, this study set out to determine whether interactivity content has any measurable impact on young adults' perceptions of internal or external efficacy or information outcomes.

Research shows that young adults regularly claim lack of knowledge about candidates and political issues as a reason why they do not vote (Kaid, McKinney, and Tedesco 2000; NASS 2000). Since recent survey research shows that young people report learning about politics from the Internet (Pew 2004), it is important to understand the conditions under which they acquire information. In this study, when young people were asked which sources would most likely supply them with information to help them make a voting decision, nonparty political Web sites ranked below only political debates as a source they would turn to for helpful information. In addition to talking with friends, young adults cited party and candidate Web sites and newspapers as particularly helpful in providing information. Most accounts show that the Internet is clearly a valuable source for young adults.

Since online chatting is the most widely used form of Web communication for young adults, it seems intuitive that young adults would use interactive features if present on political Web sites. Inefficacy is a strong predictor for non-voting. Young people do not think their votes matter or they do not think politicians care about their opinions, so they do not show up to the polls or engage in the political process. The results reported here show that interactivity, or engagement in dialogic processes, can help to increase not only internal and external efficacy, but also perceptions of information efficacy (Kaid, McKinney, and Tedesco, in press). Although participants in the interactivity condition were already significantly higher in levels of internal efficacy prior to the beginning of this study, their efficacy scores increased significantly after interacting with various Web features. The young adults in the interactive condition also became significantly more likely to indicate feelings of external political efficacy, or the belief that government would be more responsive to their opinions. Thus, engaging in dialogic processes has a direct and powerful effect on young adults' perceptions of political efficacy. Beyond internal and external efficacy, respondents in the interactive condition felt better prepared with information to help their friends decide for whom to vote and also valued more highly the importance of candidate and issue information.

Thus, it is significant to see that interactivity appears to have a significant influence on internal efficacy and its political outcomes. Participants in the interactive study were significantly more likely to indicate (internal efficacy) that "I consider myself well-qualified to participate in politics," "I think I am better informed about politics and government than most people," "I feel that

I have a pretty good understanding of the important political issues facing our country," and (information efficacy) "If a friend asked me about the presidential election, I feel I would have enough information to help my friend figure out who to vote for" and "People who are not familiar with the candidates and issues should not vote in the upcoming election." Furthermore, the information outcome scores, while high for participants in the noninteractive condition, were very high for the interactive condition and ranged from 3.99 to 4.23 on a 5-point scale. In this case, higher scores reflected increased perceptions of information outcomes.

Clearly, the evidence indicates that interactive features on Web sites help young adults feel more informed about politics and more valuable or useful to the political process. Since young adults regularly indicate lack of information and lack of efficacy as the primary reasons they disengage from the political process, the findings on interactivity are very important. For candidates and political organizations interested in mobilizing young voters, interactive Web site features appear very valuable. The data also show that young adults rate interactive Web sites much higher than noninteractive sites. Table 12.3 shows the average evaluations for each Web site included in this project. As the data show, all the interactive sites scored higher than the noninteractive sites, with only one exception. The factcheck.org site was evaluated very high among participants in the noninteractive condition. While factcheck.org is not interactive in a dialogical manner, its features are high in user-to-system

TABLE 12.3
Average Evaluations (10-point scale) for Political Web Sites without Interactivity and with Interactivity

	Mean Score
Noninteractive	
www.georgebush.com	6.26
www.johnkerry.com	6.13
English.aljazeera.net/Home Page	5.23
Abcnews.go.com/Politics	6.43
www.comedycentral	5.04
www.factcheck.org	7.94
Interactive	
www.declareyourself.com	7.09
www.ontheissues.org	8.13
www.us-election.org	7.28
www.publicagenda.org	7.37
www.mtv.com/chooseorlose	6.48
www.cnn.com/Election2004	6.59
www.rockthevote.com	6.96

interaction, as the site allows users to get verification on a wide range of political issues and statements from political candidates. Thus, if candidates or organizations want to appeal to young adult Web users, site interactivity will score valuable points among this age group. Even though message control is a very important aspect of candidate Web sites (Stromer-Galley 2000), it seems that candidates need to discover ways to integrate interactive elements into their Web design that satisfy the user and the site host.

Thus, the increase in interactivity, mostly among media and political organization Web sites, appears very favorable for young voter political engagement. Perhaps young voters are turning to the Internet for political information more frequently as a result of more interactive features on political sites. Whether young adults have recognized interactive features or not, the evidence indicates that they provide two very favorable outcomes for our political system. Interactivity appears to promote favorable information outcomes and also increases participants' internal and political efficacy.

Space limitations necessitate that this project report only a portion of the research collected on Web interactivity. Future explorations will aim to link Internet political motives or uses (information, entertainment, surveillance, etc.) with information outcomes and interactivity effects. Media cynicism and media diet will also be used to explore contingent conditions for information and efficacy effects.

As with most research, there are limitations to the design presented here. While the participants completed the project in a familiar computer lab setting, it is unlike their apartment or dorm room, where most students do their Internet browsing. While the setting might be a limitation to this study, the limits on time spent with each Web site and range of tasks were very small. The dialogic aspects of interactivity were not as process-oriented as possible over extended periods of time. The feedback loop of posting a message or sending an e-mail, getting a response, processing the response, crafting a reply, and so forth takes more time when interacting with a candidate or political organization. Most interactive sites are limited in the user-to-user real-time feedback mechanisms. Exploring real-time interactivity from user to user will also add to our understanding of information outcomes and political efficacy. If a demand factor exists, students indicating that they were more informed or more efficacious after this project, it is diminished by the differences between the interactive and noninteractive experimental controls.

While the participants evaluated the Web sites highly, and indicated they would go back to visit many of the interactive pages, it is uncertain whether the sites selected typify the types of political sites visited by young adults. While MTV, Comedy Central, ABC, CNN, and the major party candidate home pages seemed like logical choices for a young adult Internet study, it is unclear whether any of the specific projects would be pursued by participants if left to their own devices. While this study used a great deal of control on participant access, studies allowing more fluid, self-directed Internet use will provide greater levels of external validity. Tracking the types of interactive activities young adults complete on a typical basis and the effects of those activities is important not only from a developer's perspective, but also from a researcher's perspective.

Appendix

Experimental and Control Conditions

The experimental condition was designed to provide multiple opportunities for interactivity, including dialogic process communication. In the experimental condition, participants were instructed to go to several Web sites and complete several tasks. For example, participants interacted with the site for some tasks (including two quizzes and a mock vote), but constructed and sent solicited messages as well. At ontheissues.org, participants completed a personal inventory about their attitudes on a wide range of political issues. Participants' attitudes were compared to those of the leading presidential candidates. Each participant received an instant analysis of agreement percentages for themselves and each candidate for the collection of issues. On the MTV Choose or Lose site, participants visited the "You Tell Us" section, which invited visitors to post comments about their opinions on a range of political issues. The site posted comments so students could read what others had to say and participate in the dialogue. On the CNN Web site, participants read Paul Begala's debate blog and were instructed to post a response of agreement or disagreement in the "Send Your Comments" link. On the Rock the Vote site, participants visited the "Take Action" section about a campus campaign and were instructed to sign the petition if they agreed with the campaign goal. The petitions were delivered to the participants' congressional representatives.

The control condition was designed to model a one-way flow of information from source site to participant, and interactivity was limited. In the control condition, participants did not craft or send any messages. Instead, participants read stories or press releases and watched two political ads. Stories were read from Bush's site, Kerry's site, ABC news, Al Jazeera, Comedy Central, and factcheck.org.

Efficacy and Information Levels

Internal and external efficacy were assessed on the pre- and post-tests using a replication of reliable scales used previously (e.g., Kaid, McKinney, and

Tedesco 2000; Tedesco 2002) and adapted from the NES (Rosenstone, Kinder, and Miller 1997). Participants were asked to indicate their level of agreement with the following eight statements using a 5-point Likert scale, ranging from strongly agree to strongly disagree, to measure general external efficacy: (1) Whether I vote or not has no influence on what politicians do, (2) One never really knows what politicians think, (3) People like me don't have any say about what the government does, (4) Sometimes politics and government seem so complicated that a person like me can't really understand what's going on, (5) One can be confident that politicians will always do the right thing, (6) Politicians often quickly forget their election promises after a political campaign is over, (7) Politicians are more interested in power than in what the people think, and (8) One cannot always trust what politicians say. Internal efficacy was measured specifically through the following items: (1) I consider myself well-qualified to participate in politics, (2) I think I am better informed about politics and government than most people, and (3) I feel that I have a pretty good understanding of the important issues facing our country. Agreement with one of these internal or external efficacy statements, with the exception of item 5, indicates some level of inefficacy. Thus, statement 5 was recoded to have the same directionality as the other statements. The scale achieved a Chronbach's alpha score of .88.

Information levels were assessed based on a range of questions asking participants to evaluate the level of understanding and comfort with political information. The goal here was to assess the range of attitudes (level of understanding, comfort with political information, qualifications to participate in politics, etc.) participants had with political information. Expressed political information level will be assessed in relation to satisfaction with various Web sites and interactive opportunities.

At the close of the pre-test questionnaire, participants were asked about the political importance of a wide range of political activities, from contributing to political campaigns, watching news, talking about ideas with friends, and contacting political leaders to posting messages online, watching late-night comedy shows, going to rallies, and voting among several additional variables.

Participants were split between the two conditions, with an end total of 135 in the control condition and 136 in the experimental condition.

References

Acock, Alan, Harold D. Clarke, and Marianne C. Stewart. 1985. "A New Model for Old Measures: A Covariance Structure Analysis of Political Efficacy. *Journal of Politics* 47: 1062–84.

Barber, Benjamin R., Kevin Mattson, and John Peterson. 1997. *The State of "Electronically Enhanced Democracy": A Survey of the Internet.* New Brunswick, NJ: Walt Whitman Center for the Culture and Politics of Democracy.

Bucy, Erik P. 2004. "The Interactivity Paradox: Closer to the News but Confused. In *Media Access: Social and Psychological Dimensions,* edited by Erik P. Bucy and John E. Newhagen, 47–72. Mahwah, NJ: Erlbaum.

Campbell, Angus, Gerald Gurin, and Warren E. Miller. 1954. *The Voter Decides.* Evanston, IL: Row.

Congress Online. 2002. "Assessing and Improving Capitol Hill Web Sites." 28 January. Available at www.congressonlineproject.org/publications.

Delli Carpini, Michael X. 2000. "Gen.com: Youth, Civic Engagement, and the New Information Environment." *Political Communication* 17: 341–49.

DeRosa, Karen L, and John C. Tedesco. 1999. "Surveying the Spin: Interpretation of the 1996 Presidential Polls." In *The Electronic Election,* edited by Lynda Lee Kaid and Dianne Bystrom, 65–80. Mahwah, NJ: Erlbaum.

Finkel, Steven E. 1985. "Reciprocal Effects of Participation and Political Efficacy: A Panel Analysis." *American Journal of Political Science* 29: 891–913.

Hacker, Kenneth L. 1996. "Missing Links in the Evolution of Electronic Democratization." *Media, Culture, & Society* 18 (2): 213–32.

———. 2000. "The White House Computer-Mediated Communication (CMC) Systems and Political Interactivity." In *Digital Democracy: Issues of Theory and Practice,* edited by Kenneth L. Hacker and Jan van Dijk, 105–129. Thousand Oaks, CA: Sage.

Hansen, Glenn J., and William L. Benoit. 2002. "Presidential Campaigning on the Web: The Influence of Candidate World Wide Web Sites in the 2000 General Election." Paper presented at the annual meeting of the National Communication Association, New Orleans, November.

Jamieson, Amie, Hyon B. Shin, and Jennifer Day. 2002. *Voting and Registration in the Election of November 2000.* Washington, DC: U.S. Census Bureau.

Kaid, Lynda Lee, Mitchell McKinney, and John C. Tedesco. 2000. *Civic Dialogue in the 1996 Presidential Campaign: Candidate, Media, and Public Voices.* Cresskill, NJ: Hampton.

———. In press. "Political Information Efficacy and Young Voters." *American Behavioral Scientist.*

Kiousis, Spiro. 2002. "Interactivity: A Concept Explication." *New Media & Society* 4 (3): 355–83.

Levine, Peter, and Mark Hugo Lopez. 2002. "Youth Voter Turnout Has Declined, by Any Measure." Center for Information and Research on Civic Learning and Engagement. 1 December. Available at www.civicyouth.org/research/areas/pol_partic.htm.

Margolis, Michael, David Resnick, and Chin-Chang Tu. 1997. "Campaigning on the Internet: Parties and Candidates on the World Wide Web in the 1996 Primary Season." *Press/Politics* 2 (1): 59–78.

McMillan, Sally J. 2002. "Exploring Models of Interactivity from Multiple Research Traditions: Users, Documents, and Systems." In *The Handbook of New Media,* edited by Leah Lievrow and Sonia Livingstone, 163–82. Thousand Oaks, CA: Sage.

McMillan, Sally J., and Jang-Sun Hwang. 2002. "Measures of Perceived Interactivity: An Exploration of the Role of Direction of Communication, User Control, and Time in Shaping Perceptions of Interactivity." *Journal of Advertising* 31 (3): 29–42.

McPherson, J. Miller, Susan Welch, and Cal Clark. 1977. "The Stability and Reliability of Political Efficacy: Using Path Analysis to Test Alternative Models." *American Political Science Review* 71: 509–21.

National Association of Secretaries of State. 2000. "New Millennium Survey: American Youth Attitudes on Politics, Citizenship, Government, and Voting." New Millennium Young Voters Project. Available at www.stateofthevote.org (accessed October 8, 2003).

Neuman, W. Russell. 2001. "The Impact of New Media." In *Mediated Politics: Communication in the Future of Democracy*, edited by W. Lance Bennett and Robert M. Entman, 299–320. Cambridge: Cambridge University Press.

Niemi, Richard G., Stephen C. Craig, and Franco Mattei. 1991. "Measuring Internal Political Efficacy in the 1988 National Election Study." *American Political Science Review* 85: 1407–13.

Nisbet, Matthew, and Dietram A. Scheufele. 2004. "Internet Use and Participation: Political Talk as a Catalyst for Online Citizenship." *Journalism & Mass Communication Quarterly* 81 (4): 877–96.

Norris, Pippa. 2000. *A Virtuous Circle*. Cambridge: Cambridge University Press.

Owen, Diana, Richard Davis, and Vincent J. Strickler. 1999. "Congress and the Internet." *Press/Politics* 4 (2): 10–29.

Patterson, Tom. 2002. *The Vanishing Voter: Public Involvement in an Age of Uncertainty.* New York: Knopf.

Pew Internet & American Life Project. 2004. "Cable and Internet Loom Large in Fragmented Political News Universe." 11 January. Available at www.pewinternet.org (accessed April 25, 2005).

———. 2005. "The Internet and Campaign 2004. The Internet Was a Key Force in Politics Last Year as 75 Million Americans Used It to Get News, Discuss Candidates in Emails, and Participate Directly in the Political Process." March 6. Available at www.pewinternet.org/pdfs/PIP_2004_Campaign.pdf (accessed April 25, 2005).

Rheingold, Howard. 1995. *The Virtual Community*. London: Minerva.

Rosenstone, Steven J., Donald Kinder, and Warren E. Miller. 1997. "American National Election Study, 1996: Pre- and Post-Election Survey" (computer file). Ann Arbor: University of Michigan, Center for Political Studies (producer). Ann Arbor: Interuniversity Consortium for Political and Social Research (distributor).

Selnow, Gary W. 1998. *Electronic Whistle-Stops: The Impact of the Internet on American Politics*. Westport, CT: Praeger.

Sparks, Colin. 2001. "The Internet and the Global Public Sphere." In *Mediated Politics: Communication in the Future of Democracy*, edited by W. Lance Bennett and Robert M. Entman. Cambridge: Cambridge University Press, 75–98.

Stromer-Galley, Jennifer. 2000. "On-line Interaction and Why Candidates Avoid It." *Journal of Communication* 50 (4): 111–32.

———. 2004. "Interactivity-as-Product and Interactivity-as-Process." *Information Society* 20 (5): 391–94.

Stromer-Galley, Jennifer, and Kirsten Foot. 2002. "Citizen Perceptions of Online Interactivity and Implications for Political Campaign Communication." *Journal of
Computer-Mediated Communication* 8 (1). Available at www.ascusc.org/jcmc/vol8/
issue1/stromerandfoot.html.

Sundar, S. Shyam, Srimam Kalyanaraman, and Justin Brown. 2003. "Explicating Web
Site Interactivity: Impression Formation Effects in Political Campaign Sites." *Journal of Communication* 30 (1): 30–59.

Tedesco, John C. 2002. "Televised Political Advertising Effects: Evaluating Responses
during the 2000 Robb–Allen Senatorial Election." *Journal of Advertising* 31 (1):
37–48.

———. 2004. "Changing the Channel: Use of the Internet for Communicating about
Politics." In *Handbook of Political Communication Research*, edited by Lynda Lee
Kaid. London: Erlbaum.

Tedesco, John C., and Lynda Lee Kaid. 2000. "Candidate Web Sites and Voter Effects:
Investigating Uses and Gratifications." Paper presented at the annual meeting of the
National Communication Association, Seattle, November.

Index

About the Editors and Contributors

Editors

John C. Tedesco (PhD) is associate professor and director of graduate studies in the Department of Communication at Virginia Tech. Tedesco's research addresses civic engagement, civic discourse, agenda setting, and various other aspects of mass-mediated political communication in both U.S. and comparative political settings.

Tedesco has served as research coordinator of the National Election Research Team (1996 and 2000) and the UVote2004 project. Tedesco is coauthor of *Civic Dialogue in the 1996 Presidential Election* and coeditor of *The Millennium Election.*

Tedesco's research has been published in numerous journals, including *American Behavioral Scientist, Journalism Studies, Journal of Advertising, Handbook of Public Relations, Journal of Broadcasting and Electronic Media, Harvard International Journal of Press/Politics, Communication Studies, Argumentation and Advocacy, Informatologia,* and *Journal of Communication Studies.* Additionally, Tedesco is contributing author to several volumes on political communication.

Tedesco was invited by the Budapest College of Communication, the Embassy of the United States in Budapest, and the Hungarian-American Fulbright Commission as featured speaker at the conference, Communication in the Globalized World. Funded by the U.S. State Department, Tedesco delivered the featured address, "Politics and the Internet: Examining Political Mobilization and Reinforcement."

Tedesco is chair of the Political Communication Division of the National Communication Association and has served as chair of Political Communication at the Eastern Communication Association. Additionally, he is a national coordinator of the Political Communication Research Foundation and the UVote international research team and is editing a special issue of *American Behavioral Scientist* dedicated to this consortium of scholars' studies about young voters.

Andrew Paul Williams (PhD) is assistant professor in the Department of Communication at Virginia Tech, where he was awarded a 2005–2006 Dean's Faculty Fellowship in the College of Liberal Arts and Human Sciences.

His research has been published in international journals such as *American Behavioral Scientist, Harvard International Journal of Press/Politics, Journalism Studies, Journal of E-Government,* and *Mass Communication & Society,* and he has published book chapters in the political communication arena. Williams has presented numerous conference papers at international communication and political science annual meetings. He has been recipient of top-paper awards at the annual conferences of the Broadcast Education Association and the International Communication Association.

Williams's background as a communication practitioner includes his work as a reporter at regional publications such as *Financial News & Daily Record, Jacksonville Magazine,* and *The Clay County Leader.* He also has extensive experience working in public relations and marketing for numerous corporate and not-for-profit organizations, and as a communication consultant while running his own company, Andrew Paul Williams Enterprises.

Dr. Williams has been recognized for his excellence in teaching by the International Communication Association. He is chair of Political Communication at the Eastern Communication Association. Williams also serves as director of Development for the Political Communication Research Foundation and the UVote international research team. He is the faculty adviser for Virginia Tech's UVote and Public Relations Student Society of America student chapters.

Contributors

Andrea B. Baker is a PhD student in the College of Computing and Information at the University at Albany, State University of New York. Her research focus is e-government, with an emphasis on studying the impact of technology on the democratic process.

Mary Christine Banwart (PhD, University of Oklahoma) is an assistant professor of communication studies at the University of Kansas, where she teaches courses in political campaigns, politics and the media, and leadership. She has published articles and chapters on political campaigns, women and politics, and politics and the media. She is coauthor of *Gender and Political Candidate Communication: VideoStyle, WebStyle, and NewsStyle*.

Kirsten A. Foot (PhD, University of California, San Diego) is an assistant professor of Communication at the University of Washington. Her research focuses on the reciprocal relationship between information/communication technologies and society in general, and Web production practices in particular. As codirector of the WebArchivist.org research group, she is developing new tools and techniques for studying social and political action on the Web.

Christopher C. Hull (PhD, Georgetown University) is a partner in a Washington, DC, public affairs firm and the senior political editor of Tech Central Station. Before occupying his current position, Dr. Hull served three years as the majority staff director of the Iowa Senate. He worked as the press secretary for a member of the U.S. House Ways and Means Committee, as an assistant to the director of communications for a national party committee, and as a trade and foreign affairs legislative assistant to a U.S. senator. Dr. Hull worked with James P. Pinkerton at the Manhattan Institute for Public Policy Research's Washington office, assisting with research and editing for Pinkerton's book *What Comes Next: The End of Big Government and the New Paradigm to Come*. Dr. Hull graduated magna cum laude from Harvard University in 1992.

Thomas J. Johnson is professor and director of Graduate Studies at the Southern Illinois University School of Journalism. Johnson's research focuses on media history, public opinion, and political communication. He has published more than twenty refereed articles in such journals as *Journalism & Mass Communication Quarterly, Journal of Broadcasting and Electronic Media*, and *Political Communication*. In addition to several book chapters, Johnson is coeditor of *Engaging the Public: How the Government and the Media Can Reinvigorate the American Democracy* and author of *The Rehabilitation of Richard Nixon: The Media's Effect on Collect Memory*. Johnson is recipient of the School of Journalism Teaching Excellence Award and a two-time recipient of the Journalism Graduate Student Association Graduate Teacher of the Year award. Professor Johnson earned his PhD from the University of Washington.

Clifford A. Jones teaches at the University of Florida's Frederic G. Levin College of Law. His teaching and research interests include election and campaign finance law, media law, competition law, and European community law. He has authored over forty books, articles, and book chapters. He received his JD from the University of Oklahoma and his MPhil and PhD from the University of Cambridge. He is a former Fulbright scholar (University of Mainz, Germany) and former visiting fellow in the Programme in Comparative Media Law and Policy, University of Oxford.

Lynda Lee Kaid is professor of Telecommunication at the University of Florida. She previously was a George Lynn Cross Research Professor at the University of Oklahoma, where she also served as the director of the Political Communication Center and supervised the Political Commercial Archive. Her research specialties include political advertising and news coverage of political events. A Fulbright scholar, she has also done work on political television in several European and Asian countries. She is the author/editor of twenty books, including *The Handbook of Political Communication Research, The Millennium Election, Political Television in Evolving European Democracies, Civic Dialogue in the 1996 Presidential Campaign, Videostyle in Presidential Campaigns, The Electronic Election, New Perspectives on Political Advertising, Mediated Politics in Two Cultures,* and *Political Advertising in Western Democracies.*

Barbara K. Kaye (PhD, Florida State University) is associate professor in the School of Journalism & Electronic Media at the University of Tennessee–Knoxville. Her research interests include media effects and consumer uses of new communication technologies. Her work has been published in *Journalism & Mass Communication Quarterly, Journal of Broadcasting and Electronic Media, Harvard International Journal of Press/Politics, Social Science Computer Review, Journal of Promotion Management,* and *Atlantic Journal of Communication.* She has also authored three textbooks: *Electronic Media: Then, Now, and Later; Just a Click Away: Advertising on the Internet;* and *The World Wide Web: A Mass Communication Perspective.*

Kristen D. Landreville is a master's student in the College of Journalism and Communications at the University of Florida. She earned her bachelor's degree in journalism, specializing in online media, from the University of Florida. Her research interests include political communication, computer-mediated communication, and international communication. She has coauthored a book chapter in *Global Media Go to War* and journal articles in *Journalism Studies* and *Mass Communication & Society.*

Justin D. Martin is a Roy Park Fellow and PhD student in Mass Communication at the University of North Carolina at Chapel Hill. His research involves mass media coverage of political issues and events, as well as the effects of such coverage on political behavior. Also a researcher of international journalism, Martin spent the 2005–2006 academic year in Jordan on a Fulbright scholarship, studying political content in several Middle Eastern newspapers. He is a graduate of High Point University and the University of Florida.

Monica Postelnicu is a doctoral student in the College of Journalism and Communications at the University of Florida. Her research focuses on computer-mediated communication, new media, and use of Internet in political communication. She is the coauthor of several papers presented to national and international communication and political science conferences. She received her bachelor's degree from the University of Bucharest, Romania, and her master's degree from Boston University.

Steven M. Schneider is associate professor of Political Science at the State University of New York Institute of Technology, codirector of WebArchivist.org, and coeditor of PoliticalWeb.info. His research on the Web Sphere and political communication and the Web appears in such journals as *Electronic Journal of Communication, New Media & Society, Journal of Computer-Mediated Communication, Journal of Broadcasting and Electronic Media,* and *Javnost (The Public).* His research has received funding from the U.S. Library of Congress and Pew Internet & American Life Project, among others. Schneider has a PhD in political science from the Massachusetts Institute of Technology and an MA from the Annenberg School of Communications at the University of Pennsylvania.

Ashli Quesinberry Stokes is an assistant professor in the Communication Department of Virginia Tech. Her areas of interest include rhetorical criticism, public relations, and women's social and political rhetoric. Her work has been published in a variety of communication outlets, including the *Southern Journal of Communication, Public Relations Review,* and the *Encyclopedia of Public Relations.* Dr. Stokes is a former public relations practitioner who draws on this experience in her approach to scholarship and the classroom.

Jennifer Stromer-Galley is an assistant professor in the Department of Communication at the University at Albany, State University of New York. Her research interests include the political uses of and experiences with information communication technology, mediated political campaign communication, and deliberative democratic theory and practice. Her publications can be found in the *Journal of Communication, Javnost (The Public), PS: Political Science and Politics,* and *Journal of Computer-Mediated Communication.*

Kaye D. Trammell is an assistant professor in the Manship School of Mass Communication at Louisiana State University. Her research focuses on "blogs" and on the intersection of politics and computer-mediated communication. She also serves as a public affairs officer in the U.S. Navy Reserve. Her work has been published in *Journalism & Mass Communication Quarterly, American Behavioral Scientist, Harvard International Journal of Press/Politics, Journal of E-Government, Journalism Studies, Mass Communication & Society,* and the *Business Research Yearbook.* She also has written several book chapters about political content in blogs, ranging from candidate use of blogs during the 2004 election to war discourse by celebrities on their blogs. Additionally, Trammell has been recipient of top paper awards at the annual conferences of the Broadcast Education Association and the National Communication Association.